RPCM 5/23

Battle

*For Paul Nicholas Whitbread
(1956-2021)*

Battle

Understanding Conflict from Hastings to Helmand

Graeme Callister and Rachael Whitbread

Pen & Sword
MILITARY

First published in Great Britain in 2022 by
Pen & Sword Military
An imprint of
Pen & Sword Books Ltd
Yorkshire – Philadelphia

Copyright © Graeme Callister and Rachael Whitbread 2022

ISBN 978 1 39908 098 9

The right of Graeme Callister and Rachael Whitbread to be identified as Authors of this work has been asserted by them in accordance with the Copyright, Designs and Patents Act 1988.

A CIP catalogue record for this book is
available from the British Library.

All rights reserved. No part of this book may be reproduced or transmitted in any form or by any means, electronic or mechanical including photocopying, recording or by any information storage and retrieval system, without permission from the Publisher in writing.

Typeset by Mac Style
Printed and bound in the UK by CPI Group (UK) Ltd,
Croydon, CR0 4YY.

Pen & Sword Books Limited incorporates the imprints of Atlas, Archaeology, Aviation, Discovery, Family History, Fiction, History, Maritime, Military, Military Classics, Politics, Select, Transport, True Crime, Air World, Frontline Publishing, Leo Cooper, Remember When, Seaforth Publishing, The Praetorian Press, Wharncliffe Local History, Wharncliffe Transport, Wharncliffe True Crime and White Owl.

For a complete list of Pen & Sword titles please contact

PEN & SWORD BOOKS LIMITED
47 Church Street, Barnsley, South Yorkshire, S70 2AS, England
E-mail: enquiries@pen-and-sword.co.uk
Website: www.pen-and-sword.co.uk

Or

PEN AND SWORD BOOKS
1950 Lawrence Rd, Havertown, PA 19083, USA
E-mail: Uspen-and-sword@casematepublishers.com
Website: www.penandswordbooks.com

Contents

Acknowledgements		1
Introduction		3
Chapter 1	**Society**	7
	The Murder of Evesham (1265)	19
	Black Week: Stormberg, Magersfontein, Colenso (1899)	23
Chapter 2	**Grand Strategy and Politics**	29
	A Battle of Five Armies: Marston Moor (1644)	38
Chapter 3	**Leadership**	43
	Hammered by the Scots: Stirling Bridge (1297)	51
	Lions Led by Donkeys? The Somme (1916)	55
Chapter 4	**Conditions of Landscape**	61
	The Advantage of the Higher Ground? Hastings (1066)	73
	The Sun of Austerlitz (1805)	77
Chapter 5	**Battlefield Strategy and Tactics**	81
	No Hope of Safety except in Victory: Agincourt (1415)	96
	Attack them Head-on: Panjwai (2006)	101
Chapter 6	**Logistics**	107
	The Heat of War: Hattin (1187)	118
	The End of the Line: Stalingrad (1942–3)	123
Chapter 7	**Weapons and Armour**	130
	Diabolical Machines: Crécy (1346)	144
	Seeking an End to Stalemate: Cambrai (1917)	149

Chapter 8	Armies, Personnel and Training	155
	Prussian Apotheosis: Rossbach (1757)	168
	Fighting far from Home: Darwin-Goose Green (1982)	172
Chapter 9	Motivation and Morale	177
	Give unto us your Attendance: Bosworth (1485)	188
	All Hell Breaking Loose: Tet Offensive (1968)	194
Chapter 10	Non-Combatants	199
	Was There a Man Dismayed? Balaclava (1854)	210
Chapter 11	The Clash of Arms	215
	The Nearest-Run Thing: Waterloo (1815)	225
Chapter 12	Sources of Conflict	236
	Eyewitness Narratives	236
	Contemporary Reporting	239
	Official Narratives	241
	Muster Rolls, Pay Records, Supply	241
	Visual Sources	243
	Artefacts	244
	Battlefields	245

Afterword: Understanding Battle		248
Notes		253
Further Reading		266
Index		270

Acknowledgements

We would like to acknowledge our debt of gratitude to all who helped in the inception, writing and production of this book. Firstly, our thanks to Rupert Harding, Linne Matthews, and the rest of the team at Pen and Sword, whose hard work and patience have helped to make this book possible. We would also like to thank the students and colleagues, past and present, of our respective institutions – the Bromsgrove School History department, and York St John University History and War Studies – for their enthusiastic encouragement, and for discussions and debates down the years that have helped to hone some of the ideas in this book. Our thanks too to the Historiska Museet, Stockholm, and shutterstock.com for granting permission to reproduce images for this work. Finally, we would like to express our eternal appreciation to our friends and families, whose love and support means so much.

Rachael Whitbread and Graeme Callister

Introduction

Battle. Even to the most pacific amongst us, the word conjures up a thousand images: from the close-quarters combat of the medieval battlefield to the colourful serried ranks of Napoleonic armies; from the swing of sword against shield to the awesome destructive force of modern explosive weapons; from warriors sallying forth with little more than their frail human courage to soldiers surging into combat in armour or vehicles that make them appear barely human at all. Battle – the deed and the word – brings out some of the best and some of the very worst in people. Throughout history humans have used their ingenuity to find better ways to kill and maim and destroy, and battles have seen atrocities and slaughter that defy explanation. Yet battle also gives rise to feats of enormous courage and sacrifice, of comradeship and selflessness, and, paradoxically, even of touching humanity in the most trying of conditions. For participants it can be horrifying, terrifying – and exhilarating. As Sidney Rogerson, a British soldier of the First World War, remembered:

> the fact remains that, terrifying as they sometimes, and uncomfortable as they often were, the war years will stand out in the memories of vast numbers of those who fought as the happiest period of their lives. And the clue to this perhaps astonishing fact is that though the war may have let loose the worst it also brought out the finest qualities in men.[1]

There is an unavoidable degree of ambiguity about battle. Acts that would, as the old quip goes, lead to the executioner's block in peacetime are rewarded with medals and fame in war. Feats of strength, skill, endurance and courage can be admired in the abstract, but are harder to celebrate when conducted at the cost of other people's lives. Even the ingenuity of inventors and engineers in creating new machines and technologies in double-quick time can seem less praiseworthy when they are immediately put to the task of killing. Yet despite – or perhaps because of – these paradoxes and moral ambiguities, battles continue to fascinate and intrigue.

The literature of battle shares some of these ambiguities. Combat can inspire those who write about it to great literary feats, with prose or poetry that touches the soul as few other subjects can. It can equally encourage some of the tawdriest writings, including the worst kind of nationalist propagandising. On a less extreme level, the tendency of battle writing to follow the exciting narrative rather than scholarly analysis, and a tendency of some writers to glory in their subject rather more than good taste dictates, has led to a degree of disdain for the subject from some academic historians; a disdain that often does them little credit, and does little to improve the discipline.

For all its popularity as a subject, non-fictionalised battle writing of any stripe shares a common struggle, and that is simply to determine what took place on the field of combat. Battle is confused, noisy, chaotic, often limited in visibility. Most participants are focused on the immediate enemy rather than on the bigger picture. Jean Froissart, a French chronicler of the Hundred Years' War, wrote of the Battle of Crécy:

> there is no one, even among those present on that day, who has been able to understand and relate the whole truth of the matter. This was especially so on the French side, where such confusion reigned.[2]

Over four centuries later, British Field Marshal the Duke of Wellington famously saw little point in trying to recall the narrative of a battle:

> The history of a battle is not unlike the history of a ball. Some individuals may recollect all the little events of which the great result is the battle lost or won; but no individual can recollect the order in which, or the exact moment at which, they occurred, which makes all the difference to their value and importance.[3]

Only very occasionally are we lucky enough to find an eyewitness who enjoys an unsullied overview of the battle, such as William Russell at Balaclava, which was 'plainly seen from the verge of the plateau where I stood'.[4] Russell was even able to note down the order and timing of events on the constrained battlefield, although, as he ruefully remarked, 'the watch, I believe, was a little slow'.[5] Yet the participants in the battle saw much less of the events, as demonstrated by the Light Brigade's forlorn and misdirected charge; Lord Lucan simply could not see the guns he had been ordered to charge, and in his confusion took off down the valley towards the main Russian gun line. While Russell enjoyed a bird's-eye view to record the action, the participants' accounts are a tale of confusion, misunderstanding, and the noise, smoke and deadly danger of battle.

Fortunately for historians, many soldiers or amanuenses have committed their imperfect reminiscences to paper, and it is possible to cut through the confusion, the fog of war and the differences of memory to draw up a general narrative of many battles. Details can prove elusive, or remain shrouded in debate, but the broad shape of the beast starts to emerge. We can begin to analyse and, to misquote Macbeth's witches, to understand how the hurlyburly's done – how the battle's lost, and won.

There is no definitive recipe for success or failure in battle, and this book will not try to give one. Instead, it aims more modestly to invite the reader and researcher to consider a broad array of factors that influence, inform and inspire actions on the battlefield, and that have an inevitable impact on the outcome. As an introduction to the topic, the book will cover core themes of army structures and training, weapons, tactics and terrain, as well as lesser-studied influences on battle such as social organisation, grand strategy, logistics and non-combatants. Each chapter will offer an overview of how one issue feeds into our understanding and analysis of a battle, and will include lively examples from clashes – some iconic, some lesser known – to illustrate the factors in action. Often, this requires examining familiar narratives from largely under-explored perspectives.

In reality of course these factors do not exist in isolation, but are deeply intertwined. An army's structures and training will be heavily influenced by the society it represents; tactics cannot be divorced from the weaponry carried into battle; morale can be deeply affected by leadership or logistics. Each of the themes will interact with the others in a thousand small ways, and often in ways that are unique to each battle. It would be impossible (not to say a little tedious) to attempt to explore all of these connections and influences. Instead, we have contented ourselves with pointing to the most important areas of intersection.

Our analysis will focus on battles in the European world over the past millennium, from the Norman Conquest to the recent campaigns in Iraq and Afghanistan – battle from Hastings to Helmand. The broad sweep of history has seen enormous changes in almost every facet of human existence, and battle is no different. Yet there are aspects of combat that echo faintly down the ages, commonalities that join, however tenuously, the experiences of King Harold's huscarls to those of Field Marshal Montgomery's motorised infantry. Tactics and weapons change; armies become more complex, and battle even moves into another dimension with the advent of airpower; but the basic principles of battle have changed less radically. The chapters that follow will draw out these changes and continuities, and will present a picture of the wide range of factors, themes and ideas that researchers or students of war must consider to fully understand battle.

Chapter 1

Society

'One ought to seek knights on the battlefield and chaplains in churches'
Simon de Montfort.[1]

A soldier's whole approach to fighting is moulded by the society to which they belong. The fighter's understanding of the role of a soldier, the meaning of conflict, morality or rules of war, their relationship to their leaders, and even their relationship to fellow soldiers are inextricably bound to their society and culture. The underlying understandings of the world created by each society or culture, and shared by its members, help to influence how its soldiers think, react to circumstance and, at times, act on the battlefield. While training will go some way to replacing a civilian's persona with a new military identity, the militarisation of the mind rarely strays far from the values and mores of the society that it serves. Soldiers' broader life experiences are important: 'War may be all-consuming, but it is impossible to understand the experience of combat without understanding the richness of life going on around it.'[2]

Armies can also reflect their societies in a more physical sense. Most Western societies, for example, have until very recently viewed the role of the soldier as essentially masculine, overwhelmingly restricting combat roles to men. The quality of those men as soldiers has equally mirrored the condition of the civilian population, whether in terms of size and stature, physical fitness, or traits such as education and literacy. To understand a battle it can therefore be useful to understand something of the societies that put the armies into the field. Society's influence rarely determines the outcome of any battle, but it is a useful starting point for the analysis of clashes of arms.

To begin with, the make-up of an army depends largely on the society or culture that it represents. Military historian John Keegan identified six main forms of historical army organisation, each of which is, in essence, decided by the value that its society places on warfare, violence and military service: warrior, mercenary, slave, regular, conscript and militia.[3] The warrior tradition in the West largely faded with the passing of the knightly caste, although oddities showing elements of warrior culture such as the hereditary recruitment of the Russian Streltsy survived well into the early modern period. Slave armies (in the fullest sense) have played little role in European battle in the past millennium, although practices of military slavery continued in the borderlands of Eastern Europe and Asia Minor. In the Ottoman Empire, for example, *devşirme* – the taking of children in conquered territories as slaves to be turned into soldiers – continued into at least the 1600s.[4] Soldiers such as the Mamelukes were enslaved, while Russian serfs conscripted for life in the eighteenth century might as well have been. Mercenaries have been widespread, representing those who fight for pay from a state or society that is not their own. Regular soldiers also fight for pay but benefit from a place in society, even if they do not enjoy what we would now understand as full citizenship. Conscripts (by which Keegan meant men called up for limited service when they reach a certain age, even in peacetime) and militia (all able-bodied men called up for the duration of a conflict) are also members of wider society, but fight from compulsion rather than voluntarily, and as a temporary expedient rather than a profession.

The organisation of a society can be important in determining what type of army – and what type of soldiers – will take the field. For much of the High and Late Middle Ages, European societies were structured to provide monarchs with soldiers when needed. Employing a standing army was a significant drain on the coffers and a waste of valuable labour in peacetime, meaning that permanent professional forces – either in royal service or 'free companies' – were limited in size and number. Instead, social obligations were used to create armies when the necessity arose. By the time of the Norman conquest of England, much of Western Europe had developed a system of vassalage, whereby vassals were granted lands by a monarch or liege in exchange for promises of military service. This distribution of land gave vassals the resources to maintain the cripplingly expensive training, equipment, mounting and necessary entourage of the armoured knight – the dominating force on the High Medieval battlefield. In some cases the legal obligation to serve could be stronger than a mere oath of fealty, even for the knightly caste. The *ministeriales* of the German lands, for example, were a largely military class who often held privileged social rank, but who could be compelled to serve their lords or bishops 'with a serf-like status'.[5]

For the most part, vassalage provided rulers with trained and well-equipped troops for battle, although how well trained and equipped the soldiers were could depend on the wealth and resources of each region. While poorer regions by no means always produced inferior fighters, wealthier vassals could at least supply greater numbers and better equipment. Perhaps more importantly, the service owed by vassals was generally limited to only a certain number of days a year, and was gradually eroded over the centuries as vassals negotiated, bartered or bullied concessions from monarchs.[6] By the later thirteenth century, French knights' obligations had been reduced to forty days in defence of the country, or more if the king paid further expenses. Knights summoned for service abroad had to be maintained at royal expense throughout the campaign. Social obligation could still be used to muster an army – for example with the later French use of the *arrière-ban* to summon all subjects, not just vassals – but money was by now arguably more important.

If knightly vassals provided the theoretical backbone of an army, they were usually supplemented by a larger force of non-noble infantrymen. Although by the twelfth century there was a theoretical division of society into those who prayed, those who fought, and those who laboured, the strict hierarchisation continued to allow the use of labouring peasants as humble foot soldiers. These were for the most part levies, summoned only when needed. Rarely would they have formal military training, and it is no coincidence that some of the more effective infantry weapons of the period resembled the agricultural implements that the levies were more used to handling. Some societies, however, did insist that all men trained to arms, offering a potentially significant advantage in providing skilled men for the battlefield. From the thirteenth century, all Englishmen were obliged to practise archery, a command reiterated by Edward III to his sheriffs in 1363:

> every able bodied man on feast days when he has leisure shall in his sports use bows and arrows, pellets or bolts, and shall learn and practise the art of shooting … as the people of the realm, noble and simple,

used heretofore to practise the said art in their sports, whence by God's help came forth honour to the kingdom and advantage to the king in his actions of war, and now the said art is almost wholly disused ... whereby the realm is like to be kept without archers.[7]

Such training was not unique to England; in the Low Countries and some Italian states, companies of crossbowmen became known for their skill and training. In Switzerland, a culture of exposing boys to warlike games and insisting that men 'daily exercise' was the foundation for the cohesion that allowed Swiss pike squares to dominate the late fifteenth-century battlefield.[8]

Although universal training created a large pool of potential fighters, in practice relatively few men actually fought. Societies simply could not survive if a significant portion of the population were dragged off to war, which effectively limited the size of forces that could be raised. Moreover, as with knightly vassals, the service that could be compelled of ordinary folk often diminished over time. In England, towns and counties could still be obliged to provide men, but individuals could pay scutage instead of personal service, with the money raised used to fund professional soldiers who would be both more effective and better motivated.[9] Although levies were still used, especially in civil conflicts, most of England's forces in the Hundred Years' War were professionals or mercenaries. This reflected a wider shift in many European armies towards professionalism, partly driven by a strengthening of central royal authority and, in many places, the weakening of legal social obligations. These changes – both social and military – contributed to the growth of mercenary companies of the later medieval and early modern periods.

By the latter years of the early modern period, few societies were organised around the idea of military service. Obligated service in the form of conscription was still used to great effect in countries such as Sweden, Brandenburg-Prussia, or Russia, and many countries retained compulsory militias for local defence, but most regular forces relied on volunteers. Even here, however, social organisation had a clear continuing influence on the shape of armies. Officers usually came from the nobility or landed gentry, as both a vestige of traditional values of military service and a reinforcement of elite status. In Prussia, for example, the noble Junker class provided the army with officers; in France before the Revolution, four generations of nobility were required to gain a king's commission. In the ranks, the harshness of conditions and low pay in most armies meant that recruits tended to come from the poorer, and in some cases most desperate, levels of society. The Duke of Wellington notoriously referred to his soldiers more than once as 'the scum of the earth', lamenting that many joined up primarily for the daily drink ration.[10] Even by their own people, soldiers were often feared and despised.

The late eighteenth century, however, saw a marked revival of the classical notion of the citizen-soldier, which had lingered in only a few early modern states, and was now linked to growing revolutionary notions of popular government. This ultimately had a profound effect on how societies provided themselves with armies. Revolutionary France, faced with war against almost all of Europe, proclaimed the whole population requisitioned to aid the war effort through the *levée-en-masse* of 1793, and so successful did it prove that the idea of the nation-in-arms was born. For a short time the French army even flirted with soldiers electing their officers. However, by 1798, the makeshift measure of the *levée* was replaced by a more systematised method of conscription, whereby every man was envisaged as owing service to his nation. Napoleon, coming to power the next year, adopted and expanded this system of annual conscription to great effect, mobilising some 2.3 million soldiers over a fifteen-year period, giving him the manpower to conquer Europe from Lisbon to Moscow. This draft was never popular, but the combined forces of coercion and habit eventually embedded it largely successfully in the French population.

What began as mass mobilisation to serve a popular government thus became systematic conscription in service of a non-democratic state, although Napoleon and the enemies who copied him often took pains to portray compulsory service as a patriotic duty. It was in this vein that it was continued through the nineteenth century; societies grew to accept that men should be glad to give service to their homeland, and peacetime conscription, often for limited periods, was introduced in several states, creating large armies and huge reserves of trained manpower. As nationalist rhetoric grew through the century, unevenly accompanied by greater levels of popular representation, the social acceptance of soldiering as a service to the nation became more prominent. Some, such as many African-Americans, volunteered in the hope of improving their civil rights.

This is not to say that social attitudes always approved of military service. When William Robertson, who would eventually rise all the way to field marshal, enlisted in the ranks of the British army in 1877, his mother bitterly proclaimed that she was ashamed and would rather see him dead than in a red coat – although Britain was one of the few countries to resist introducing conscription. Yet even in Britain the distrust of soldiering was overcome in bursts of patriotic enthusiasm during the Boer War and, to a much greater extent, the First World War. Men who marched into battle on the veld or in Flanders often did so believing in the cause of king and country.

Britain was perhaps unusual in retaining volunteers all the way through to 1916. Most other states resorted to conscription much earlier, and it is clear that by the twentieth century most European societies were accepting of the idea of universal male service, especially in times of major conflict. Moreover, the states of Europe now had the administrative and coercive means to make the idea of universal service a reality. Yet even with these egalitarian ideas of service, hierarchies remained. In most states officers continued to be drawn from social elites, or at least from those with access to higher levels of education. Where compulsory service was non-universal, the weight continued to fall as it always had on the poorest and least educated. The wide-ranging exemptions from the US draft during the Vietnam War, for example, caused some resentment amongst those who felt unfairly targeted for service.

Soldiers are therefore a reflection of the society from which they emerge. Social structures, ideologies and forms of government shape the basic outline of an army – who is in it, who leads it, and the cause for which it fights. More important, however, is how this translates into action on the battlefield. In some cases there is a direct impact, especially before armies had a permanent infrastructure in place to train or nourish their soldiers in any real sense, meaning that combatants would better reflect the physique and skill-at-arms of the society they represented.

Recruits especially tend to reflect the fitness of their society, above all in periods of compulsory service. In Napoleon's France, for example, fully one-third of conscripts were rejected on medical grounds as being unable to withstand the 'rigours of war', even though health and height requirements were hardly exacting. Those who remained were often still physically unimposing specimens. In desperate times, such as during the invasion of France in 1814, conscripts were hurled into combat with little time for training or physical development, leaving their units as very much a cross-section of civil society. The level of rejections from military service can also give an insight into the general health of an army; the number of British recruits rejected in the First World War fell steadily throughout the conflict not because of better health, but because men of lesser fitness were increasingly accepted into service. Conversely, Britain's post-Second World War national-service army saw rejections rise from 11 to 26 per cent in thirteen years, a reflection of ever-rising health and IQ requirements. By the abolition of national service, soldiers were, on average, healthier and more intelligent than ever.[11]

In cases where conscripts could be properly trained and fed, the results could be astonishing. Lieutenant Charles Carrington of the Warwickshire Regiment complained that the conscripts of 1916 were 'the refuse of our industrial system', but commented that:

> when they came to us they were weedy, sallow, skinny, frightened children ... But after six months of good food, fresh air and physical exercise, they changed so much their mothers wouldn't have recognised them. We weighed and measured them and they put on an average one stone in weight and one inch in height.[12]

But in armies that had neither the time nor resources to feed and train recruits, a society's health would be laid bare on the battlefield.

Social norms also have a clear effect on levels of obedience, subordination and cohesion in an army. As with physical fitness, this is something that can be reconditioned by training and the creation of a military culture, but often the values of civil society are reflected in those of the army. This is strongest where formal military hierarchies are weakest. The clan system of early modern northern Scotland, for example, gave Scottish fighters a strong sense of cohesion and communal loyalty, even in the absence of formal military structures and training. On the opposite side of Europe, the Cossacks of the Russian steppes formed similarly close-knit units, bonded together by family, community, and the harshness of life rather than any strict disciplinary regime. Into the early 1900s, the Boer communities of southern Africa were bound by kinship, personal loyalties and the need for mutual support in the hostile environment of the veld – traits that carried over into their commandos.

Elsewhere, habits of deference and obedience could translate from civil to military life. Entrenched loyalty to an abstract institution – religion, ruler or republic – could make men more pliable once in uniform, but it only took them so far. The disintegration of the Russian army in 1917, the mutinies in the French army in the same year, and the failure of the German army in 1918 point to the limits of obedience to intangible people or ideas. Ingrained everyday customs were perhaps more important. Noble leaders of medieval armies were able to command obedience through their social status, without the need for formal military rank structures. In a more recent example, it has been argued that the habits of obedience of Britain's industrial workforce – which in the early twentieth century remained larger than that of any other European power – was a key factor in the British army being the only one not to suffer a major mutiny during the First World War.[13]

In a similar vein, ideas adopted from civil society largely underpin the beliefs and moral codes that soldiers take onto the battlefield. Social attitudes dictate whether war is celebrated or abhorred, and whether the soldier is to be admired or shunned. Combatants' understandings of violence, morality, mortality, and the rules of war will always have an influence on how they fight. Most Western societies have associated battlefield action with heroism and, even when soldiering as a profession was unfavourably viewed, have held up conquering warriors as worthy of emulation. Some have even portrayed war as something to be enjoyed. Nineteenth-century Britons often spoke of war in the same terms as the hunting or sports field. Even amidst the horrors of the trenches, soldiers still referred to war as a 'game': the editorial of *The Somme Times* (a renaming of the more famous *Wipers Times*) in July 1916 concluded: 'So here's to you all, lads, the game is started, keep the ball rolling and remember that the only good Hun is a dead Hun.'[14] Although the publication was intended as a light-hearted interlude for troops at the front, the jocularity of the tone belies the deadly seriousness of battle.

Basic understandings of violence and death will influence whether combatants approach battle with enthusiasm or trepidation, and will generally come from wider social attitudes and beliefs. Equally, whether soldiers fear, respect, or despise an enemy will largely stem from prejudices inherent in their society, alongside any previous experience of fighting that particular foe. These attitudes might inform whether soldiers panic and flee at the sight of the enemy, or whether they are encouraged to stand and fight, and will influence their approach to killing, taking prisoners, or treating the wounded. Expectations of the enemy will also inform a soldier's choice between surrender or fighting to the death; British soldiers were much more likely to surrender in the Boer War, for example, than in any of their recent campaigns against the Zulu, Matabele, Ashanti or Mahdists, as they believed (rightly) that the Boers were more likely to accept surrender rather than slaughtering them.

Sometimes the influence of social attitudes is most obvious where there is a clear clash of cultures. Japanese soldiers' approach to combat in the Second World War, for example, was far removed from that of their Western enemies, with Japanese units sometimes fighting quite literally to the last man, and inflicting atrocities on Allied prisoners they considered unworthy of respect for having capitulated. Jack Sharpe of the Leicestershire Regiment recalled being told 'that no Japanese soldier with a body as strong as mine would allow himself to become a prisoner'.[15] Second Lieutenant John Randle remembered British troops being appalled by Japanese behaviour, but that they also replied in kind:

> With the exception of one officer, the Japs butchered all our wounded. News of this got back to us and conditioned mine and the battalion's attitudes towards the Japs. We were not merciful to them for the rest of the war. We didn't take any prisoners.[16]

Soldiers will generally act with greater restraint fighting those viewed roughly as equals, and less mercifully when the enemy can be labelled as something intrinsically dangerous or irredeemably different, whether traitors, heretics or savages. Examples of this abound from the Crusades to colonial campaigns, and from the Wars of Religion to the Eastern Front in the Second World War. Supposedly inferior people were often subjected to massacre or atrocity in a way that supposed cultural equals were not.

Until the twentieth century, the measure of whether societies (and therefore soldiers) saw others as civilised was often bound to religious belief. Religion could be an important factor in how soldiers conducted themselves in battle, underpinning moral principles and placing constraints on their actions. Whether holy days, spaces or people are held as sacrosanct, or whether soldiers are affected by superstitions or portents, largely depends on the piety and religious conventions of their society. In the medieval world, for example, places of worship were considered spaces of sanctuary and were theoretically inviolate, although the wealth of monasteries and churches made them tempting targets for marauding soldiers, and churchmen were frequently found in battle. Warrior bishops were common in medieval Germany, and the formal prohibition on English clergymen taking up arms rarely prevented those so inclined from fighting.[17] At Myton-on-Swale (1319), churchmen were so prevalent in the English army that it became known as the 'white battle' due to the colour of their vestments. In modern conflicts clergymen have tended towards non-combat roles, although they are often more prominent in fighting in irregular forces. Most modern armies also tend to try to avoid targeting religious sites, even if this stems more from consciousness of the outrage that damage can provoke than from any strictly religious motivation.[18]

Religious observance can also affect an army's tactical position or its soldiers' readiness to fight. Holy days held sacrosanct can make frontline units more susceptible to surprise attack, as seen with Trenton (1776), Tet (1968) or Yom Kippur (1973). The Tet Offensive was all the more surprising because in previous years both sides had observed an effective holiday truce. Less spectacular but more frequent is the tacit understanding in forces of similar religious views that holy days should be peaceful, of which the unofficial truce on parts of the Western Front at Christmas 1914 is perhaps the most striking example. At times, European forces have also declined to fight on the Sabbath; the chronicler Cousinot claimed that at Orléans (1429), Joan of Arc advised against engaging the retreating English, unless they turned to attack, because it was a Sunday.[19]

Beyond this, religious beliefs are a crucial component of the moral codes with which societies try to regulate warfare from time to time, even if soldiers in the heat of combat often stray beyond what is technically permissible. Formal written laws are a modern innovation, but widely understood rules of combat stretch back through the centuries. St Augustine wrote of the principles of just war in the fifth century, and St Thomas Aquinas in the thirteenth.[20] The values of *jus in bello* (just conduct in war) proved hard to pin down, but most Christian and Western societies shared broadly similar ideals. Richard II's 1385 ordinances for his army invading Scotland are typical of the few medieval codes of conduct in relating to the treatment of the church or non-combatants, rather than strictly to men in battle, but there were clearly some expectations of what should or should not happen on the battlefield.[21] Indeed, the chivalric ideal is an example of a standard to which combatants were supposed to adhere. Henry V's killing of prisoners at Agincourt (1415) was subject to contemporary commentary and recrimination because it was deemed (largely by his enemies, it must be said) to have breached the standards of expected behaviour.

Codes of conduct nevertheless tended to do relatively little to restrain soldiers in medieval and early modern battle. If surrendering noblemen were generally taken prisoner, it was likely the prospect of a healthy ransom rather than moral scruple that stayed the would-be killer's blade. Impoverished levies received no such favour. There was little obligation to treat enemy wounded with any sort of consideration; indeed, for many of the badly wounded, a knife to the throat was considered a kindness. In religious or civil conflicts, heresy or rebellion were punishable by instant death. Combatants could therefore expect little quarter. Similarly, a fortification that refused to surrender when summoned was liable to be sacked and its garrison put to the sword. All of this was accepted (and expected) behaviour.

Rules of combat evolved alongside changing social sensibilities. The sheer brutality of some sixteenth- and seventeenth-century conflicts prompted some thinkers, especially in Germany, to reconsider what should be acceptable in war. There was certainly agreement that non-combatants should be more protected from violence, although this was ignored in practice by armies of all countries. It is a moot point whether civilians would have noticed any discernible difference between the English *chevauchées* in France during the Hundred Years' War, the Swedish in Germany in the Thirty Years' War, Napoleon's legions in Spain during the Peninsular War, or the German army in the USSR in the Second World War. In all cases, civilians were plundered, molested, violated and murdered with abandon. On the battlefield a clearer set of values nevertheless began to prevail. Men of all ranks who surrendered expected, by the eighteenth century, to be taken prisoner, and to be treated with a degree of humanity. Wounded enemies were likewise to be cared for within the medical practices of the day. For the most part these rules were adhered to, although there were always noteworthy exceptions. Napoleon ordered the execution of 3,000 Turkish prisoners at Jaffa in 1799, while in 1812, Wellington's soldiers subjected the (allied) Spanish city of Badajoz to an atrocious sack, despite their officers' attempts to stop them.[22]

That these things happened highlights the limits of legal codes in restraining soldierly conduct, but that they were considered atrocities also shows that values were changing. By the nineteenth century, the idea of 'no quarter' had been largely abandoned, and the torture or mistreatment of prisoners of war was generally frowned upon. At Geneva in 1864 and The Hague in 1899, treaties were drawn up that specifically limited mistreatment of prisoners, the wounded and non-combatants. At St Petersburg in 1868, the international community agreed to renounce exploding small-arms ammunition. The Treaty of The Hague, expanded and extended in 1907, went further in forbidding the use of certain weaponry, including aerial bombardment, poison gas and soft-tip bullets. These treaties were limited in both scope and signatories, but reflected the prevailing spirit of the age. Further conferences at Geneva in 1929 and 1949 led to more explicit rules on the treatment of humans in war, and renewed prohibitions on the range of weaponry considered acceptable.

The idea that battle became somehow more humane because of these treaties is questionable, certainly considering the experiences of the two world wars, and of some of the conflicts since. Almost all of the protocols of The Hague were breached in the First World War – and almost always on the initiative of high command rather than soldiers running amok. The idea of the nation-at-war blurred the battlefront and the home front, allowing anybody to become a legitimate target. Prohibitions on munitions placed few operational limits on armies' firepower, while bans on operational actions – such as carpet-bombing civilian areas – tend to forbid activities that are of limited military value. Rules around the treatment of prisoners or enemy casualties likewise do little to affect the decisions of soldiers in combat, as the battle has generally been decided once prisoners are taken. Nevertheless, the contemporary battlefield is regulated as never before, with comparatively strict rules of engagement dictating how soldiers should engage the enemy.

The Murder of Evesham (1265)

Medieval England was not rife with armed conflict. The reign of Henry III (1216–72) was one of widespread peace and, although it began with the Battle of Lincoln in 1217, battles for much of the period were generally fought in Wales or on the Continent, rather than home soil. The notable exception was the Second Barons' War (1264–5), a bloody civil conflict that pitched relatives and comrades-in-arms against one another for power and liberty in the kingdom.

The conflict was initiated by divisions in noble society: Henry III's financial demands on his nobles combined with his promotion of foreign relatives – the Savoyards of his wife Eleanor of Provence's family and the Lusignans of his mother's second marriage – over English magnates. This was all played out in the context of Henry's father's own overbearing rule: King John had alienated many of his own nobles to such an extent that they forced him to sign the Magna Carta to protect their rights and liberties. It was only John's death in 1216 that prevented further rebellion when he reneged on the charter's conditions; rebel nobles had even gone so far as to suggest that the French crown prince, Louis (eldest son of Philip II), become king of England in John's place. It was against this political and social backdrop that English earls, led by Leicester, Gloucester and Norfolk, forced Henry to sign the Provisions of Oxford in 1258 – effectively passing political power to these overmighty subjects.

Simon de Montfort, Earl of Leicester, was soon to play a leading role in further rebellion. Married to the king's sister, Montfort was one of the leading magnates in the country and a proven military leader. Victory at the Battle of Lewes on 14 May 1264 and the capture of both King Henry and Prince Edward (later Edward I) meant that 'the barons of England adopted [him] as the leader by whom they were ruled'.[23] In his role as English leader, Montfort ruled through a council of nine magnates and called a parliament, with every borough and county to send two elected representatives, although in reality most power lay in his own hands.[24]

This, however, alienated rebel nobles who had presumed they would gain greater autonomy and authority. In particular, the Marcher lords along the Welsh border were angered by Montfort's settlement with the prince of Wales, Llywelyn ap Gruffudd – an enemy that those same lords had spent years fighting. It was no coincidence, therefore, that the royalist leaders at Evesham were two Marcher lords: Roger de Mortimer and Gilbert de Clare, Earl of Gloucester, the latter defecting from Montfort's cause at Easter 1265. Furthermore, the escape of Prince Edward from Montfort's hands at Hereford, after he evaded guards while out riding, provided royalists with a figurehead around whom to unite.

Mortimer and Gloucester could not rely on royal writs to summon troops to fight for the king, as Henry III was in custody. Instead, they recruited those who would fight for Henry out of loyalty or were disaffected with Montfort's regime. These included 'the Marchers ... and fugitives, and the friends of the prisoners' who would have joined them with retinues and men-at-arms.[25] Royalist knights would have been trained and experienced, with many having fought at Lewes the previous year.

Montfort's core support came from his family and his own knights, as trained and experienced fighters. For Evesham, however, he also sent out royal writs to summon both nobles and lesser gentry to fight for him, underlining his view that he formed the legitimate government of the realm. On 30 May, a royal writ was sent to 'tenants in chief, bishops, abbots, earls, barons, soldiers and all others, except those for the Earl of Gloucester', summoning them to muster in Worcester.[26] How many turned up to fight for Montfort is uncertain – although relatively lacklustre support from the English is perhaps suggested by his need to supplement his forces with Welsh foot soldiers sent by Llywelyn ap Gruffudd; their presence on the battlefield only antagonised the royalists further.

Montfort was mindful that his control of England hung by a thread; the armed supporters of the Marcher lords and Prince Edward had unified and marched after him across the West Midlands, attempting to cut him off from his son and reinforcements at the Montfort castle of Kenilworth. Pursued by the royalists through the night, Montfort reached Evesham around 6 am on 4 August. His men were exhausted after a night march and little food or rest for several days; they pleaded with him to 'place us in the church and the tower ... until your host is reinvigorated'.[27] Montfort's army therefore sheltered in the abbey and surrounding parkland.

The choice of abbey and church grounds to rest reflects the role of the Church during Montfort's rebellion and in wider thirteenth-century society. In a general sense, religious buildings were sanctuaries that could protect those within from royal censure; those fleeing arrest were supposedly safe within ecclesiastical walls, both in a legal sense and in a practical one as religious buildings were often well defended. In the case of Montfort specifically, however, his rebellion against Henry III enjoyed substantial support from English religious society. Montfort himself was seen by his supporters as a crusading knight, fulfilling God's holy purpose and reflecting contemporary society's obsession with crusade; his men even wore white crosses on their right arms.[28] Bishop Cantilupe of Worcester counselled Montfort before the battle and said Mass to his army; Cantilupe and four other churchmen were later suspended from office for supporting the rebels.[29] Church support was motivated not by Montfort's political actions, but by his accepted piety and specifically his support of reform of the English church.[30] By linking with the reform faction, Montfort was able to use divisions in religious society to engender further support.

Of course, the use of white crosses by Montfort's men – echoed in red crosses worn by the royalist forces – may have had a more practical application. Particularly in civil conflicts, identification of the enemy during battle could be challenging: they dressed and spoke similarly, and fought with identical weapons. In order to separate friend from foe, therefore, visual symbols served a useful purpose.

As Montfort's army caught their breath in Evesham Abbey grounds, royalist forces arrayed on Green Hill above the town. Montfort's forces marched out of Evesham Abbey northwards, rejecting the opportunity to flee from battle – for Montfort realised that his army could not escape and, without his army, his cause would be lost. Shortly before battle was joined, a thunderstorm and torrential rain soaked the gathering armies, providing 'a harbinger of the painful event that was to take place'.[31] Foul weather events were often noted by medieval narrators as *signa*, signs of trouble to come, reflecting that society's interest in natural portents of important events.[32]

Once battle was joined, it quickly became clear to the rebels that this clash was highly unusual. Firstly, the focus on Montfort as rebel army leader was crucial to the royalists' battle plan. Fuelled by long personal rivalry, Mortimer was already out for Montfort's blood. Before the battle, Mortimer, Edward and Clare selected twelve 'of the strongest and most intrepid' men-at-arms, and ordered them to kill Montfort during the battle, 'break[ing] through the ranks forcibly and rapidly in such a way that they would look at no one nor let anyone come between them until they reached the person of the earl'.³³ Not only was Mortimer's personal hatred of Montfort almost certainly a factor in this plan, but to kill the rebel leader would also likely win the battle – and the war – for the royalists. As soon as battle was joined, this small group of men made a direct line for Montfort and eventually, after several hours of combat, caught him. It is possible that this hit squad was led by Mortimer himself, motivated by personal animosity, as a 'lance struck [Montfort] through the neck, and it was Sir Roger de Mortimer, for he could be recognised by his armour and shield-straps'.³⁴ As Montfort fell from his horse, the rest of the hit squad surrounded him on the ground and butchered him, cutting off his head, hands, feet and genitals. As a final gruesome act in his personal grudge, Mortimer gifted the head to his wife – who had perhaps led the defence of Wigmore and Radnor against Montfort's sons the previous year.³⁵

Evesham also differed from the convention of battles at the time as no right to surrender was afforded to the rebel knights. This is evidenced by the sheer scale of death among the magnates in the rebel ranks: thirty-six important nobles were among the rebel dead, and contemporary accounts claim that over 160 knights were killed. Such a death toll was highly unusual; knights could usually surrender in order to be ransomed for exorbitant amounts of money.³⁶ At Evesham, such surrenders were not accepted and knights were deliberately cut down. Such was the political upheaval caused by Montfort's rebellion that Edward and his commanders wanted to execute as many of the rebel lords as possible, despite Edward's later claims that his uncle Montfort's death was against his wishes.³⁷ Such a death in battle would certainly solve a problem for Prince Edward; a trial for Montfort would have been without precedent and would have provided him with a platform to garner further support, whereas death on the battlefield would get rid of Montfort and his supporters once and for all.

What followed was a massacre of the rebels that Robert of Gloucester, writing in the later thirteenth century, described as 'the murder of Evesham, for a battle it was none'.³⁸ The killing did not stop on the battlefield, as rebels were slaughtered as they fled and even as they took shelter in the abbey and church. The killing here was so extreme that one contemporary described how:

the choir of the church and the inside walls and the cross and the statues and the altars were sprayed with the blood of the wounded and dead, so that from the bodies that there were around the high altar a stream of blood ran right down into the crypts.[39]

For such slaughter to be committed inside a religious building – normally protected by sanctuary – demonstrates just how far beyond the societal norms of thirteenth-century battle Evesham was. Neither the knightly brotherhood nor the sanctity of the church was respected, reflecting perhaps the political disorder of the time, the animosity between army leaders and for the Welsh supporting Montfort, and the need to avoid a lengthy and uncertain legal process towards rebels who might otherwise have escaped.

Although the Barons' War was to have long-lasting consequences for the stability of the realm with continuing disorder and resistance, Evesham was decisive in bringing to an end the period of rebellion and attempted reform which had begun in 1258. Evesham was remarkable for how it reflected mid-thirteenth-century society in England, but also how it broke and reformed societal norms and expectations.

Black Week: Stormberg, Magersfontein, Colenso (1899)

When the South African Republic and Orange Free State declared war on Britain in October 1899, few expected a long, drawn-out conflict. The Boers of the two republics believed that Britain lacked the stomach for a lengthy fight and would come to terms after a military reverse or two, as they had after Majuba (1881) in the First Anglo-Boer War. The British believed that their opponents were little more than uncultivated farmers, who would not stand long against disciplined and organised troops. Both sides soon found that they were wrong. Far from throwing in the towel, Britain responded to early defeats – especially the 'Black Week' catastrophes of Stormberg, Magersfontein and Colenso in mid-December 1899 – by flooding in reinforcements and resources, until they possessed a force in southern Africa of almost 250,000 men, a juggernaut able to crush the two independent states. Before that juggernaut got rolling, however, the Boers were to prove skilful and tenacious fighters, inflicting a series of stinging and costly defeats on the British army.

The war lasted two-and-a-half years, and those thirty months of conflict highlight the importance of social condition, attitudes, norms and practices in shaping soldiers on and off the battlefield. Rarely had two Europeanised forces with such different social structures clashed, and the differences of approach to battle in many ways mirrored the differences in social organisation of the two combatants.

The disparities between the two societies were stark. Britain, with a population of around 40 million, was relatively highly urbanised and industrialised, and sat at the centre of a global empire. The two Boer republics had white populations numbering under 400,000 (and only white people could hold citizenship in these republics – people of other skin colours were kept legally and physically subordinate), were predominantly rural, boasted little appreciable industry aside from mining, and wanted little enough to do with the outside world. The British public and soldiery certainly saw this as a conflict between a modern, civilised, industrial nation and a pair of rural backwaters.[40] The commander-in-chief of the army in 1899, Sir Garnet Wolsley, dismissed the Boers as 'the only white race ... steadily going back to barbarism'.[41]

Despite their differences, both societies responded with a degree of enthusiasm to the outbreak of war. In the Boer republics a spirit of independence – and a belief in the need to fight for it – was integral to national identity, and helped to convince people that the war was both necessary and just. In Britain, the widespread sense of national pride and faith in the moral rectitude of the British imperial 'mission' helped to create a patriotic desire to do one's bit. Anti-war sentiment was drowned out in a cacophony of support, with anti-war speakers often shouted down or even assaulted.[42] The popular press further stirred up jingoistic emotions.

The eager volunteering showed a country whose soldiers were largely enthusiastic for war, but also highlighted issues within Britain's industrial society. Army medical inspectors were shocked to discover that many thousands of men who answered the call for recruits early in the war were unfit. In Manchester it was reported that almost three quarters of the 11,000 who volunteered in 1899 were rejected on medical grounds.[43] Although such statistics were extreme, with overall rejection rates eventually settling at closer to one third, there followed something of a crisis of confidence.[44] The apparent ill-health of the population, combined with a series of military reverses that included the unprecedented surrender of over 2,000 men, rattled the British public.⁴⁵ The high rejection rate of recruits was almost certainly occasioned by unfit men volunteering as a route out of poverty, but concerns over Britons' fitness for international contest would eventually prompt the government to investigate 'physical deterioration' in the British population.

The fact that Britain's army relied largely on recruits from the poorest in society was just one of many differences between British and Boer militarism. Although small by Continental standards, Britain's professional standing army was as large as the entire white Boer population, and included a full complement of combat arms and support services. It was heavily hierarchised, directed by a dedicated general staff, and led at regimental level by professional officers. For many of those officers a commission was a social statement as much as a vocation, marking them out as gentlemen and providing a convivial social milieu in the officers' mess. Obedience was prized over innovation, and society expected of its troops the values that they believed had led to victory on the field of Waterloo: stoicism under fire, casual disregard for personal safety, and unfailing obedience to command. There was also a sense that going head-to-head with the enemy could be enjoyable, with one officer commenting that open battle had 'some sport about it too'.⁴⁶

The Boer republics, on the other hand, had no standing army other than a professional corps of artillery. Instead, their military needs were fulfilled by the system of commandos. Once the order for mobilisation went out, all able-bodied men over the age of twelve in each district assembled for duty in the commando. A full-time field cornet organised the assemblage, with other officers elected for the duration of the campaign. There was no formal system of compulsion. Networks of kinship, friendship, mutual trust, and the need for mutual protection bound the men of the commandos together into solid combat units. Those who owned them provided their own weapons and horses, while others were issued Mausers from government arsenals.⁴⁷ The fighting attributes valued by the Boers were those with which they were most familiar from the hunting field: patience, marksmanship and economy with their men's lives. The need for cooperation and mutual support they had learned in the laager, in battle against indigenous African warriors.

The values that each society gave to its army extended to the tactics of the battlefield. The British army, built on social and military traditions of deference and discipline, still went into battle in linear formations. Although khaki had replaced red coats two years earlier, men were rarely expected to use camouflage or stealth. Officers, marked out by distinctive uniforms and weaponry to denote status, were expected to lead from the front, keeping close control until near enough to the enemy to order the charge. In the Boer forces, on the other hand, command relied on consent as much as compulsion. They preferred to fire from cover and at relatively long range, aiming to break up attacks before they could close and inflict casualties. There were no real formations and far less control from officers. The Boer republics benefited from a 'rifle culture', in which target shooting and marksmanship were widely practised and popular activities.[48] This was easy to translate onto the battlefield. Men lay down and took cover when firing; standing in the open within rifle range of an enemy was thought stupid rather than brave. At Colenso, for example, Major General Neville Lyttelton, commander of British 4 Brigade, complained: 'I never saw a Boer all day till the battle was over.'[49]

British tactics were in part based on previous experience of colonial wars. Against the Zulus at Ulundi in 1879 or the Mahdists at Omdurman in 1898, the formation of mass infantry squares in the open had allowed British discipline and firepower to win the day. Although the Boers were equipped with modern firearms and artillery rather than predominantly bladed weapons, British soldiers and commanders assumed that they would be overcome in the same manner. When that proved not to be the case, the British blamed the Boers for not adhering to the unwritten rules of colonial combat. Lord Kitchener accused the Boers of 'skulking', grumbling that 'They are not like the Sudanese who stood up to a fair fight. They are always running away on their little ponies.'[50] The British put the outmanoeuvring of their forces down to low cunning rather than tactical brilliance on the part of the Boers.[51]

The battles of Black Week underlined the two societies' differences in approach. The British defeats were largely due to poor generalship and outdated tactics in the face of modern weaponry, which stemmed in part from Britain's social and cultural values. General Buller and his subordinates' approach relied on traditional tactics and a belief that the doughty character of the British soldier would see him through. At

Magersfontein and Colenso, attacks were made in close order against entrenched or hidden Boer riflemen. In the former, Major General Wauchope advanced his Highland Brigade to within 400 yards of the Boer position in extremely close order before trying to deploy; the failure of the attack was predictable. The Boers relied much more heavily on individual initiative, with men in action selecting their own targets and rates of fire. This usually allowed a more effective fusillade, as it did to deadly effect against the Highlanders at Magersfontein, although at Colenso the lack of discipline led the burghers of Louis Botha's force to open fire on Major General Hart's 5 Brigade at longer range than their commander had planned; casualties were heavy, but perhaps not so heavy as they might have been.[52]

While more reliant on discipline and control, the British army still prized individual bravery. The type of insouciance in the face of the enemy portrayed in memoirs of Napoleonic officers had become the standard against which British society measured a man's courage. When Colonel Long at Colenso deployed his artillery batteries within easy rifle shot of the Boer lines, the gunners for some time served their pieces with outwardly calm efficiency even as their comrades fell around them; when the guns ran out of ammunition, three officers of Buller's staff, a corporal, and six men volunteered to ride into the heavy fusillade to try to bring some of the weapons to safety. The three officers and corporal were awarded Victoria Crosses for their gallantry, although the action cost Lieutenant Freddy Roberts (only son of the field marshal) his life.[53] Thomas Pakenham wrote that Long's deployment showed 'one of the great traditions of the British army: courage matched only by stupidity'.[54]

While the British grew to respect the Boers' fighting ability, and eventually adapted their tactics to good effect, they never lost the supercilious sense of moral superiority over their foe. Despite their own atrocities – of which the maltreatment of civilians in concentration camps was the ultimate nadir – British soldiers despised the Boers for uncultured and even uncivilised actions in battle. In some cases British troops complained that Boer riflemen would pick them off at long range, and then surrender the moment their position was breached. It seemed to them unfair that the Boers did not allow themselves to be killed in retribution for firing on the attackers. More insidiously, once the British army had got the hang of the open-order advance, the Boers were accused of raising flags of truce to lure British soldiers out into the open, only to shoot them down without warning. Many of the documented accounts of this practice amount to second-hand rumour, but British and imperial soldiers believed it enough that many surrendering Boers were bayoneted rather than being taken prisoner, in retribution for their supposed crimes.

While the battles of the Boer War were far from decided by society, culture or social conditions, it is clear that these issues had an impact. The size, strength, organisation, tactics and values of each army reflected the society that produced it, and these in turn went some way to influencing how the armies acted on the battlefield.

Chapter 2

Grand Strategy and Politics

'War is not merely an act of policy but a true political instrument, a continuation of political intercourse, carried on with other means'
                                                               Carl von Clausewitz.[1]

It is almost a cliché that soldiers are constantly hampered by political interference. From the *Dolchstosslegende* – the 'stab-in-the-back' myth to explain German defeat in the First World War – to the disillusionment of American Vietnam veterans, the failure of politicians to support their troops has been loudly proclaimed as a reason for reverses in war. Often this is an attempt to rationalise or mitigate the collective trauma of military defeat.[2] Yet it is also a reflection of the vital importance of political decision-making and grand strategy for military operations, and ultimately for the battlefield itself.

As important as grand strategy appears, the term has defied attempts to coin a universal definition. In general, it refers to the means by which a state attempts to achieve its aims. In the broadest sense these methods can be peaceable as well as military, encompassing systems of alliance, diplomatic pressure, trade, 'soft power', aid, or simple bullying. There is a direct correlation between strategy and warfare insofar as conflict is usually entered into with the aim of improving a strategic situation, as famously explored by Clausewitz, but the relationship between grand strategy and battle (that is to say actual combat, rather than war more broadly understood) is a little more complex. Battlefield success does not always guarantee a more favourable strategic situation, nor does defeat necessarily imperil the wider cause. This can be the case even in major theatres of operations. In his invasion of Russia in 1812, for example, Napoleon was victorious on the battlefield but could not translate tactical success into strategic advantage. Tsar Alexander's refusal to negotiate, and the Russian army's ability to withdraw into the country's vast hinterland, left Napoleon's victories hollow, and the campaign failed spectacularly. Entire wars can be fought successfully on the ground and lost elsewhere, as Harry Summers's anecdote of a conversation in Hanoi in 1975 highlights:

> 'You know you never defeated us on the battlefield,' said the American colonel.
> The North Vietnamese colonel pondered this remark a moment. 'That may be so', he replied, 'but it is also irrelevant.'[3]

Battlefield victory was not the same as success in war. Such an outcome has been repeated countless times in military history.

A key reason for this is often simply that the grand strategy is faulty, and that battlefield victory is not enough in itself to alter the enemy's political position or to bring a victorious peace. In 1812 Napoleon had no clear strategy beyond a misguided hope that crushing the Russian army would force the Tsar to negotiate. It is axiomatic that counterinsurgencies are not won on the battlefield, even when there is a conventional aspect to the war. It can also be the case that success on the field of combat does not alter the operational situation of a campaign enough to lead to a decisive outcome. In 1870, for instance, French troops at St Privat slew almost 8,000 Prussian guardsmen and 'left a deep scar on the consciousness of the European military establishment' because of the deadly effect of modern rifles against attacking infantry, but the action did little to alter the complexion of a rapidly failing campaign.[4]

Nevertheless, combat has remained an important means of conducting strategy. For all that they are fraught with uncertainty, decisive battles do occur, and can achieve what other approaches to a problem cannot. William I's ascent to the English throne would have been impossible without Hastings; the Treaty of Troyes, which finally gave official acknowledgement to the English kings' claims to the French throne after nearly eighty years of trying, was only possible because of Henry V's crushing victory at Agincourt. Modern warfare has often become much more multi-dimensional, with military action just one string to a belligerent's bow, but even here we see decisive battles. German victory in the Battle of France in 1940 led to stunning strategic results that Germany could not have obtained in any other way. Such rapidly conclusive affairs are few and far between, but can make battle (rather than a drawn-out campaign or wider war) an attractive prospect. In some instances, seeking battle can be a strategic end in itself. At Bosworth (1485), both Richard III and Henry Tudor sought a speedy confrontation, as only victory in combat (preferably encompassing the death or capture of their rival) would secure their claim to the throne.

Indeed, battle as a deciding factor in war – rather than, say, the slow burn of an economic blockade, the attrition of lengthy campaigns, the destruction of infrastructure, or the use of diplomatic pressure and isolation – is more likely when strategic goals are limited or more focused. The overthrow of a monarch or regime, especially in the medieval or early modern worlds, could be accomplished with a single, well-directed battle; conversely, rebellions could be ended in the same manner. The death of Simon de Montfort at Evesham (1265) effectively ended the Barons' Revolt, the strategic aim of Prince Edward simply having been to crush and decapitate the enemy army. By contrast, Montfort's equally impressive victory at Lewes the previous year had not led to such a decisive outcome, despite the capture of Henry III and Prince Edward, because his strategy encompassed a far wider range of political goals that could not be attained through combat alone. Lewes brought breathing space, but not strategic victory.

Battle can also be used for political rather than strictly strategic reasons. It is well accepted that war is useful for rallying the support of the populace or boosting the popularity of a regime, especially in the world of nation-states when justified as a 'defensive' measure. From the Franco-Prussian War to the Falklands, regimes of all types have benefited from this phenomenon – although in both cases while the victors reaped the rewards, the losing regime fell in very short order. A victorious battle is the icing that tops that particular cake, allowing a government to bask in the reflected glory of its armed forces. Yet battle has long been desirable to leaders for its capacity to reflect honour and glory on the victor. Henry VIII's wish to be seen as a true renaissance prince by showing military prowess and chivalric heroism led to a strategically pointless campaign in France in 1513, culminating in a scrappy engagement that became known as the Battle of the Spurs. Henry nevertheless made much of his victory, using it to bolster his image as a warrior-king. Perhaps he had learnt from the mistakes of his father, whose French-bothering campaign of 1492 had exacted a large payment to make him go away, but no battle and therefore no military glory. Henry VIII's vain desire for battle actually put England in a difficult strategic position. With its king gallivanting on the Continent, Scotland took the opportunity to invade from the north; it was to Henry's good fortune that the competent Earl of Surrey was on hand to raise a northern army and rout the Scottish invasion at Flodden.

While battle is clearly important to politics and strategy, strategic and political decisions also play their role in shaping the course and outcome of battles. Grand strategy tends to be important in forming the underlying conditions for battle. It will usually dictate overall aims or objectives of a conflict or campaign, and so the reasons to fight. Strategic decisions will be behind the allocation of troops, equipment, supplies and additional support to the field army. Political considerations can place limitations on the actions of commanders and soldiers, especially when fighting on nominally friendly territory or attempting to avoid alienating either a civilian population or the wider international community.

Strategic or political decisions will also determine whether an army fights alone or with allies, and whether it fights for itself or for the good of a coalition. Alliances in war can offer huge advantages, but composite allied armies in actual combat do not always add up to the sum of their parts. Simply getting coalesced forces to a battlefield might be difficult, as allies often have rather different strategic objectives, especially if their armies are under separate command. Once in battle, relying on cooperation between different armies can be fraught with problems, not least issues of overall command, differences in training, equipment, experience, and potential barriers of language and communication. In a clash at Rouvray in 1429, a strong Franco-Scottish force was routed because of a total failure to cooperate; the French preferred to bombard the English with artillery, but the Scottish force, lacking its own guns, decided to launch an independent frontal assault. French equivocation as to whether to follow this rash move meant that the English were able to isolate the two forces and defeat them in detail. When such problems are solved, and when commanders are willing to work together, alliances can bring great benefits to the battlefield: the Duke of Marlborough and Prince Eugene, for instance, enjoyed a strong bond that saw their Anglo-Austro-Dutch armies achieve great victories at Blenheim (1704), Oudenarde (1708) and Malplaquet (1709), while the Second World

War Anglo-American alliance muddled along sufficiently well, sharing resources, expertise and experience to largely mutual benefit.

The resources allocated to a field force will go some way to influencing its approach to battle. Grand strategic decisions will affect army size, the quality of troops, their equipment, and available supporting units, and even the experience and quality of their commander, all of which have an important bearing on an army's operational and tactical options. The main Soviet forces in the initial incursion into Afghanistan in late 1979, for example, comprised four relatively weak motor rifle divisions, including many reservists from Central Asia who the Politburo hoped would be more acceptable to the Afghan population, with little air support and few helicopters. Although always intended as a limited deployment, the poor quality of the force essentially restricted it to garrisoning major cities and lines of communication rather than proactively engaging in combat, giving the Mujahadeen time to grow significantly in strength and reach in the first year of the conflict.[5] It was only when Moscow fed in new troops and sufficient helicopters that Soviet forces could engage the enemy on their own terms. Even then, it was deemed politically expedient to keep total troop numbers down to around 100,000 in order to maintain the illusion that resistance was minimal.[6] Such strategic decisions had a major influence on what could or could not be achieved on the battlefield.

Issues of troop quality and equipment can be as much a matter of long-term planning as wartime decision-making. A government that plans to rely on conscripts and reservists rather than full-time professionals may have no choice but to send less-trained and less-experienced men into combat, for example. Perhaps more importantly, especially since the later nineteenth century, equipment procurement strategies make a major difference to the forces available for a campaign. Although in the past century or so the British army has tended not to stray too far from the crest of the technological wave, procurement policies have at times left its operational forces at a clear disadvantage. The penny-pinching of successive British governments in the fifteen years after the First World War, understandable though it was, meant that the army was relatively poorly prepared and equipped when war broke out in 1939. In a slightly different vein, the failure to anticipate the needs of counterinsurgency operations in Afghanistan and Iraq in the early 2000s left British troops with a dearth of appropriate fighting vehicles, placing limitations on their tactical capacity and contributing to higher than necessary casualties.

Commanders with fewer resources, or with little hope of major reinforcement, will have to take greater risks if they wish to maintain an offensive or act as the aggressor on the battlefield. When successful this could bring great rewards. When unsuccessful, aggression with inadequate force could lead to catastrophe. A case in point is the Battle of Poltava (1709), where Sweden's Charles XII launched his army against a Russian force that outnumbered it three or four to one. Perhaps relying too far on the training, experience, and audacity of his men to win the day as they had at Narva (1700), Charles attacked a series of prepared Russian positions. After significant early progress, casualties mounted and the assault stalled with fatal consequences. Without reserves, and with no reinforcements to fall back on, Charles's army was virtually wiped out, leading to the collapse of Swedish military dominance in northern Europe.

More prudent or cautious generals might decline to take such risks, sitting on the defensive or attempting to divide enemy forces before engaging them in detail. Such attempts to negate an enemy's numerical advantage or to try to preserve an army intact would impose their own operational limitations. Lord Wellington's approach in the early years of the Peninsular War was marked by caution rather than excessive boldness; mindful of the need to preserve Britain's only major field army, especially in the period 1809–11, he engaged in largely defensive battles at Talavera (1809), Bussaco (1810) and Fuentes de Oñoro (1811). In April 1810, the Secretary of War instructed: 'a very considerable degree of alarm exists in this country respecting the safety of the British Army in Portugal ... I could not recommend any attempt at what might be called desperate resistance.'[7] Wellington, with perhaps a degree of irritation at the fretting of politicians, moved to reassure him: 'I am not so desirous, as they imagine, of fighting desperate battles; if I was, I might fight one any day I please.'[8] Only once he had achieved numerical parity and established the fighting credentials of his army did Wellington engage in more consistently offensive actions, winning impressive victories at Salamanca (1812) and Vitoria (1813).

On the other side of the coin, commanders who are plentifully supplied and supported by reserves – or who have state resources at their disposal, like Frederick the Great, Napoleon, or even Charles XII, for all that he did not ultimately use them effectively – can afford to be more profligate, knowing that losses will be replaced. Frederick the Great's battles were unusual in that Prussian casualties were often higher than those of his opponents, even when he was the victor.[9] This is not to suggest that he was uncaring of his men's lives, but simply that he could afford to be more aggressive as he could ensure that losses were replaced. Some commanders certainly were more callous. Napoleon perhaps falls into this category, claiming arrogantly in 1813 that 'a man like me cares little for the lives of a million men', but it is noteworthy that his early battles were characterised by greater tactical innovation and proportionally lower casualties.[10] The bloody slugfests of the later empire coincided with a significant dip in the quality of his army, even as it grew significantly in size. A political willingness to accept casualties certainly absolves a commander of the need to avoid combat, and can encourage foolhardiness. In Italy's 1896 Abyssinian campaign, General Baratieri was encouraged to take the offensive at Adowa after receiving a message from his prime minister to the effect that Italy was ready for any sacrifice. He launched his heavily outnumbered command into an attack on Abyssinian forces and was quickly crushed.

Commanders will also be far more willing to commit hardware and weapons systems to battle if they know that losses can be replaced, as it effectively changes the cost-benefit ratio of using up kit. Often this is a logistical issue, but it can equally be a matter of strategic planning. Ensuring sufficient industrial capacity to supply military need was vital to Allied success in both world wars. American productive power was crucial, but also important were the British shadow factories, or the USSR's Herculean efforts to relocate industrial capacity beyond the Urals – both results of strategic decisions. Production that kept up with or surpassed losses did not guarantee victory, but allowed Allied commanders to accept a higher rate of consumption of machines and munitions, giving them somewhat wider tactical options. Where domestic production is impossible or insufficient, strategic use of allied resources can be vital. Israel's securing of immediate American resupply of arms and equipment to make up for losses during the early days of the Yom Kippur War allowed their Defence Force to release its reserves for a counteroffensive in mid-October 1973, turning the tide of the conflict. The fresh supplies of equipment allowed a more offensive approach that better suited Israeli doctrine, and afforded a degree of battlefield success that would otherwise not have been likely. However, availability of equipment had to be matched by a willingness to commit it to a theatre of operations. The British government's decision not to reinforce air units in France in late May 1940, for instance, hampered evacuation operations at Dunkirk; Admiral Ramsay's report praised the 'gallantry of our outnumbered airmen' but noted with a touch of asperity the navy's 'sense of disappointment and surprise at the seemingly puny efforts to provide air protection'.[11] The irritation of naval personnel was more profound as it was clearly a strategic decision rather than a lack of equipment that left them exposed to German air attack.

Issues of personnel and supply aside, strategic instructions to army commanders probably have the most immediate effect on the battlefield. Operations most usually have a mix of military and political goals, and understanding battle can involve exploring any political motives that pushed the armies to seek combat despite potential military disadvantages. These are as varied as the wars themselves, but common themes include fighting to secure politically or symbolically important territory, supporting an ally, the need for a battle to bolster home morale, or the need to engage troops to claim a more secure place at the negotiating table. Political pressure for results might compel a commander to feel the need to fight despite being outnumbered, underequipped, underprepared, or on unfavourable ground.

Examples of political or strategic influence pushing armies to battle abound. Medieval crusades to the Holy Land were unusually driven by political-ideological motives, but provide good examples of grand-strategic desire to secure territory (from both sides) overriding strictly operational considerations. The Battle of Arsuf (1191) is just one instance, fought because Richard the Lionheart's crusading army had fixed its eye on Jerusalem, and Saladin's Muslim forces were determined to prevent its recapture. In the constant jockeying for territory in the later Middle Ages, sieges of strategic or symbolically important cities could be the cause of decisive clashes, as relieving forces often felt compelled to march to battle; the English defeat at Orléans in 1429, or the destruction of Charles the Bold's Burgundian army at Morat (1476) were both caused by the besiegers' desire to strike a symbolic as well as military blow by capturing their target, although both failed spectacularly. In the eighteenth century it was considered sloppy to fight a battle without an immediate strategic aim, such as the defence or capture of a city, or the expulsion of the enemy from a specific territory. Fighting simply to destroy the enemy's army or even to win the war by a knockout blow 'was usually put some way down' the list of priorities.[12] Even in the world wars, battles were fought for specific strips of territory that perhaps did not objectively merit such attention, most notably in the militarily preposterous German assault on Stalingrad in 1942.

At times, underlying strategic aims can influence combatants' tactical approaches on the battlefield, especially if the enemy army is itself the strategic target. It was usual in medieval power struggles for rival leaders to ride into battle, which made them a tempting target for the enemy. Small groups of men were specially tasked to take out both Montfort at Evesham and the Earl of Warwick at Barnet (1471), although in the latter case Edward IV's intent seems to have been to capture rather than kill. At Bosworth, Richard III made a bid to end the battle (and the war) by charging straight at Henry Tudor and his retainers, only to be surrounded and killed in turn. Richard had not been indulging in idle hyperbole when he reputedly proclaimed, 'this day I will die as a king or win'. In other instances strategic reasoning might make an enemy army itself a target for destruction, beyond the operational consideration of removing an opponent's ability to make war. A handful of battles have aimed at extermination for ideological reasons. The destruction of rebellious or heretical forces could be a strategic goal in itself, as demonstrated by the merciless behaviour of soldiers at the opening of the Albigensian Crusade in southern France (1209). Whether or not the crusading commander Abbot Amalric actually responded to a question of how to distinguish Catholic from heretic with the infamous line 'kill them. The Lord knows his own', it sums up the brutality of his army's approach.

More common, however, are tactics adopted to erode the enemy's will and ability to fight – tactics aiming to achieve longer-term strategic benefits rather than shorter-term operational advantage. Tactics of ambush in guerrilla clashes tend to serve this purpose; picking off enemy soldiers or destroying outposts will generally have little immediate impact on the operational situation, but will hurt the enemy through attrition and loss of morale. On a greater scale, larger battles of attrition are usually fought for their strategic rather than strictly military value. Perhaps the most striking example is Verdun. Realising by 1916 that the greatest threat to Germany was the industrial and maritime strength of Britain combined with the military might of France, German Chief of Staff Erich von Falkenhayn devised a plan to draw the French into a counteroffensive that would shatter either their country's army, or their morale, or both, driving a wedge between the allies and forcing France out of the war. The brutal attrition of the French army seemed to him the best way to achieve this: 'if we succeed in opening the eyes of [France's] people to the fact that in a military sense they have nothing left to hope for ... breaking point would be reached and England's best sword knocked out of her hand.'[13] Launching an offensive at the Verdun salient – surrounded on three sides by German troops – would allow Germany to amass such a preponderance of firepower that France would be obliged either to accept a humiliating defeat, or 'to throw in every man they have. If they do so the forces of France will bleed to death.'[14] Few battles have so openly embraced a grand strategic aim of pure bloodletting and destruction of life as Verdun.

On the other side of things, decisions taken at strategic level might also restrict an army's tactical freedom of action. Counterinsurgency combat is especially prone to troops feeling that they are being kept on a leash, above all when they believe that the tactical initiative has been handed to the insurgents. In the early years of the Algerian War (1954–62), the French army felt constrained by government preference for a system of garrisons and small offensive forces, which they felt placed them at a permanent disadvantage in combat. It was only with the Challe Plan from late 1958 that they began to regain the operational initiative – albeit at the cost of popular support.[15]

Grand strategy will rarely prove the deciding factor in battle, but its importance in shaping combat is clear. Strategic decisions influence the size, organisation, and equipment of field armies; they can dictate the targets and aims of a campaign; and they can lead to pressure to engage in battle or adopt tactics that are not the most appropriate from a purely operational perspective.

A Battle of Five Armies: Marston Moor (1644)

The Battle of Marston Moor, fought near York on 2 July 1644, was one of the most important clashes of the civil wars that wracked the

British Isles in the mid-seventeenth century. In a strategic sense it cost Charles I control of northern England and showed the strength of the Parliamentarian-Scottish Covenanter alliance. Although undermined by defeats in the south of England in the short term, the Parliamentarian-Covenanter victory laid the seeds for later triumphs, not least in giving further valuable battlefield experience to Sir Thomas Fairfax and Oliver Cromwell.

The battle was the product of high politics, alliances and grand strategy. Five distinct armies took part: Parliament's northern army under Lord Fairfax (father of Sir Thomas) and Eastern Association army under the Earl of Manchester joined the Earl of Leven's Scottish Covenanters, while on the royalist side, Prince Rupert's field army linked with the northern forces of the Earl of Newcastle. Remote political influence was exerted on commanders on both sides. Charles I had clear influence over the royalist generals, while the Parliamentarian-Covenanter forces were subject to political control from the Committee of Both Kingdoms, newly formed to coordinate the allied war effort.

The wider strategic situation in 1644 favoured Parliament. Until the previous year Newcastle's northern royalist forces had been holding their own, but the Parliamentary alliance with the Scottish Covenanters tipped the balance. News of a large Scottish army moving south in early 1644 compelled Newcastle to divide his forces. Taking part of his army to screen the Scottish advance, he left significant forces to deal with Fairfax further south. However, this left him too weak to fight the Scots on equal terms, and the defeat of a southern detachment at Selby on 11 April left York under threat. The juncture of Leven and Fairfax's armies pushed Newcastle back into York itself, where he was besieged, although he did dispatch his cavalry under Lord Goring to join the royalist field army under Rupert. Manchester's arrival with his Parliamentarian army, which moved up from Lincolnshire in early June, allowed the complete investment of the city, although an attempted storming through the walls of St Mary's on 3 June failed.

York had been a royalist stronghold throughout the Civil War, but more than that it was the symbolic capital of the north and second city of England. It remained a major population centre, locus for trade, and seat of the second most important archbishop in the Church of England. It held enormous importance to Charles I both strategically and politically, and he had no intention of losing his northern prize. A conference between the king and Rupert in late April had decided that the latter should march north to the relief of the city. Yet the situation in the south left few men to spare, so Rupert marched with a small force via Lancashire in order to recruit more men along the way. The extemporisation of an army from strategic need placed his forces at a mild organisational disadvantage compared to their more established foes. Rupert's appearance in Lancashire in late May nevertheless spooked the Committee of Both Kingdoms, which suggested that troops should be withdrawn from the siege of York and sent over the Pennines to deal with him. Preferring to maintain the siege rather than frittering away their forces in detachments, the allied commanders in the north ignored the committee's messages.

Rupert, on the other hand, was bound rather more closely to follow royal commands. On 14 June he received a missive from Charles urging him to greater action:

> If York be lost, I shall esteem my crown a little less, unless supported by your sudden march to me, and a miraculous conquest in the south, before the effects of the northern powers can be found here; but if you beat the rebel armies of both kingdoms which are before it, then, but otherwise not, I may possibly make a shift to spin out until you come to assist me: wherefore I command and conjure you, by the duty and affection which I know you bear me, that you immediately march all your forces to the relief of York.[16]

The broader strategic motivation behind Rupert's moves is clear. He was to march without further ado, and without pausing to gather or train further forces. Although only explicitly ordered to relieve York, the impetuous Rupert understood Charles's letter to include an injunction to defeat the Parliamentary-Scottish army in battle. He was therefore determined to force a general engagement. As Lord Colepeper warned the king, 'upon this peremptory order he will fight, whatever comes on't'.[17]

The wider strategic situation was crucial in dictating the quality and objectives of Rupert's army in the early summer of 1644, and in drawing together the armies of Leven, Fairfax and Manchester against which he would fight. Rupert arrived in North Yorkshire at the end of June; the allied armies now felt compelled to lift the siege of York and move against him, concentrating their forces towards Long Marston a few miles from the city. Moving his army to the opposite bank of the river Ouse, Rupert made a successful dash for York, where he was able to join up with Newcastle's infantry.[18] According to Simeon Ash, Manchester's chaplain, this disappointed the Parliamentarian troops who had hoped for battle.[19] They would not have long to wait.

In both camps there was now some disagreement amongst senior officials as to what to do next. Rupert's enthusiasm for a battle was not shared by Newcastle, who preferred not to engage the more numerous allied troops. The prince solved the impasse by unilaterally assuming command and ordering Newcastle to join him.[20] On the allied side, there was a disagreement between the Parliamentarian commanders who wished to challenge Rupert's army, and the Scottish contingent who wished to withdraw and screen Rupert from moving south. The disagreement highlighted some of the divisions between the allies, with Ash acerbically commenting that the Scots were in favour of 'retreating to gain (as they alleged) both time and place of more advantage'.[21] Yet it seems that the Parliamentarian commanders were willing to follow the experienced Leven's advice. As they told the Committee of Both Kingdoms following the battle, Rupert's relief of York:

> made us resolve, the next morning to march to Tadcaster, for stopping of his passage southward; and the armies being so far on their way, as the van was within a mile of it, notice was sent to us by our horsemen, who were upon our rear, that the Prince his armie, horse and foote, were advanced the length of Long Marston Moore, and was ready to fall upon them, whereupon we recalled the armie [22]

The movement southward had in fact left the allied army strung out and vulnerable, but Rupert's army was not fully arrayed to take advantage. He had only that morning met Newcastle in person to browbeat him into joining forces for a battle. By the time he was in position in the later afternoon the allied army had reassembled opposite his own.

The armies that drew up at Marston Moor on 2 July 1644 were certainly a product of political and strategic manoeuvring. The Parliamentarian-Covenanter army of approximately 27,000 men was arrayed as an integrated force, with infantry in the centre under Leven and cavalry on the flanks under Cromwell and Thomas Fairfax, but overall command appears still to have been exercised by Leven, Lord Fairfax and Manchester equally. The royalists boasted perhaps 18,000 men of Rupert and Newcastle's armies, now under the firm command of the prince, but many of the troops were relatively recent recruits, and some of Newcastle's more experienced men remained in York.

It is unclear whether the lack of a supreme allied commander delayed their attack on the royalist lines. Lion Watson, the Parliamentary Scoutmaster General, asserted that the forces were fully assembled by five in the afternoon and stood waiting for two hours before the engagement began, although the allied commanders claimed that they were not fully in position before seven.[23] Either way, the delay persuaded Rupert that a battle was unlikely that day and he retired for supper; Newcastle returned to his carriage to smoke. The allied advance therefore caught them unawares.

Grand strategic or political considerations had little effect on the fighting that ensued. As firing became general along the line it was the tactics of unit commanders, and the skill and bravery of their men, that dictated the course of the day. The royalists made good headway for some time, driving in the enemy infantry and throwing back Fairfax's cavalry on the allied right. Yet they were unable to press their advantage beyond the allied baggage train. Wheeling around from the left, Cromwell's cavalry assailed the royalist infantry from the rear, turning the tide of the battle and scattering regiments who had thought victory was within their grasp. As night fell, the royalist army disintegrated. Some men were cut down in the rout; according to Watson, many more fled back to the homes from which they had been recruited only weeks previously.[24] Rupert was able to rally only a small portion of his army as he escaped northwards. With the royalist field army destroyed, York surrendered two weeks later.

Marston Moor was a battle fought for political reasons, in a campaign launched for political-strategic advantage. It showed the benefits of close allied cooperation, and the dangers of divided command. Allied grand strategy afforded the Parliamentarian-Covenanter commanders a stronger and more experienced army than that available to Rupert and Newcastle. The courage and tenacity of royalist troops went some way – but not quite far enough – to overcoming this disadvantage. Ultimately, however, the battle transformed the strategic complexion of the war in the north, and laid the foundations for the even more far-reaching Parliamentarian victories of the following year.

Chapter 3

Leadership

'Leadership is a word and a concept that has been more argued than almost any other I know'
                                                            Dwight Eisenhower.[1]

Leadership in battle is a much broader concept than may first be assumed. Not confined purely to generals and army commanders – although including them – military leadership encompasses those in command of men from an entire army to a small unit. Generally speaking, the number of officers at any specific rank decreases the higher that rank is. The majority of leaders in a battle are therefore the 'middling ranks', those who command small groups of men. In medieval armies, particularly those until the fourteenth century, these middle ranks were usually the lords and knights who had been summoned to form the army. Each would command a group of his supporters, ranging from only one or two, to several hundred. This group would then be placed under the command of another prominent lord, who would command a section of the army known, somewhat confusingly, as a 'battle'. There were usually three battles in a medieval army: one in the centre, with one on each side. These battles would march as units, with the right battle usually forming the vanguard at the front of a marching army, and the left comprising the rearguard.

In more modern armies the range of ranks and command structures has multiplied, and generally become more permanent. Since the seventeenth century, each unit in an army's hierarchy has tended to have a commanding officer of a certain rank, equivalent to others commanding similar-sized units, from junior subalterns at platoon level to generals at brigade or division. To prevent chaos reigning with this array of men of rank, armies tend to adhere to the principle of the chain of command, whereby soldiers should receive orders only from their immediate superior officers. At the lower level, junior officers are assisted by non-commissioned officers (NCOs), who also play a vital role in leading soldiers in battle.

Leadership on these different levels presents different priorities and challenges. As well as the size of a command, the size of the battlefield will also affect the way that leaders go about their business: leaders that can see every aspect of a battle as it unfolds on a small field in front of them will face very different challenges, priorities and objectives to a commander in the context of a large battlefield or campaign.

The qualities of leaders can influence battle in myriad ways. Their background and personality can impact how they are perceived by their troops, and how they understand battle. Their professional knowledge and competence can play a part in great victories or can contribute to devastating defeat. They have the power to inspire their troops, or to provoke fear and opprobrium from those under their command.

In earlier centuries, leadership of military forces in battles often fell to those who carried social as well as military status. In many countries, this included the monarch or his representatives, who themselves were often drawn from the nobility or armigerous society. In some countries, this dependency on the nobility for military command continued well into the modern period. In Russia, for example, although the formal requirement for army officers to be noble had been removed by Peter the Great in the early eighteenth century, during the early months of the First World War the officer corps was nevertheless drawn predominantly from noble families. In more modern armies, however, leadership is usually given based on ability rather than birthright. Leaders' backgrounds are far more varied, and they bring with them to leadership a greater understanding of the men and women under their command.

In medieval contexts, the entirety of the leadership structure for battle was present on the battlefield itself. Everyone from the commander of the army to smaller unit commanders – the equivalent of junior officers – would be present on the field of battle and usually personally involved in the fighting. Examples abound of commanders, even those royal leaders, participating in the press of combat – although common sense would dictate that many leaders preferred a safer position from where they could observe the contest. From King Harold at Hastings, who met a bloody end in battle either at the tip of an arrow or the blade of a sword, to the ill-fated charge of Richard III against Henry Tudor and his retinue at Bosworth, royal commanders could not always command from a position of safety. They were usually very much in the thick of the action.

In modern warfare, battle leadership may be some distance removed from combat – or away from the battlefield altogether. Modern militaries often utilise a system of mission command – the delegation of tactical decisions to those who can carry them out, usually unit commanders with their troops in the combat zone. This initiative requires discipline and professionalism; battle leaders can leave battlefield decisions to their subordinates, knowing that their training and preparedness will equip them to make choices best suited to conditions on the ground. As such, in modern warfare this greater independence of battlefield commanders allows leadership to come from the bottom up, as well as the top down.

Mission command, as an official approach, began in Prussia following defeat against Napoleon in 1806–7, after which Johann David von Scharnhorst, August Graf Neidhardt von Gneisenau and Carl von Clausewitz began a review of Prussian battlefield command. They found that French success was aided as 'the exercise of initiative by junior officers was tolerated ... the result was an operational tempo which left the incredulous Prussians bewildered.'[2] In 1837, the Prussian field service regulation was updated to include the ability of commanders on the battlefield to make tactical decisions. This mission command has continued to develop throughout the twentieth and early twenty-first centuries, aided by advancements in communications technology that allow unit commanders not only to make tactical decisions on the field of battle, but to communicate these to the battle commanders behind the lines.

While junior officers have therefore benefited from growing freedom in decision-making in recent centuries, the overall leadership of a battle has also continued to be of enormous strategic importance. Battle command, or a commander's overall control of the battlefield, remains critical in deployment and operational orders. This also includes an ability to visualise an end goal for military action, and oversee the deployment and action of troops to achieve this goal. This does not mean, of course, that other members of an armed group are not aware of wider targets or objectives, but rather that commanders are best placed to coordinate efforts towards an overall goal.

Battle command demands of leaders a number of decisions. These can include strategic decisions on the aims of a battle; tactical decisions on how a battle will be fought; and practical decisions on the timing and location of combat. One of the Duke of Wellington's greatest victories, at Salamanca in 1812, saw Wellington successfully dictate the course of a battle and help to ensure his forces' victory. Having gained the ridgeline in the early phases of the battle, Wellington defended it against French attack by ordering Portuguese reserves to reinforce his centre, catching the French by surprise. He then moved in person to the weak left flank, directing cannon to shift position so that they were at right angles to the advancing French. Combined pressure of infantry and artillery, along with a charge by British heavy cavalry, shattered the French left, leading to the wider rout of their army. Wellington here demonstrated qualities required in a battlefield leader: awareness of the whole battle, tactical command, and adaptability when faced with new challenges as the conflict unfolded. And Wellington led from the front; although grazed on the thigh by a bullet during the battle, he kept command until the final French retreat. Wellington was also helped at Salamanca by the failure of French leadership. Their commander, Marshal Marmont, was seriously wounded early in the battle and unable to lead, as was his immediate subordinate General Bonet; command instead passed to General Clausel, who was unprepared for command of the whole French force.

Occasionally, battle command also requires leaders to distance themselves from conflict in order to focus on a more long-term goal. In 1944, for example, despite hoping to lead the Allied invasion of Normandy, General Patton was instead publicly assigned command of a purely fictitious Allied force preparing for a non-existent invasion of the Pas-de-Calais, to distract the Germans from the true Allied focus. It was only after the landings in Normandy in June 1944, when the First Army broke through German lines, that Patton commanded the very real Third Army through the breach into northern France.

Some of the key tactical and strategic decisions that leaders are responsible for making in battle relate to the timing, location and adaptation of battle to suit one force at the expense of the other. The timing of battle is, wherever possible, a decision taken by a leader to best suit his or her own forces. It is the ability of the leader to place a battle into a wider strategy that enables them to time that conflict. Staying with the example of D-Day, supreme Allied commander General Eisenhower chose the timing of the Normandy invasion, personally taking the decision on 5 June to launch the invasion the next day despite weather projections not being wholly favourable. 'This is a decision I alone can take,' Eisenhower told his staff. 'After all, that is what I am here for.'[3]

Leadership also imbues battle commanders with the ability to control the information that is given to the soldiers under their command. This can have an important impact on morale: soldiers may be kept in the dark about particularly dangerous operations while they are being planned, or may be disheartened by bad news from elsewhere on a campaign. At Waterloo, for example, Napoleon told the French army that the troops visible on the horizon were French reinforcements there to swell their ranks. The truth, which Napoleon hid from his men for as long as possible, was that the troops were actually Prussians whose arrival ensured the destruction of the French army.

As well as communicating with their own men, leaders tend to be in a position to provide points of contact with the enemy. Their wider battle control allows them insight into strategic goals that can be negotiated with opposing commanders; their leadership allows them to speak for the army under their command. In 1812, the Prussian commander with Napoleon in Russia, General Yorke, negotiated his own armistice with the Russians – much to Napoleon's consternation. It was Yorke's hatred of the French that, once they began to lose, pushed him into changing sides, but his position of authority allowed him to take his army with him. In rather different circumstances, Lord Stanley at Bosworth in 1485 negotiated with both Richard III, his king, and Henry Tudor, his stepson, before deciding to throw his army's support behind the latter.

There are, however, additional less tangible roles that leaders must serve. The most important of these is perhaps ensuring their soldiers' welfare, whether through logistical preparation at higher command or seeing to the physical and mental fitness of troops at a more junior level. This role has certainly developed over time but those who cared for their men often reaped the benefits. Frederick the Great gave careful thought to administration, even pausing at a 'period of dire emergency' in his 1757 campaign to ensure his men were issued with new uniforms.[4] Yet history is replete with examples of slapdash logisticians and aloof subalterns, whose troops frequently paid the price for their lack of attention. In most modern armies this would be unthinkable. A key role of modern platoon commanders is to ensure the well-being of their troops, from helping with personal issues to conducting foot inspections while in the field.

A further key role of battlefield leaders is providing a figurehead for soldiers under their command. Leaders can engender almost mythic status among their troops, particularly those leaders associated with previous military success. It was perhaps no surprise that, given his extensive military victories in the 1790s and 1800s, Napoleon prompted such responses among his men. A French sergeant at the Battle of Leipzig in 1813 remarked that:

> No-one who has not experienced it can have any idea of the enthusiasm that burst forth among the half-starved, exhausted soldiers when the Emperor was there in person. If all were demoralised and he appeared, his presence was like an electric shock. All shouted '*Vive l'Empereur*' and everyone charged blindly into the fire.[5]

The mere presence of a noted military leader on a battlefield can therefore act as a morale boost and crucial inspiration to troops. Some commanders took this further, walking among troops on the eve of battle to reassure tattered nerves and focus men on the task ahead. Although Shakespeare's *Henry V* may use artistic licence when it depicts the king in disguise, wandering among his troops on the eve of Agincourt (1415), other commanders certainly did mingle with their soldiery before combat commenced. Frederick II, for example, walked amongst his men through the Prussian camp on the evening before the Battle of Leuthen (1757), and Napoleon famously mingled with his men in a torchlit procession in the freezing darkness of early December before Austerlitz in 1805.

Leaders can also increase their ability to inspire their troops with words before battle, lifting spirits or allaying fears of impending combat. Pre-battle addresses from army commanders were a feature of some medieval battles: Edward III before Crécy in 1346, and Henry V before Agincourt are two well-known English examples. Speeches before battle may not usually be enough to force men to fight; often, however, they are not attempting to whip up a frenzy of military machismo. Rather, a leader's words before battle usually seek to cut through fear and focus soldiers on the task at hand. Colonel Tim Collins, for instance, achieved worldwide fame with his improvised speech to troops on the eve of the Iraq War. Given to the 1st Battalion, The Royal Irish Regiment battle group on 19 March 2003, hours before British soldiers entered into battle, the speech made headlines around the world as a measured plea for soldiers to focus on their mission. Letters have also been used to serve a similar purpose – especially when modern technology can be used to disseminate the missive to thousands instantaneously. The day before beginning their own assault into Iraq, every member of 1st Marine Division received a letter from General Mattis. 'On your young shoulders rest the hopes of mankind,' he reminded his troops, before encouraging them to focus 'for the mission's sake … carry out your mission and keep your honor clean.'[6] The lasting nature of a letter means that soldiers are able to carry it with them; its impact can therefore persist throughout military action lasting days or weeks.

As well as inspiring others with spoken or written word, commanders can have a crucial impact by leading by example, motivating soldiers to fight and aiding morale. Leaders in medieval battles were sometimes keen to be seen leading from the front. Edward the Black Prince commanded his own battle at Crécy, and Henry V commanded the central battle at Agincourt; both were described as being at the front of their forces, in the press of the fighting. Indeed, the Black Prince's engagement with the enemy was so extreme that, at one stage, other English commanders asked Edward III to dispatch additional soldiers to go to his aid. The king, anxious for his son to win his first significant battle on his own merits, told them to stay put. In early modern warfare army commanders generally began battles to the rear of firing lines but could eventually find themselves forward – either by design or as a result of the push of battle and confusion of combat.[7] This sometimes led leaders into danger: the Duke of Marlborough was almost killed when his horse was shot from under him as he led a cavalry charge at the Battle of Ramillies in 1706, a fate also suffered by Gebhard von Blücher at Ligny in 1815. Gustavus Adolphus, Sweden's great military leader of the Thirty Years' War, was actually killed at Lützen (1632) having led his horsemen into the fray. Many corps, divisional, brigade and regimental commanders were killed leading from the front throughout the age of linear battle.

It is of course not only the actions of an army's highest commanders that can control and inspire men. The actions of junior officers are crucial to delivering exemplars of behaviour and reassurance in battle, from the sangfroid of subalterns at Waterloo to the calm stoicism of junior officers in the First World War. Even at Poitiers in 1356, with the by-now-experienced Black Prince commanding the army, chronicle accounts of the battle are replete with honourable deeds of more junior English leaders. Geoffrey le Baker pauses in his description of Edward's own prowess to remark on the leadership shown by Robert Ufford, Earl of Suffolk, who commanded the rearguard:

> Passing through each line, he encouraged and urged on individuals, saw that fiery young men did not advance against orders, and that the archers did not waste arrows; his courageous spirit added fire to his venerable voice.[8]

The inspirational value of leaders in battle, combined with their martial abilities and command, make them natural targets as the focus for enemy attack. By removing a commander from the field of battle, an enemy removes the person most able – both in terms of command legitimacy and in training – to pose a threat to them. The targeting of well-known and recognisable commanders was a feature of medieval warfare: the wearing of crowns into battle by royalty in particular, provided a visible identifying symbol by which they could be targeted by enemy troops. Henry V had a battle helmet at Agincourt, for example, covered in precious jewels, that provided a useful target for French knights in combat; afterwards, it was found 'broken and depeased in the fielde by the violence of the enimie'.[9] The targeting of officers continued into the modern period – as did, in the early modern period at least, the use of uniform to identify commanders from those they led.

This changed somewhat with the advent of accurate long-range rifles in the nineteenth century. Officers then became targets not simply at close quarters, but from some distance, and so began to disguise their status by removing outward signs of rank. Even other recognitions of officer status, such as being saluted, was at this stage enough to endanger officers' lives.[10] The lack of visual symbols of status had some apparent drawbacks: in the Dunkirk evacuation of 1940, for example, Vice Admiral Ramsay opined that soldiers in the army had no discipline because officers appeared indistinguishable from their men, while the smartly dressed naval officers commanded automatic obedience.[11] This protection of officers' identities on the battlefield nevertheless continues into modern armies, with little to distinguish the combat uniforms of officers from the men and women they command.

As well as inspiring their own troops, however, leaders can intimidate the enemy into defeat – or at the very least into changing their operational behaviour. Such was Napoleon's reputation as a general by 1813 that the powers coalesced against him did not trust even their preponderance of numbers, and came up with a stratagem to withdraw from battle when faced by the emperor and fight only when certain he was not on the field. Their first departure from this so-called Trachenberg Plan led to a crushing defeat at Dresden in August 1813; only when their strength was overwhelming were they finally able to overcome him at Leipzig in October. Nevertheless, Napoleon's reputation remained; even his ultimate conqueror Wellington claimed that 'Napoleon's hat is worth 40,000 men' on the battlefield.

Hammered by the Scots: Stirling Bridge (1297)

Edward I's reputation as 'hammer of the Scots' is a sobriquet he gained in later centuries based on his victories and his harsh handling of Scottish politics north of the border. An event less likely to make headlines south of the border, perhaps, was the Battle of Stirling Bridge: an English defeat at the hands of a Scottish army considerably smaller, poorly armed and inexperienced in set-piece battles.

It is perhaps in the absence of Edward from the battlefield that Stirling Bridge allows an in-depth study of the commanders that did fight that day, no longer able to hide in Edward's shadow. Blame for the English defeat has been laid by historians at the feet of their commanders, in particular John de Warenne, Earl of Surrey, and Hugh de Cressingham. Similarly, the victory of the Scots has been credited to their commanders: Andrew Moray, a Scottish nobleman, and a certain William Wallace. Stirling Bridge therefore affords a valuable opportunity to explore the importance of leadership in the outcome of battles, as much by demonstrations of effective leadership as examples of poor commanders.

The first crucial influence of leadership on Stirling Bridge has to be the absence of the leader that the English were ostensibly fighting for: Edward I himself. The king was an experienced and effective military commander, and had he been present on the campaign that culminated at Stirling Bridge, it seems likely that some of the blunders and confusions of the English forces would not have occurred. Edward, however, was fighting in Flanders in 1297 when news arrived that the Scots were threatening rebellion and even outright war.

Wily military strategist that he was, Edward had already put in place a command structure able to address any uprisings in Scotland decisively, without the need for his personal leadership, before his departure to Flanders. It seems somewhat likely that Edward, keen to beat the French and prove himself a Continental commander, had abandoned Scotland at this juncture to men whom he trusted to manage the business of governing the country in his absence. In doing so, Edward appears to have underestimated the Scottish forces that were rising against him. He certainly underestimated their leaders, men more than capable of uniting and commanding a sizeable Scottish force in military manoeuvres and campaigns of their own.

Nevertheless, the men whom Edward placed in charge of Scotland were highly experienced, and Edward clearly believed them capable. John de Warenne, sixth Earl of Surrey, commanded the English force at Stirling Bridge. Surrey was sixty-six years old by the time he led the English contingent north from Berwick towards the Scottish host waiting for them at Stirling. Despite his advancing years, Surrey was an experienced and seasoned warrior. During his long military career, he had fought at the battles of Lewes, Evesham and Chesterfield in 1264–6, and Dunbar in 1296, as well as fighting on Edward's Welsh campaigns in 1277, 1282 and 1283. Given his experience, Edward had created Surrey 'Warden of the Kingdom and Land of Scotland' in 1296, effectively meaning that Edward handed the country north of the border to Surrey so that he could, guilt-free, go off and fight the French.

Surrey was not as overjoyed as might have been expected from an important and politically influential position, and after a few months in position as Warden he returned to England, claiming that the cold, wet Scottish climate was bad for his health. As we will see, poor health may well have impacted on Surrey's effectiveness as a leader at Stirling Bridge, so perhaps his comment on his reasons for leaving Scotland does hold some weight.

One of Surrey's key advisors in his position as Warden of Scotland was Hugh de Cressingham, a member of the Exchequer and part of the household of Queen Eleanor. He was appointed Treasurer of the English administration in Scotland in 1296, and seems to have been eager from the outset to closely control the purse strings of Surrey's wardenship. Certainly, by the Stirling Bridge campaign in 1297, he was so fiscally controlling that it was his wish to end the campaign with a swift victory, rather than Surrey's to delay the battle until a more favourable position could be found, that ultimately led to English defeat. Cressingham was given command of the English vanguard at Stirling Bridge, despite his very limited military experience.

As with all military commanders, the impact of leadership on Stirling Bridge began days, weeks or even months before the battle itself. The Scottish commanders Wallace and Moray had begun recruiting men to their cause in the preceding months and years. Andrew Moray, son and heir of a local lord, had fought and been captured at Dunbar in 1296. However, he had somehow managed to escape and began raising rebellion in spring 1297. By August of that year, several northern towns and castles had fallen into his hands.

William Wallace was completely unknown until he incited rebellion in 1297; there is a brief mention of a 'William le Waleys, thief' in a court roll from 1296, but no concrete evidence to suggest that this was the same man who led the Scots at Stirling Bridge. He was, most likely, a younger son of Alan Wallace of Ayrshire, which also coincides with the locale of William Wallace's early rising.[12] Despite his uncertain background, Wallace was clearly imbued with a sense of effective leadership. Walter of Guisborough wrote that he 'united the people' of Scotland against their enemies.[13]

In response to the risings of Wallace and Moray, who were soon to unite into one force of approximately 6,000 light infantrymen under their dual leadership, Surrey was forced to return to Scotland with an English host of approximately 7,000 men, including at least 300 heavy cavalry. English numbers were supplemented by a handful of Scottish combatants, including Malcolm, Earl of Lennox, and James Stewart, the High Steward of Scotland. They left Berwick in late August, joined at this point by Cressingham. The primary objective of the English force was to relieve Dundee; the city remained in English hands but was becoming an isolated island in the midst of lands taken or claimed by Wallace, Moray and their supporters. In order to reach Dundee, however, Surrey and Cressingham would be forced to take their army over Stirling Bridge – the most easterly crossing place of the formidable Forth.

Here we see the Scottish commanders already one step ahead of their English opponents. Moray and Wallace took their forces to Stirling Bridge and arrived slightly ahead of the English host. They arrayed their troops to the north of the bridge, choosing as their own command post the Abbey Craig, an area of high ground with a clear view of the bridge and likely battlefield – as well as the English force's arrival.

From this strategically advantageous position, the Scottish commanders watched the English attempt to cross the bridge twice, each time being called back as the English commanders appeared to prevaricate. Quite why Surrey did not commit to a clear strategy from his arrival at Stirling Bridge is unclear, although it is likely that he was at odds with Cressingham. The Treasurer, conscious of the cost of maintaining a full English host in Scotland for any longer than necessary, was eager to attack the Scots immediately and pushed the council of war into agreeing to a swift attack. The experienced and more tactically astute Surrey would have been more cautious. The bridge across the Forth would force them to cross in pairs, effectively nullifying their numerical advantage if the Scots attacked before the entire English force could cross. Another English commander highlighted this threat, and offered to take an English contingent over a nearby ford and encircle the Scots. However, such was Cressingham's haste to attack that the council supported his decision and the orders were given. Cressingham himself commanded the English vanguard that finally, on the third attempt, crossed the bridge and began forming up on the northern bank.

Of course, the inevitable ensued. Wallace and Moray allowed a small portion of the English army to cross the bridge – many of Cressingham's vanguard – before they attacked. The Scots also seized the bridgehead, cutting off the English vanguard from any hope of support from the remainder of their army on the southern bank. The English who had already crossed, including Cressingham, were surrounded and slaughtered. Seeing the disaster unfold before him, Surrey ordered the bridge destroyed so that the Scots could not give chase to the main cohort of the English army. Surrey then turned around and led the army back southwards.

One of the continuing puzzles of Stirling Bridge is why a military man as experienced as Surrey would have allowed such a haphazard, disorganised attack. Why not delay, and wait to see how the Scots reacted to the English arrival? Or take up the commander's offer to explore an encirclement of the Scottish host via the ford, only two miles further west? The reason for Surrey's mistakes is given in contemporary chronicles as his laying in bed during the day, effectively sleeping through his own war council and waking only to give the nod to the battle plan already, presumably, having been agreed by the other commanders. It seems difficult to consider that this apparent laziness would come from a man who, despite his advancing years, had played an active role in almost a dozen other battles and campaigns during four decades of military experience, including seeing active fighting only the previous year at Dunbar.

It seems more likely that Surrey was, in fact, ill – as he had alluded to the previous year – which would explain why he was unable to sit in his own campaign's war council and had to instead simply agree to a plan hatched by the less-experienced Cressingham and others. It was this absentee leadership – an echo of the absence of Edward himself – that effectively crippled the English at the same moment as Scottish leadership was cohesive, inspirational and effective.

Stirling Bridge is therefore understood not only as a battle heavily determined by its military leaders on both sides, but also by the absence of a military leader whose presence may well have influenced the outcome of the battle. In the end, neither Surrey nor Cressingham were as inspiring, capable or coordinated as their Scottish counterparts Moray and Wallace. Their leadership left the English forces confused and indecisive, whereas the leadership of the Scots commanders both inspired and effectively organised their men into a decisive victory.

Lions Led by Donkeys? The Somme (1916)

The first of July 1916 has gone down in myth as one of the greatest failures of generalship in British military history. Obeying orders passed down from 'chateau generals', some thirteen British divisions attacked entrenched and fortified German positions along a fifteen-mile front roughly straddling the Albert-Bapaume road, near the gently meandering river Somme. The British infantry, many belonging to Kitchener's 'New Army', were told to advance at walking pace in good order towards the German positions that would, they were assured, have been destroyed by a week-long preliminary artillery bombardment. The men of the first waves were to secure their objectives in the German first and second lines, advancing behind the continuing artillery barrage that would disrupt enemy counterattacks. Reinforcements were scheduled to consolidate the gains, with cavalry waiting in the wings to exploit the expected breakthrough.[14] All had been prepared by the general staff for a successful and potentially war-changing offensive.

The reality was, of course, very different. Far from finding the enemy positions destroyed, advancing troops emerged from their trenches into a hail of machine-gun, rifle and artillery fire. Some units were virtually wiped out. The 1st Newfoundland Regiment, advancing at Beaumont-Hamel, lost seven eighths of its strength, including all of its officers; the 103rd (Tyneside Irish) Brigade in the 34th Division, ordered to advance in open country from the British second line rather than moving up through the support trenches, lost over 2,000 casualties, including the brigadier and three of four battalion commanders, one of whom was killed. By the end of that sultry summer's day, nearly 58,000 men of the British army lay dead, dying or wounded on the fields of northern France, one third of whom would be recorded killed in action.

This example of the Battle of Albert, as the first day of the Somme is officially known, was a human tragedy, and it is one that is frequently invoked in support of the 'lions led by donkeys' thesis of First World War generalship. The Battle of the Somme is certainly instructive of many of the key features of leadership in modern warfare.[15] Like almost all First World War battles, the role of the general was far removed from that undertaken by Napoleon a century earlier. By 1916, the sheer size of the battlefield meant that it was impossible for any single man to see more than a fraction of the combat. As such, the role of the general officer at army, corps and even divisional level was no longer to direct affairs by responding rapidly to events, or to inspire his men in action, but to plan, prepare and ensure that contingencies were provided for. Some brigade and divisional commanders were able to call off second-wave attacks on 1 July, especially where casualties were highest and the first attacks failed to get beyond no man's land, but in most instances they lacked a clear picture of developments beyond the front line, and simply sent in reinforcements according to the preordained schedule. The extreme difficulty of advancing telephone communications beyond no man's land meant that generals frequently remained without news for hours after battle was joined; direction of the action and responses to circumstance therefore tended to fall to officers at battalion or even company level.

The Somme put these evolving command networks through the sternest of tests, and showed their inadequacies. The BEF had expanded almost beyond recognition from the professional force of 1914, and many of the officers at all levels were inexperienced at their new level of command. The commander-in-chief himself, Douglas Haig, had been a lieutenant general and corps commander at the start of the war. Most of the divisional commanders had been recently promoted or in some cases transferred from non-combat arms; in the New Army divisions that made up a large part of the British forces, professional officers and NCOs were few and far between.

The general staff's planning for the offensive was nevertheless, in some regards, quite meticulous. Although Haig hoped for a major breakthrough, General Sir Henry Rawlinson, commander of the Fourth Army, insisted on thorough planning and more limited initial objectives. In recognition of the difficulties of command and control, detailed schemes were drawn up dictating the objectives of the thirteen attacking divisions, and schedules of reinforcements were drafted to ensure that the success of the first waves could be maintained. This was a departure, and perhaps an improvement, on previous practice. The offensive was also preceded by a week-long artillery bombardment intended to obliterate German forward defences and second lines, for which a staggering 1.7 million shells were procured.

The fact that these detailed objectives and optimistic hopes were not fulfilled highlights one of the failures of leadership at the Somme. For while the scale of the preparatory bombardment was truly terrifying for the German defenders, it did little physical damage to the deep concrete bunkers in which the men sheltered. The shrapnel shells employed to cut the wire also had little effect. Yet these facts were either not filtered through to army headquarters – certainly a failure of intelligence gathering – or were roundly ignored. John Keegan accused the general staff of a 'complacent misapprehension' of the situation.[16] Part of the reason for this may have been political; a British offensive was desperately needed to relieve pressure on the French line at Verdun, and no significant delay could be brooked. Part may have been a simple inability to conceive of anything surviving such an unprecedented (for the British army) bombardment.

An accusation frequently levelled at generals on the Somme was that they were too detached from the front line to know what was really going on. The charge of detachment is somewhat justified, but this was largely driven by the necessities of command responsibilities rather than any collective disinclination to get their hands dirty. Whereas Napoleonic soldiers might have expected a general to set an example on the battlefield, men at the Somme did not. A general at headquarters could do his job; a general near the trenches was little more than a hindrance. Moreover, the British army had lost several experienced generals killed in action already in the war, and could scarce afford to sacrifice a few more to fruitless expeditions up to the line while bullets were flying. Some nevertheless went up to the front. The 34th Division's commander, for example, Major General Ingouville-Williams, was seen on 1 July acting as a stretcher-bearer, evacuating some of the casualties that his disastrous decision had caused; he would be killed three weeks later by artillery when examining the terrain over which his troops were scheduled to advance.

The general officer's role at the Somme was nevertheless mostly limited to broader considerations of strategy, logistics and planning. Leadership of men into battle devolved to more junior officers, the quality of whom varied enormously in the British army at the Somme. Until the huge casualties of 1916, the main qualification to become an officer in the 'new' battalions was attendance at a suitable public school. These gentlemen, used to civilian leadership of men accustomed to deference, could make good officers. Some took the time to know their men, took steps to ensure their welfare off the battlefield, and took their limited training seriously. Others were aloof, uninterested in their men, and unfamiliar with their new profession. Yet on the whole, it seems that soldiers trusted and were willing to follow their officers into combat. The junior officers on the first day of the Somme also had few tactical decisions to make, as their advance in waves had been dictated by corps and army command. Their primary duty was to lead their men into action; for all their lack of training and experience, the public-school officers had been brought up on tales of Waterloo, and were conditioned to believe that above all an officer should lead by example.

There were a great many examples set on 1 July 1916, and the battalion officers of the British army paid a high price indeed. In one famous episode, Captain Wilfred Nevill of the 8th Battalion, East Surrey Regiment encouraged his men to charge German positions at Montauban by booting a pair of footballs ahead of the advance; Nevill was killed up against the German wire, but his men (and the footballs) made it to their first objectives. Up and down the line company officers and subalterns put themselves at the forefront of the charge and, if less inventive than Nevill, showed similar courage in inspiring their men to the attack.

Once the enemy front line was gained, leadership once more became crucial. Even where German defences had been thinned by the bombardment, the infantry tended to arrive disorganised and in small groups and, unless quickly put into some order, were highly vulnerable to counterattack. In several instances where resistance was fiercest, officers had to be sent from reserve cadres to organise the front lines, as all of those in the initial advance had become casualties.[17] The officers who commanded these smaller groups at their objectives often did so isolated from the wider battle. German counter-barrages into no man's land interdicted reinforcements or communication with higher command, and the nature of the fighting meant that lateral observation of the battlefield was severely limited. The huge offensive on a fifteen-mile front therefore degenerated into a series of small-unit clashes, in which leadership frequently fell to junior officers or NCOs. Cut off from orders, reinforcement and resupply, unable to recall their own artillery barrage to clear further enemy strongpoints, and already suffering from heavy casualties, these officers faced the unenviable choice of pressing on according to pre-battle orders, or consolidating their position and awaiting further instruction. Frequently they chose to dig in. The leaders at the front acted with immense courage and no little initiative, but they still expected to be part of a chain of command and to receive new orders that reflected the realities of the offensive. That such orders were not forthcoming in any timely fashion was another of the failures of the Somme.

The first day of the Somme reflects an army's leadership in continued transition. General officers at army and corps level concerned themselves mostly with strategy, planning and setting the pieces in place for a coordinated offensive between infantry, artillery and support services.

Their direction of combat once the machine guns rattled into action was minimal. Increasingly, however, leaders at divisional and brigade level were also reduced to waiting for news from the front and were unable to respond with any rapidity to events. Battalion and junior officers bore the burden of immediate command under fire, and often did so in effective isolation from the rest of the battle around them. Yet this essential devolution of responsibility was not matched by any change in command culture; the instinct to follow pre-set orders, or to seek further instruction from higher up the chain of command once plans fell into disarray, remained strong. The severe difficulty of communication between front and rear lines once the offensive was underway contributed to a loss of momentum in the offensive. Also strong was the culture of leaders setting a physical example for their men, with company officers at the Somme showing immense courage in leading from the front and sustaining commensurately crippling casualties.

Chapter 4

Conditions of Landscape: Climate, Weather and Terrain

'I have trained the officers to judge the terrain and occupy it advantageously'
Frederick the Great.[1]

While issues of social organisation, political influence and leadership inform the context of a battle and can be crucial to its outcome, the physical landscape and conditions of combat play a key role in its course and conclusion. The climate, weather and terrain of a battle have a significant impact on military planning and operations, from placing physical limits on soldiers' endurance to conferring strategic advantage or disadvantage. While terrain and extreme weather events have generally been taken into account when identifying the causes of battlefield victory or defeat, the wider impact of the interplay between climate, weather and terrain on all combat has often been overlooked.

Climate and weather are absolutely crucial to setting the parameters for a battle. Climate here is understood in a broad sense, and includes average weather patterns, temperature, precipitation and humidity; long-term conditions such as drought or dustbowl; the effect of the seasons, hours of daylight, phases of the moon, or tides; and any other facets of the natural environment that might impact on a battle. This might include the availability of foodstuffs, fresh water, local flora and fauna (the unfortunate intervention of a swarm of irate bees at the Battle of Tanga in 1914 springs to mind), or air quality.

Even in such a small cockpit of conflict as Europe there are enormous climatic variations, from the baking heat of a Mediterranean summer to the bitter freezes of a Baltic winter – and the variation grows when European armies expand out of the continent's confines. For much of the continent the weather is neither wholly reliable nor particularly predictable; while extreme weather events are relatively rare, a mild winter thaw can be as likely as a cold mid-summer deluge. Such variable climate and weather can have an enormous impact on battle, from affecting the practical ability to fight, morale and ability to adapt to changing circumstances of combat of individual soldiers, to influencing weapons systems, army movement, supply and communications.

The most recognisable way that weather influences battle is by impacting the ability of soldiers to move, operate or wield weapons, and withstand the rigours of combat. In the latter instance, prevailing temperatures and conditions can pose serious challenges to a soldier's effectiveness. Although it is by no means always the case, exhausted soldiers tend to struggle to maintain military efficiency or cohesion in the face of the enemy. Fighting in cold weather – or consistent exposure to water – will rob men of stamina and will impair their physical and mental faculties. Although major examples such as Napoleon's retreat from Moscow in 1812 or the destruction of Paulus's command at Stalingrad in 1942–3 give ample proof of the destructive force of extreme cold, more modest dips in temperature also have great importance for men in battle. A 2017 study focusing on soldiers in the Norwegian Arctic suggested that, during cold-weather operations, combatants expend 10–40 per cent more energy than in temperate operations, primarily due to the additional weight they must carry in clothing and equipment, and the effort of walking, skiing and working in snow and treacherous terrain.[2] Not only does this additional energy expenditure accelerate the development of fatigue, but it can also lead to thermal strain and a decline in core temperature that can make physical movement more difficult. It can also, of course, reduce temperatures in the body's extremities, especially when digits are at rest or stop moving, increasing susceptibility to frostbite or cold trauma and reducing their dexterity and tactile sensation – including their ability to handle a weapon.

While cold and other weather conditions can be overcome in part through clothing or equipment, there is a constant balance to be struck between countering the effects of severe weather and contributing to them getting worse. Carrying heavy coats may protect the body from the worst effects of frostbite, but the additional weight would mean that combatants need more energy to complete the same tasks as effectively. Furthermore, some fighting equipment makes the impact of cold considerably worse. Armour chilled and drew heat from the body, even through layers of padding, meaning that those who fought at armoured battles in frozen conditions such as Lake Peipus (1242) or Towton (1461) would have had to contend with protection that may have prevented fatal injury, but actively made combat more physically exhausting.

Extreme heat carries similar dangers, draining energy rapidly and leading to physical exhaustion. The Battle of Hattin in 1187 offers an example of the potentially disastrous impact on combatants. Marching across a hot, arid plain to relieve the besieged city of Tiberius from Saladin's army, a force of 20,000 European crusaders ran out of water, as they had not been able to plan a route that would incorporate a fresh supply. Their plight worsened overnight when they still had no water, and their heat exhaustion and dehydration – exacerbated by heavy armour – was a crucial aspect in their defeat in the hills surrounding the village of Hattin, where Saladin's army had been able to drink and refresh themselves. In a more recent example, the aridity of the landscape around Gallipoli contributed to the high levels of British casualties in 1915, and helped to reduce the campaign to an impotent stalemate.

The debilitating impacts of extreme heat and cold are still problematic in modern conflict zones. During the Battle of the Bulge (1944–5), many wounded Americans froze to death before they could be evacuated, and thousands of GIs were treated for cases of frostbite and trench foot. Even in the twenty-first century, extreme weather cannot be fully compensated for. In US manoeuvres near Najaf in Iraq (2004), dozens of combatants were treated for the effects of heat stroke in the burning sun. The timing of combat operations can serve to alleviate some of the impact of climate and inclement weather – the initial invasion of Iraq in March 2003 allowed troops to avoid major combat in the hottest months, for example – and because of this, operations can be brought forward or delayed to avoid poor conditions. However, complete removal of weather as a risk factor is rarely possible; in Iraq, several American service personnel died of heatstroke and other related problems.

Weather will also have an effect on morale, which can be an important influence on the battlefield. The effect is normally one of simple creature comfort; miserable conditions make for miserable soldiers. Historically, the time of year has been an important factor in combatants' morale; there is evidence from the Middle Ages to the French Revolution to suggest that the enthusiasm of levies for military adventures wanes dramatically when the harvest needs gathering, which could have a key impact on the quality and quantity of troops available.[3] In some cases levies were dismissed entirely, such was the importance of the harvest to both the army and civil society; before Hastings, King Harold was compelled to release his fyrd, having a significant effect on the strength of his forces on the battlefield.[4]

Weather and climate also impact on the effectiveness of weapons and military technology. Most hand-to-hand weapons will operate with few problems in all but the most extreme of conditions, but the impact of weather on projectile weapons can have an important influence on the battlefield. Modern weapons with more moving parts are particularly susceptible to failure in extreme conditions of wet, heat or cold. In the latter case, in addition to frozen fingers losing dexterity and function, frozen weapons can malfunction or fail altogether. When a percussive weapon is fired at sub-zero temperatures, the barrel will rapidly heat and risk breakage, while 'sweating' weapons – those taken from cold exterior conditions to warm shelters – will freeze when taken back out into the cold, resulting in their internal mechanisms freezing together and failing. In violently cold conditions such as those faced by the German army in the USSR in winter 1941, lubricants and gun oil can freeze, leading to jams and stoppages. The negative impacts of cold do not only affect projectile weapons. At Bolimov on the Eastern Front (January 1915), German forces deployed shells loaded with xylyl bromide, but due to the cold weather the gas froze, preventing it from being fully effective. The early use of gas was in fact particularly susceptible to weather conditions. Before the perfection of artillery delivery systems, the use of gas relied on wind, which had disastrous effects for the British army at Loos in September 1915, when dozens of tons of chlorine gas blew back towards their own lines.

Projectile weapons have also proved susceptible to rain and damp conditions, especially throughout the early modern period due to the impact of moisture on black powder. Black powder, first famously used in European battle in the English cannon at Crécy in 1346, must be kept dry in order to ignite, and heavy rain could make reloading a difficult process. By the early eighteenth century, when muskets had become almost universal, rain could be expected to affect both armies equally, although those with a greater tactical reliance on firepower might be expected to struggle more. It was only with the advent of the percussion cap in the early nineteenth century that gunpowder weapons could reliably be used in heavy weather, and not until the needle guns and cartridge rifles of the later nineteenth century that troops could be confident of their weapons in wet and dry conditions.

While weather and conditions can clearly be inhibitors of weaponry, they can have a role in actively enhancing weapon performance. Atmospheric conditions can affect the range and accuracy of firearms, sometimes to their advantage. Projectiles shot with the wind are naturally at an advantage, benefitting from additional force. At Towton, for example, the Yorkist army benefited significantly from a tailwind that allowed them to shoot with relative impunity at the Lancastrian forces, whose return volleys into the wind did not have the range to reach their targets.

This example also shows that weather is not always a levelling factor, and that it does not always affect both sides exactly equally. Indeed, in some cases, especially where there is a technological differential, weather can significantly benefit one force over another. Such was the case at Crécy, where a heavy rainstorm fell on the opposing armies just before combat commenced. Contemporary accounts agree that when battle was joined the Genoese crossbowmen in the service of France proved unable to shoot their bolts into the English lines. The traditional interpretation has been that the crossbow strings had become saturated in the wet, and thus stretched, lacking the tension to project the bolts; English longbowmen did not face this problem as they carried their weapons unstrung. More recently, however, Kelly DeVries argued that the Genoese used a bowstring protected by a leather wrap – shielding the crossbows from the rain. Instead, DeVries believes that the rain and mud meant that the Genoese were unable to step into the stirrup required to reload their crossbows, leaving them unable to shoot at the English.[5] Whichever explanation is used, it is evident that the weather conditions proved decisive in turning the tide of the battle in England's favour before the two armies had actually clashed.

In the twentieth century, weather and conditions also became vital to the availability and effectiveness of air support. These conditions do not have to be over the battlefield; ice, fog, storms or high wind over airfields can prevent aircraft from taking off in the first place, and can make the return treacherous for those that do become airborne. In the Battle of the Bulge, for example, heavy snowfall and high winds kept Allied air support grounded, allowing the German army to advance without aerial harassment – although the poor road conditions did serve to hamper and slow their movements. Even modern jet aircraft require the cooperation of the elements. In October 1995, NATO air strikes as part of Operation Deny Flight during the Kosovan conflict were frustrated due to poor weather conditions.

One of the chief reasons for the negative impact of weather on air manoeuvres is the detrimental effect on visibility. Low cloud or fog over targets will reduce the effectiveness of air support, especially where precision is required. Even modern radar systems and laser-guided munitions can struggle in certain conditions, and any study of battle involving air units must take into account the three-dimensional variables of visibility. This is of course also the case for ground operations, with the lack of visibility through rain, snow or fog a significant factor in being able to site and aim weapons. Such was the case in the Battle of the Bulge, when the chilled climate of the Ardennes meant that visibility was almost reduced to zero. Moreover, ground battles in the age of gunpowder frequently became obscured by the clouds of smoke emitted by the massed firearms, which would tend to linger stubbornly over the field unless dispersed by a stiff breeze. Smoke from grass fires started by explosives could also add to the man-made fog of war, with examples from Talavera (1809) to D-Day attesting to its influence in reducing battlefield visibility.

The most common impediment to visibility is of course darkness. The onset of night has tended to prove a limiting factor in combat, with generals often unwilling to commit to large-scale fighting in the dark. In set-piece battles before the twentieth century, nightfall would frequently bring fighting to a close, allowing the bested army to slip away. Should the outcome remain in the balance, fighting would often die down for the night as troops rested and waited to renew the struggle on the morrow. Occasionally, overnight manoeuvres were attempted, although with very mixed success. The Jacobite army spent the night before Culloden (1746) marching fruitlessly on an attempted raid on the Duke of Cumberland's encampment, serving only to exhaust themselves and contributing to their defeat the next day. Daylight in general can influence battles in other ways. German gunners on the Western Front would usually be most active in the early morning, for example, because it gave them the best light for practising their art.

A lack of visibility leads to myriad problems on a battlefield. It affects everything from command-and-control to the ability of individual units to engage the enemy. Friendly fire incidents are most common when visibility is poor, as are incidents where enemy units move to close range undetected because they are assumed to be friendly. Poor visibility can also lead to ill-directed attacks or manoeuvres, with sometimes devastating consequences. At Eylau in 1807, a sudden snowstorm blowing in the face of the advancing French led Marshal Augereau's corps to drift mistakenly into the killing zone of the massed Russian artillery, suffering horrific casualties at point-blank range. Their plight was exacerbated by the 'friendly' fire of their own gunners, who could not recognise their own men through the snowstorm.

Alongside visibility, climate and weather can have a deadening effect on the acoustics of battle, making it difficult for supporting forces to follow the adage of 'marching to the sound of the guns'. Staying with the example of Eylau, although Marshal Ney was within marching distance of the battlefield, the heavy snow muffled the sound of gunfire, and he was completely unaware of events until a messenger reached him once the battle was well underway. Ney's arrival won Napoleon the battle – but only just; snow had almost cost Napoleon his victory. A similar situation had also occurred the previous year at the Battle of Jena-Auerstädt (1806), when the heavy air had apparently prevented Marshal Bernadotte from hearing the guns of Napoleon's army, and he had thus not joined the fray.

While lack of visibility or poor acoustics can be a clear hindrance on the battlefield, it can also be turned to an army's advantage. Conditions and climate in general provide the opportunity for adaptive tactics that incorporate weather events into a plan of battle. An obvious way to do this is to use weather or climatic conditions to disguise troop movements or to hide portions of a military force. This was used with particular effectiveness at Towton, when the Duke of Norfolk and his 5,000 men remained hidden by the blizzard conditions until they were almost upon the Lancastrian forces. The manoeuvring of troops behind screens of smoke or fog is a rough but effective means of gaining tactical advantage.

Movement on the battlefield in general can be heavily affected by climatic conditions, with the changing seasons and weather altering landscapes from pleasant plains to baking dustbowls, impassable quagmires, or frozen wastes. In farmland, the time of year will dictate whether agricultural land is ploughed or fallow, full of crops or barren, which will go some way to changing the underfoot conditions of the terrain. Reduced mobility due to conditions could prove fatal in stalling attacks, preventing reinforcements, or cutting troops off from support services. At Agincourt (1415), the cloying mud caused by torrential rain meant that the French cavalry became a sitting target for the English bowmen; the ubiquitous mud of Passchendaele caused by unseasonable and unceasing rain in the late summer of 1917 not only prevented men on the front lines from advancing effectively, but impeded the siting of artillery and made the task of ferrying supplies to the front lines fraught with danger. Private S.C. Lang recalled:

> It was raining and misty everywhere and we had to travel on duckboard tracks ... The mud dominated everything in that attack ... We could have gone on and on and on, there was nothing to stop us except a sea of mud through which no gun could possibly be dragged.[6]

Napoleon notoriously had to delay the start of the Battle of Waterloo until late morning because mud from the previous day's storm prevented his troops and guns from moving into position – a delay that arguably cost him the battle. The difficulties of movement are often even more marked when weather leads to unusual conditions of terrain: the Battle of the Ice at Lake Peipus was fought on an ice-covered lake, causing enormous difficulties for the combatants in simply keeping their footing.

Such conditions would not affect all combatants equally. Troops on the defensive tend to be more static and therefore less affected by conditions that render movement difficult – although the inability to manoeuvre can also lead to an army being caught in an unfavourable position and forced into battle. On the battlefield, heavier units such as cavalry or later artillery tend to find movement in poor conditions more difficult than individual foot soldiers.

Along with weather or season, the time of month can be important, especially in night fighting or amphibious operations. Moon cycles could have a significant impact on the viability of night-time manoeuvres, and the impact of tide has been crucial in waterborne operations from General

Wolfe's assault on Quebec in 1759 to the D-Day landings of 1944. In the former, the combination of tide, moon and direction of moonlight have been found to have had a critical impact on the success of Wolfe's bold (some say foolhardy) strategy, and according to one interpretation may explain Wolfe's inactivity in the days leading up to the attack, as the night of 12/13 September was the only one in the entire year when such perfect conditions would exist.[7] On D-Day, the Allies required a low tide just before sunrise to be accompanied by a full moon – conditions that were rarely available. Moreover, they required good weather for the sea crossing, enough daylight to secure a beachhead, and a long enough post-landing campaigning season to make significant headway before the onset of winter; all of which pointed to June. The success of the Allied strategy was therefore very much dependent on climatological conditions coming together on 5, 6 and 7 June 1944. However, even here there were problems. Poor weather caused the postponement of operations from 5 to 6 June. The rapidly rising tide on the Normandy coast also created difficulties; the destruction of German beach obstacles was not complete by the time the tide covered them, and the troops on the landing craft often disembarked into deeper water than they were expecting, leading to several losses in the assault parties.

Weather could also have an important impact on the movement of supplies, infrastructural support, and reinforcements for battle. The seasons heavily influence the abundance or scarcity of locally available food, forage and water, which before the twentieth century tended to be of prime importance to armies in the field. Especially cold or hot weather leads to a dearth of supplies; particularly in the medieval and early modern periods, this would mean that supplies were running low and more time on military campaign would have to be spent gathering food rather than seeking out one's enemy. Severe weather in the modern period can detrimentally affect the ability of supplies to reach combatants – thick snow, high winds or conversely boiling temperatures can all hamper relief efforts.

Although it can have an implication on an army's ability to effectively fight a battle, weather can be overcome by meticulous planning, logistical support, and careful use of terrain. Extreme weather can also of course be avoided by restricting campaigning seasons to more temperate times of year. When weather affects both sides in battle equally, it is often the side who best overcomes these challenges – often by maximising the terrain available – that is able to establish an advantage.

The influence of terrain on battle has long been recognised: Carl von Clausewitz even claimed that it has a 'decisive influence on the engagement, both as to its course and to its planning and its exploitation'.[8] The primary reason for terrain's apparent influence on battle is that it can act as a force multiplier. This effectively means that it allows an army to gain greater results with fewer resources. That effect can of course be achieved in other ways – through weaponry or training, for example – but terrain provides a free and widely accessible resource that requires only intelligent generalship to exploit. Terrain is in some ways intimately linked with battlefield strategy and tactics, as the landscape of a battle sets the physical parameters for the conduct of operations. It can, in some circumstances, offer an equalising effect for mismatched forces; in other cases, it can confer a decisive advantage on either an attacking or defending army. On a wide-open plain, the army with superiority in mobility, numbers, weaponry, training or discipline will be able to use that advantage to the full; terrain simply offers a way of disrupting, neutralising or enhancing those advantages.

This begins with the alignment of forces, at both the grand tactical (army) level, and at the minor tactical (battalion, company, platoon) level. At the risk of stating the obvious, armies that make effective use of terrain are aligned to maximise their own advantages, while minimising those of their enemy. As battle is joined, the side that can make best use of terrain at the point of contact will more often than not come out on top.

Within this general idea of maximising advantage, terrain can be used for a number of purposes. Perhaps the most obvious is to use terrain to anchor a defensive position. The exact way of doing this will naturally depend on how a force is likely to be attacked, but the basic principle always remains that a tactical strongpoint should offer protection to its defenders, render mobility more difficult for the attackers and, if possible, should favour the defensive weapons systems or technology. In the modern era this includes ensuring excellent fields of fire and ideally the creation of a 'killing ground' into which the enemy can be lured, but can also involve neutralising the effects of more advanced or deadly enemy technology. Examples of this abound, from the use of elevation and muddy conditions to neutralise heavily armoured horsemen at Crécy, to insurgent use of jungle or mountainous terrain to nullify the effects of helicopters and smart munitions over the past half-century or so. Terrain can also be used to protect an army's most vulnerable areas, most notably in allowing a force to anchor its flanks to prevent enfilade or envelopment.

A good position is one that adheres to these general principles rather than to any specific type of terrain. In the pre-modern era, for example, the most accessible defensive position was an open hilltop; it allowed for the deployment of closely formed tactical units, served to slow (even if only a little) an enemy advance, and gave a minor advantage in any clash of steel. Once precision long-range rifles, artillery and, later, aircraft came to dominate the battlefield, a hilltop on its own became a much less hospitable place, serving to do little other than make its defenders a target unless bolstered by field fortifications or defended by superior firepower.

Higher ground nevertheless remains a key element of defensive terrain. It presents an obstacle to advancing troops, gives the defender enhanced visibility and lines of sight, and often offers a better field of fire. However, its advantages need to be qualified. Sloping ground might serve to slow defensive reinforcements as much as enemy attackers, and its sheer height can make it a better target. Heights can also isolate units from supply, communication, and effective lines of retreat or counterattack. A defensive position might also prove too strong, leaving an enemy to decline battle – which may or may not run contrary to the aim of the campaign. Moreover, anchoring an army on higher ground can have the effect of making it too static, and handing the initiative entirely to the enemy. This can be fine if the defender wishes to remain in place and the enemy commits to a full-frontal assault (think Waterloo), but is less useful if it leaves the enemy free to manoeuvre without interference. James IV's carefully prepared positions on Flodden Edge (1513), for example, proved useless when the Earl of Surrey simply manoeuvred around them, forcing James to realign his army in a much less favourable location.

There are many other types of terrain that can confer defensive advantage, depending on the situation and the enemy. Broken ground will prove difficult for formed units, horses or even vehicles to traverse, but may just serve to provide cover for advancing open-order infantry. Wet, boggy or sandy ground can hamper enemy movement, but might prove less effective if the defender is relying on explosive shells to stop the advance. It may also make a counterattack significantly more difficult.

Mountainous country and woodland have historically proven horrendously difficult to fight through (look no further than Delville Wood on the Somme, or any of a dozen horrific encounters on the Italian front in the First World War), but can be as deadly for defender as for attacker. Rivers, streams and ditches provide natural lines of defence which, while rendered occasionally useless by ice, such as during the French invasion of the Netherlands in 1795, tend to confer a significant tactical advantage on the defender. It is rare for a commander to be presented with the perfect terrain for his designs – although the best commanders and armies will adapt to the situation.

While terrain is primarily a force multiplier for the defender, it can also be exploited by the attacker. The simplest expedient is to manoeuvre an enemy into a position where the above advantages – of movement, cover, weapons, and technology – are with the attacker rather than the defender. This relies perhaps on sloppy opposition generalship, but history abounds with such examples, from Ulm (1805) to Sedan (1870). Presuming, however, that the enemy has a modicum of strategic sense and does not land himself in the proverbial *pot de chambre*,[9] an offensive force might seek to exploit terrain in other ways. The most common is perhaps to use terrain to shield or conceal an attack, whether on a grand tactical or minor tactical level. This can involve manoeuvring with a screen of woodland, behind elevation, or simply using folds in the ground. The latter – essentially small pockets of land hidden from line of sight by slight vagaries in topography – are often overlooked in the study of battle as it is impossible to pick them out from most maps, and their effects often go unremarked in accounts of battle already confused by the fog of war.

Alongside concealment for manoeuvre, an attacking force might also exploit terrain for cover from defensive weapons. While a good defensive position should ensure a clear field of fire, a tactically adept attacking force would seek to make use of any features of terrain that offered protection. This is both easier and more prevalent with more modern open-order fire-and-move tactics; the example of Majuba (1881) is perhaps one of the best illustrations where an attacking force made substantially better use of terrain for concealment than the defenders. Attackers might also use stealth and stratagem to overcome disadvantages of terrain; the Jacobite forces at Prestonpans (1745), for example, were able to use local knowledge to find a route through a marsh protecting the Hanoverian position, and launched a dawn attack that utterly routed their enemies.

Beyond topography, armies must also take into account the changing condition of the ground, which can be as important as contours in giving advantage in battle. Poor weather can turn inviting plains into marshy quagmires, impeding movement and dealing a decisive blow to any attack. Attacking forces at Agincourt and the latter stages of the Somme both suffered from this in different ways. Patches of marshy ground can have an equally devastating effect on a charge, as Richard III found to his ultimate cost at Bosworth in 1485. Freezing conditions can turn significant barriers of water into minor obstacles, while an unseasonable thaw or flood can reverse this spectacularly, demonstrated by Napoleon's difficult recrossing of the Berezina (1812).

Man-made change is also important. Open fields can become serious obstacles when ploughed, while something as simple as unharvested crops can affect the field by providing cover or impeding movement. At the opening of the Battle of Quatre Bras in the Waterloo Campaign, a few battalions hidden in the tall crops caused the French commanders to fear that the allies were present in far greater numbers than was actually the case, buying the Duke of Wellington desperately needed time to bring up reinforcements. Recent research on Crécy also suggests that an unseasonably cold summer had left the late-ripening wheat as yet unharvested at the time of the battle, allowing Edward III to hide archers amidst the tall stalks.[10]

Modern technology and transport has, of course, made great strides in overcoming some of these issues of ground and topography, not least through aerial deployment, airstrikes and precision munitions. Yet even here terrain can have a decisive influence on the outcome of combat. Urban terrain can negate many of the advantages of air support, for instance, as seen in the Battle of Mogadishu (1993). As in other periods of rapid technological development, it is the responsibility of modern battlefield commanders to work out how to use terrain to maximise their own advantage, while negating or reducing those of the enemy.

The Advantage of the Higher Ground? Hastings (1066)

If the weather had been fair, William Duke of Normandy's invasion of England would have occurred in late summer 1066. He was preparing for the Channel crossing in late August, and according to multiple contemporary chronicle accounts, wanted to cross to England before the harsher autumn weather. However, the famous invasion did not take place until mid-October, as a consequence of storms and northern winds: one contemporary chronicler described how September was 'cold and wet and the sky was hidden by clouds and rain'.[11] Indeed, this unfavourable weather – confirmed by modern climate science – delayed William's invasion for a month as he waited to cross the Channel.[12]

With the delay caused by the unusually stormy weather, the actual confrontation between William and English king Harold Godwinson was fought not on a late summer's day, but on 14 October. The English forces, led by Harold, had marched from northern England after defeating the Norwegians at the Battle of Stamford Bridge near York, and arrived from the north or north-west on the evening of 13 October. William, meanwhile, marched northward from his camp, situated near Hastings to the south-east.

As the English force arrived at the area first, they were able to initially survey the area where battle would occur and select the strongest possible tactical position. They chose a location 'on higher ground, on the hill near to the woods through which they had come'.[13] Such topography suited the battle tactic that Harold had perfected at Stamford Bridge, and that had proved so successful: use natural shelter from which to surprise the enemy, and defeat them from higher ground without having to engage on a level battlefield.

The paucity of geographically accurate sources from the period means that historians and archaeologists are left to surmise – with varying degrees of certainty – the actual location of the English and Norman lines. Although the site of the battlefield is uncertain, recent studies have identified four possible locations by using topographical descriptions gleaned from contemporary narratives. All four feature the description of the battlefield terrain found in the contemporary sources: a hill, close to a woodland, overlooking a lower-lying area. Recent work at the intersection of battlefield study and geographical survey has revealed that the landscape of the small town of Battle and the surrounding countryside may in fact have changed relatively little over the past millennium, suggesting that the current landscape remains an important and credible source of investigation as to the development and outcome of the battle.[14]

At the time of the battle, precipitation levels were high – perhaps as a consequence of the very storms that had delayed the Normans from crossing the Channel. Fresh water would therefore have been readily available to both Norman and English armies near Hastings.[15] The subsequent ease of access to fresh water may have impacted William's decision to remain near Hastings in the days prior to the battle, fortifying the Normans' position at Pevensey and waiting for Harold to come to them, rather than marching north in search of immediate confrontation. As a result of their tarry, William and the Norman forces came from the south-east along the main road which began just to the north of Hastings. The road itself is a vital clue as to the location of the battle site: it provided a clear track for the Norman army to follow, and pointed the way directly to London for William – and thus towards his enemy and the throne that he wished to claim.

Once the Normans sighted the English forces positioned on the high ground, the need to fight up the slope would have been clearly evident to William: he consequently arrayed his forces in preparation for committing his foot soldiers and mounted knights, keeping the projectile bombardment for later in the battle when he presumably hoped to fight the English on level terrain.

However, the strategic position of the English forces on the hill allowed them to rebuff the first Norman attack. The Normans attempted to use missiles, but the angle of trajectory uphill was too great to afford them significant success. The Norman foot soldiers advanced for an initial attack, but were beaten back by English missiles, which would have been given additional range downhill.

After failing to break through the English ranks, the Norman foot soldiers retreated to allow for an attack by William's cavalry, who also failed to get the English off the hill. The English forces used their elevated position to repulse numerous Norman attacks, taking advantage of the ineffectiveness of Norman projectile weapons up the hill as well as the dominance of their own weapons down the slope, combined with the exhaustion of a Norman force who had to climb the mound to attack. The English were clearly aware of the pre-eminence of their position in regard to the terrain of the battlefield: one contemporary chronicle states that 'the English were greatly helped by the advantage of the higher ground, which they held in serried ranks without sallying forward'.[16]

It was at this point in the battle, with the English seemingly able to defend the high ground indefinitely, that some of William's army decided to turn tail. Contemporary chronicles describe how, seeing the English win the early confrontations, some of the Norman foot soldiers and even knights – in particular the Bretons – panicked and started to retreat. Furthermore, a rumour spread throughout the Norman forces that their duke and commander had fallen.

Noting this collapse of a portion of the Norman line, and believing that their tactical advantage was paying off, the English advanced a contingent of their forces down the hill. Although Harold's brothers may have participated in this advance, Harold himself was apparently not among them, preferring to remain at the summit in order to retain the tactical overview afforded by the position that would allow him to continue to control the field of combat.

During the English advance, a number of William's men continued to flee. It was at this point that William began rallying his men to repel the English attack. Throwing back his helmet, he assured his men that he was well and then led them in a blistering counterattack. Seeing the effectiveness of his forces against English fighters who had come down off the summit of the hill, William appears to have used this English attack – and the brutally effective Norman counterattack – to inform his approach for the following few hours. As the afternoon wore on, the Normans used the tactic of feigned retreat to lure portions of the English forces from the hill, into William's foot soldiers and heavy cavalry. The tactic was a simple one, but proved effective in nullifying the English force's topographical advantage – William may have used it multiple times throughout the afternoon.[17]

As the battle reached early evening, however, William's lure had only succeeded in winning skirmishes against the English forces. Harold and much of his force, including his elite troops – the huscarls – remained positioned on the high ground and were resistant to giving it up. At the same time, the Norman forces – who had repeatedly had to rush uphill and then turn around in their efforts to convince the English of their retreats – were beginning to tire. Knowing that to continue the attack into the night would be impossible, and without wishing to leave the battlefield without assured victory, William attacked with all of his remaining units around dusk. The Norman archers were ordered to shoot their arrows in the air to blind the enemy, and it was during this attack that Harold was killed. The manner of his death is open to speculation.

Conditions of Landscape: Climate, Weather and Terrain   77

The *Chronicle of Battle Abbey* describes him being killed by a chance blow in the foot combat when the Normans peaked the ridge.[18] Other contemporary narratives describe how he was wounded by an arrow in the eye and then killed along with his brothers by Norman knights.[19]

Seeing their king and commander fall, the English fled the battlefield. Once again, their knowledge of local terrain and the surrounding area may have proved advantageous: English forces apparently used the network of marshes and ditches to cover their escape, and it is likely that the woods that had protected their advance to the battlefield now covered their disordered retreat: with the Normans giving chase, 'only darkness and flight through the thickets and coverts of the dense forest saved the defeated English'.[20]

The Battle of Hastings therefore offers a clear example of the impact of terrain and weather on a medieval battlefield. High ground was prized as a more defendable position, although adaptive tactics could be used to nullify its impact. While inclement weather may have delayed the military campaign leaving Normandy, heavy rainfall also provided William's men with fresh water once they landed in England, and meant that escape for the vanquished English was aided by flooded terrain that the Normans could not easily traverse. The English mastery of the terrain at the start of the battle proved crucial to their early dominance, whereas William's mitigation of this advantage saw his forces eventually triumph.

The Sun of Austerlitz (1805)

The Battle of Austerlitz is generally considered to be Napoleon's masterpiece.[21] It confirmed to Europe Napoleon's status as a great battlefield commander, and is often held up as one of the greatest examples of operational art. Yet even in such a triumph, factors of terrain, climate and weather would play a significant role in the course and outcome of the battle.

The battle itself took place on 2 December 1805. Earlier that year, Napoleon had abandoned plans to invade England and swung his *Grande Armée* from the Channel coast down to southern Germany to face the growing threat of Austria and Russia. Having destroyed the main Austrian field army in Germany at Ulm in October, Napoleon chased the Russian army and the remaining Austrian forces into Moravia (modern-day Czech Republic), where eventually, in late November, they turned to fight. By this stage Napoleon's strategic position had become precarious, and he was eager to seal the campaign rapidly with a victorious battle.

The influence of climate and topography is evident even before combat was joined. Although the relatively benign climate of Moravia allowed Napoleon to maintain his men even into the depths of November, the onset of winter with his army so far from its supply depots also contributed to his strategic vulnerability, which made a swift battle essential. Seeking to encourage his enemies to fight, Napoleon put on a deliberate show of weakness, including making use of terrain by staging a disorderly withdrawal from the Pratzen Heights, the higher ground dominating the future battlefield.[22] By surrendering the high ground to the allies, Napoleon ensured that they would feel confident enough to give battle. Napoleon then arrayed his army with its strength on the left and centre, leaving the right (which covered the all-important communications route with Vienna) deliberately weaker. This had the effect of encouraging the allies to take the initiative in moving against the French right, leaving themselves vulnerable to a counterpunch in the centre that could split their army.

The Austro-Russian plan to exploit Napoleon's apparently faulty dispositions was to move the bulk of their forces in five columns against the French right, hoping to crash through the weakened lines, cutting Napoleon off from retreat or reinforcement, and to roll up his army. The pivot for the manoeuvre would be the Pratzen Heights. It was, in fact, a sound enough plan, although Napoleon further counted on assistance of terrain in the shape of the villages of Tellnitz and Menitz, Sokolnitz Castle and village, and the Goldbach stream, which all created natural strongpoints to anchor his right. The flank was further protected by the marshy ground around the large Satschan and Menitz ponds, which effectively blocked any allied manoeuvres further around his right. Napoleon's left was anchored on Santon Hill. He also found a useful vantage point on Zurlan Hill, a slight rise in the centre of the French lines, from where he could oversee and command the battle.

Climate played a further role before day had even dawned on the morning of the battle – quite literally, because the fact that the battle was fought in early December meant that the sun rose late, and that there would be only around nine hours of daylight in which to fight. In order to buy themselves time to carry out their plans, the allies were forced to begin their manoeuvres against Napoleon's right in the pitch dark of a freezing pre-dawn, leading to inevitable delays, significant confusion, and some exhaustion amongst their troops, exacerbated by less-than-stellar staff work. As the sun rose, a heavy fog enveloped the battlefield and added to the confusion and poor visibility.[23]

This contributed more than a little to the lack of immediate success against the French right. The allied forces began to move into action at around 6 am, but by daybreak they had made little progress, with the French falling back slowly rather than being overwhelmed. The advancing allied columns were hampered by the poor visibility and struggled to deploy for action, although the fog worked to their advantage when two French units engaged in a brisk exchange of friendly fire in the gloom, leading to their premature abandonment of the village of Tellnitz. However, from the early morning, French reinforcements began to arrive from the south, further bolstering this apparently weak flank of their army.

The fog also contributed in no small part to the success of Napoleon's masterstroke, which came shortly after 9 am. Knowing that his enemies had moved in force against his right, leaving the higher ground lightly defended, Napoleon gave orders for Marshal Soult's IV Corps to assault the Pratzen Heights to seize the crucial central position. The terrain of the battlefield was also vital here. The higher ground, once captured, would allow Napoleon to consolidate his centre and reorientate his line to roll up one half of the enemy army, while also giving some protection against allied countermoves. The lingering fog hid the advancing troops, who were able to move to within a short distance of the Austro-Russian lines unnoticed, gifting them an enormous advantage and robbing allied commanders of time to orchestrate effective countermeasures. Moreover, as Soult's forces reached the crest of the heights, the fog lifted to be replaced by the fabled 'sun of Austerlitz', removing a potential obstacle to the French commanders' control of the struggle in the centre.

The fighting on the heights was hard and bloody. Both sides threw reserves into the fray, and for some time the struggle ebbed and flowed. Perhaps the freezing conditions contributed to the relative success of some of the cavalry charges, as infantrymen fumbled at the locks of their muskets with frozen fingers, but this is more a matter of extrapolation than hard evidence. More certainly, the gradients of the slopes favoured

Napoleon; the gentler slope on the French side of the heights did relatively little to inhibit reinforcement, while the steeper, at times almost precipitous inclines of the allied side impeded his enemies' movements.

At last, by early afternoon, Napoleon's grip on the higher ground was secure, and the allied army was effectively cut in two.[24] The central position of the heights further gave Napoleon flexibility to alter his plans; there is evidence that he initially intended to turn to crush the Austro-Russian right, but changed in view of circumstance to eliminate their left. As he moved against the allies to the south, he was able to use the higher ground as an artillery platform to bombard their remaining troops. The fighting was again intense, but eventually the allied forces broke, withdrawing in some disorder. Thousands of troops took advantage of the opportunity afforded by freezing conditions to escape across the icy ponds and marshes that might, at another season of the year, have proved impassable. Rumours of thousands of men drowned as French artillery smashed the ice are almost certainly exaggerations. By 4 pm, a combination of falling darkness and a sudden snow squall put an end to the active fighting; the remaining allied forces were able to withdraw, while the French were too weary – and the conditions were too poor – for an effective pursuit.

Austerlitz remains one of the great examples of operational battlefield success but, as the above shows, the conditions of battle – the climate, the weather, the terrain – were crucial to its outcome. Napoleon made best use of the strategic strongpoints on the battlefield, and (whether by luck or judgement) his plans were best suited to the climatic conditions and the vagaries of the weather. The later dawn, the early morning fog, and the late morning sun all conferred strategic advantages that the emperor was able to exploit to the full. The conditions of Austerlitz by no means won the battle, and much less determined an inevitable outcome, but they contributed significantly to the way in which the battle was fought, won, and lost.

Chapter 5

Battlefield Strategy and Tactics

'Tactics is the art of using troops in battle; strategy is the art of using battles to win the war'
                                        Sir Archibald Wavell.[1]

Strategy and tactics are at the heart of every military operation. They provide the basis for the aims, intentions, manoeuvres and formations of armies on the battlefield; they can dictate how armies try to exploit terrain, how they use their weapons, and fundamentally how they seek to force victory. This arguably makes them the most important factors in assessing how armies or units act on the battlefield up to the moment of engagement, 'since everything that occurs is ultimately manifested on a tactical level'.[2] American military theorist Stephan Biddle argued that in twentieth-century battles, 'force employment has played a more important role than either technology or preponderance [in numbers]' – a suggestion that remains largely valid for combat in earlier periods.[3]

The contention that strategy and tactics in a broad sense play a major role on the battlefield can be accepted as fact. Yet a focus on tactical evolutions to understand battle brings its own problems. In examining grand tactics, it is too easy to imagine combat as if it were conducted on a tabletop rather than a battlefield, with chess pieces rather than soldiers. Antiquarian accounts of battle often narrate all-seeing general officers giving orders, units moving as a block to obey them, and foes being suitably vanquished, ignoring the chaos, noise, smoke or fog of war of the battlefield. While the linearity of eighteenth- and early nineteenth-century warfare lent itself to tales of great generals winning glorious victories with their grand tactics, the reality was often very different. The grand tactics of generals were put into practice using an array of minor tactical systems, or sometimes with little in the way of a system at all. Before the seventeenth century few battles saw anything like an image of a general studiously moving blocks of troops around a battlefield, except in the most rudimentary sense.

Strategic and tactical arts have evolved enormously over the past millennium, often in line with developments in weaponry or technology, but also to take into account army size, structure, and leadership. Minor tactics have changed beyond recognition as the tools of combat have developed in range or lethality. Yet in a broad sense, there remains a degree of continuity in some of the basic principles of military operations. Even where tactics did not develop beyond the truly rudimentary, armies or units have faced the same basic vulnerabilities – on the flanks, for example – that have invited enemy exploitation.

It is worth beginning with a brief note on the meaning of strategy and tactics, which are widely used but not universally defined terms. Essentially, operational strategy refers to the coordination of military assets on a large scale, and tactics deals with how soldiers attempt to carry out their tasks on the battlefield. Nineteenth-century military theorists generally used strategy to mean moves made on campaign and tactics to denote movements in the face of the enemy, but it is also important to delineate between political strategy ('grand strategy') and operational strategy, and between actions of large formations (corps, divisions, brigades) and those of smaller units (battalions, companies, platoons) on the battlefield. 'Grand tactics' is usually used to denote the overall moves of large formations on the battlefield, and minor tactics refer more to the formations or movements adopted by individual units as they make contact with the enemy.

There are myriad factors that will influence the tactics employed in battle. Many of these are explored elsewhere in this book: army sizes; topography or climatic conditions; the personality and ability of leaders; and the weapons used. However, there is another crucial influence on tactical decisions: the aims of the combatants, or in other words, what they seek to achieve from the battle in question. For example, a commander who aims to annihilate his enemy will employ different tactics to one who simply wishes to manoeuvre them out of position; a commander who wishes to take control of an enemy-occupied area will employ different tactics to a commander who needs to pin an enemy in place. In their most basic terms, the majority of tactics employed in battle can be categorised as either those to attack an enemy, offensive tactics, and those used to protect something, be it a position, another armed force, or a strategic initiative. Despite this delineation, combat situations often require a combination of these two approaches. A single battle can contain numerous phases in which the aims of commanders on both sides change; often, the victorious party will be the army able to respond most effectively to the tactics of the opposition.

The grand tactics adopted in battle are to a large extent dependent on the weapons and equipment that an army has at its disposal. The combination of different forms of arms, generally including sidearms that are carried by troops alongside projectiles or airborne missiles, has evolved since the medieval period to incorporate new technologies and techniques. At their heart, however, the grand tactics of manoeuvring combined forces on the battlefield remains one of the most complex aspects of battle.

An examination of the development of combined-arms tactics in medieval England provides an interesting example. As William of Normandy conquered England in 1066, he brought with him a style of cavalry-based combat and use of archers in battle that contrasted to English tactics of the time, which were invariably dominated by infantry who fought on foot. The joining of England and Normandy, however, led to the melding of their martial strategies to create a new system of warfare. This approach, the combination of arms, often had a devastating effect in battle. At Tinchebray in 1106, for example, Henry I fought on foot alongside his infantry forces against his brother, Duke Robert of Normandy, as did many other knights on both sides of the encounter. Henry also maintained a cavalry presence on the battlefield which would be decisive in his victory, as it attacked the flank of the enemy line when the foot soldiers had been weighed down into a stalemate.[4] Less than twenty years later, another Anglo-Norman army – at Bourgthéroulde in 1124 – combined dismounted knights and infantry alongside archers. Led by Odo Borleng on behalf of King Henry, these combined arms initially attacked a force led by Norman rebel Waleran de Beaumont with volleys of arrows before an infantry charge.[5]

The combination of infantry, cavalry and archers continued to develop in England through the twelfth and thirteenth centuries. Although the grand tactical use of combined forces on the battlefield did prove effective in many engagements, in others the system fell down. At Bannockburn in 1314, England fielded a large army – perhaps 15,000 men – combining archers and cavalry, but the charging horsemen quickly found themselves impaled on the pikes of the Scottish schiltrons.[6] Sending his archers to support, Edward II was horrified to see them cut down by the Scottish cavalry in turn. The lack of coordination between these two groups directly contributed to England's defeat, and underlined how a combined force using its disparate elements effectively – as the Scots did their foot soldiers and cavalry – could outmanoeuvre a more numerous opponent, as well as highlighting the tactical challenges of cavalry charges against tightly packed pikemen or men-at-arms. In the fourteenth and fifteenth centuries, through the period of the Hundred Years' War, it became more common for English armies to combine archers with dismounted infantry forces.

The emergence of this 'English system' was to dominate military strategy and grand tactics throughout the next century in Western Europe, as armies increasingly combined archers and men-at-arms on foot. An early demonstration of quite how effective this approach could be came at Halidon Hill (1333), when Edward III routed a Scottish army so decisively that one chronicler claimed that after the battle, 'there was hardly a Scot remaining who had the ability, knowledge and wish to assemble an army'.[7] Edward adopted a hilltop position and, ordering his men to dismount, arrayed them with men-at-arms at the centre, flanked by longbowmen. Using their lances perhaps like pikes, Edward copied the tactic employed so effectively against his father's forces at Bannockburn in combination with archers directing arrows towards the enemy flanks and rear.[8]

The English system is only one example of combined-order tactics employed throughout Europe by the advent of gunpowder on Late Medieval battlefields. These new technologies were incorporated into mixed armies and integrated into tactical planning – in some countries, more successfully than others. Burgundy and France, for example, who had seen the effectiveness of the English system first-hand, successfully incorporated handgunners and pikes into their armies so that, by the mid-fifteenth century, they surpassed the English in flexibility; reliance on the old system of archers and dismounted infantry cost England at the Battle of Castillon in 1453, yet would dominate the Wars of the Roses for the remainder of the century.

The effective combination of arms on the Continent was especially important to counter the emerging formation of the pike square, which by the later fifteenth century was proving to be a potentially devastating entity on the battlefield. Pike squares' strength lay in numbers, which gave weight to an attack; discipline, which prevented the square pulling apart during an advance or becoming compressed when assaulted; weapons and armour, which gave significant striking power while protecting against many traditional weapons; and the formation, which could defend itself on all sides and move in any direction. Traditional thinner infantry lines could not withstand the mass of a pike square's attack, and cavalry were unable to make an impact against the arrayed hedges of pike-heads. Improvements in armour made archers far less effective against breast-plated pikemen, while firearms could do damage but were too slow and cumbersome to stop a square's advance.[9] Victories like that of the Swiss over the Burgundians at Nancy in 1477 showed the power of the pike against traditional arrays of cavalry, infantry and archers.

To stop a pike square therefore required a more coordinated approach to combined-arms tactics. Attacks against a pike square's flanks or rear would do little damage but could force the square to halt its advance to turn its pikes outwards; mobile cavalrymen were best suited to this task, especially when they later developed the caracole. With the square stalled, firearms – which packed a much greater punch than bows – could pour shot into the massed ranks, the depth of formation here proving a disadvantage as every shot could take out a number of victims. With ranks thinning, the square might resume the advance, in which case it was best met with prepared positions and obstacles, or by another formation of pikemen. At Marignano (1515), the effective combination of French guns, cavalry, and allied Landsknechts was able to defeat a disciplined and determined army of Swiss pikemen, marking the beginning of the end of their mystique.

Effective combined arms therefore became a necessity for any army by the later fifteenth century. And with pike squares becoming vulnerable to suitably coordinated enemies, pike formations themselves were increasingly integrated into mixed-arms units. To protect against the possibility of vexatious flank attacks and unanswered bombardment, blocks of handgunners were interspersed with pike formations. Spanish tercios and German or Swiss Landsknechts became dominant forces on the battlefield by adopting formations that combined pikemen, gunners, and often swordsmen to provide a vital blend of striking power, weight of numbers, flexibility and protection.

The advent of the bayonet-tipped musket by the end of the seventeenth century meant this blend of factors could be achieved without combining with pike or swordsmen. Yet mutual support between infantry, cavalry and artillery was still important to battlefield success. A major problem was communication and timing; with army sizes expanding, soldiers now fighting in scores of separate units rather than one contiguous line, and battlefields increasingly shrouded in thick palls of smoke, getting formations to work in unison could be desperately difficult.

Issues of communication continued to dog combined-arms operations well into the twentieth century. In the First World War, for example, coordinating artillery barrages with advancing infantry was notoriously difficult. The introduction of aircraft and tanks added additional complexities, sometimes exacerbated by inter-corps and eventually interservice rivalries. There were, however, some notable successes, such as the opening of the Battle of Cambrai (1917), which saw tanks, aircraft, infantry and artillery combine to great effect in an assault on the German lines. Yet it was in minor tactics that the combinations were becoming increasingly important. German stormtrooper tactics, which proved so effective during the 1918 Spring Offensive, were based around coordinating shock artillery bombardments with small group infantry assaults, which themselves combined a range of different weapons, from machine guns to mortars, grenades, rifle grenades and standard rifles.

As weapons systems became more advanced, so coordination became ever more vital. On a grand tactical level, integration of infantry, artillery, armoured vehicles and airpower was increasingly crucial for successful – and lower-cost – attacks. The unsupported waves of infantry occasionally hurled against the Germans by the Red Army in 1941 led mostly to utter failure and enormous casualties.[10] Their combined tactics later in the war were notably more successful, and generally less costly. Even the most technologically advanced weapons struggle to operate alone. As fearsome as tanks have been since the 1940s, for instance, they remain vulnerable without adequate infantry and even air support.

The most successful operations for any party during the Second World War were those where firepower, mobility and manpower were effectively combined. While German blitzkrieg is often associated with its armoured spearhead or innovative use of new arms such as paratroopers, it could only work with sufficient aerial cover and infantry support, with the various elements working in close cooperation. The Western allies after 1942 especially sought to confront the enemy with a wall of explosive and steel rather than flesh, requiring attacking troops to operate in conjunction with significant firepower from ground and air forces. The combination of air and land (and to some extent sea) has proved ever more crucial for advanced militaries in the twentieth and twenty-first centuries, with close air support and strike aircraft able to give huge battlefield advantages if properly coordinated. The capability of airpower to disrupt and destroy enemy formations has been proved time and again – with Desert Storm arguably its conventional apogee – but it is only by working in tandem with ground forces that it can prove a definitively battle-winning weapon. As Canadian Lieutenant Colonel Lavoie said of his experiences in Afghanistan in 2006, 'you cannot win with airpower alone.'[11]

Ensuring effective combinations of arms can rely on commanders ensuring the effective concentration of forces. At an operational level, this boils down to a general bringing all available units to the battlefield in good time. Napoleon made it a maxim that 'when you have resolved to fight a battle, collect your whole force. Dispense with nothing. A single battalion sometimes decides the day.'[12] There is a constant temptation for all generals to fritter away forces in guarding lines of communication, or taking minor targets, or protecting against hypothetical contingencies. Frederick the Great counselled his generals:

> In a war of *defence*, we are naturally induced to make detachments. Generals of little experience are anxious to preserve everything, whilst the man of intelligence and enterprise regards only the grand point, in hopes of being able to strike some great stroke, and suffers patiently a small evil that may secure him against one of more material consequence.[13]

The ability to convince an enemy to disperse or divide his forces is equally useful. Well-executed concentration can allow a general to achieve local numerical superiority even when heavily outnumbered in the wider theatre, as demonstrated to great effect by Frederick himself in the Seven Years' War.[14]

Once an army is concentrated and closes on the enemy, it will be in a position to engage them in battle. Sometimes both armies are eager for combat; at other times, one force might have to take quick offensive action to pin the enemy in place and prevent their withdrawal. Whichever is the case, offensive tactics – moving to attack the enemy – are crucial to opening an engagement.

The most basic offensive tactic is the frontal assault. This may take the form of a headlong charge, using cavalry or infantry, or a slower but deliberate attack straight at the enemy centre, perhaps preceded by bombardment with whatever projectiles are to hand. Throughout much of the medieval period, for example, French cavalry often opened battles with a direct charge at the enemy's front lines. While potentially devastating, such as at Patay in 1429 or Formigny in 1450, this tactic was open to risks including ground conditions, infantry defence, and projectile attack – as demonstrated so effectively at Crécy (1346) and Agincourt (1415). Frontal attacks continued to be a favoured tactic through the early modern period – notably with pike squares – and into the nineteenth century with the massed attacks of Napoleonic armies. In both instances, formed units would make a steady advance directly towards the enemy, charging only at the last moment to preserve cohesion and strength. Preliminary bombardments to disrupt the defenders' cohesion were increasingly used, but the need to avoid hitting advancing troops meant that they could rarely be sustained during the attack. Many of Napoleon's bloodiest battles – Eylau, Wagram, Borodino – saw mass frontal attacks on enemy positions, relying on weight of numbers and fighting ability to bludgeon the enemy into submission.

In more modern battle, such a headlong charge onto the enemy lines is rarer, but nevertheless featured in conflicts of the twentieth century, in both a grand tactical and minor tactical sense. The 'going over the top' from the trenches in the First World War featured huge numbers of combatants, on both sides, charging across no man's land, while the D-Day landings in 1944 required some straightforward and bloody attacks on established defensive positions. In both cases, assaulting troops were supported by significant preliminary bombardments to 'soften' targets; once the assault began, fire was shifted to interdiction barrages of the enemy's depth positions to prevent reinforcements and prepare the ground for follow-up attacks. In tactical terms, a frontal assault is best encapsulated as a penetration of the centre, which succeeds by exploiting a gap driven into the centre of an opposing force.

Such a direct frontal attack is not, of course, guaranteed to be victorious. Indeed, some medieval manuals of war advised avoiding manoeuvre entirely, as the side that moved first was most likely to lose.[15] If the enemy is expecting such an assault, they will take measures to prevent their front lines being breached. The English at Bannockburn in 1314 experienced first-hand the devastation that may be wrought on a cavalry charge by men-at-arms bracing pikes, and was almost certainly an influence on Edward III's tactical developments in the Hundred Years' War when he abandoned English cavalry charges for infantry and archer combat.[16]

A slightly more subtle offensive tactic is to threaten or attack the flanks, which are usually an army or unit's most vulnerable spot. At the core of this vulnerability is a straightforward calculation of numbers and direction: formations are easiest to assail from the side, as the edges of a formation can bring fewer men or weapons to bear against the enemy. The flanks are also usually the most difficult to reinforce from central reserves. Because of the vulnerability and opportunity offered, military commanders from antiquity onwards sought to bolster their flanks with stronger or more mobile units, or sought to anchor flanks on fortifications or impassable features of terrain. Frederick the Great was again vocal on this topic, declaring in his *Political Testament* of 1752: 'I have trained the officers to judge the terrain and occupy it advantageously, especially to secure their flanks.'[17]

The advantages of attacking the edges of an enemy's army are manifold. At the very least, pushing back an enemy flank compels them to realign the axis of their defences in order to maintain the line, thus putting their army off balance. In many cases a compromised flank can oblige an army to withdraw from prepared positions to avoid any risk of encirclement or enfilading fire. A major threat to a flank can force an enemy to redeploy reserves to prevent a breakthrough, reducing their freedom of action or ability to reinforce the line elsewhere. Of course, flanking movements hold their own risks. The defending force can use interior lines to strengthen their front, while attacking components can get separated from one another and defeated in detail. Yet if well executed, the results can be spectacular. It was through attacking the Burgundian, French and Hungarian flanks that the Ottoman forces were victorious at Nicopolis in 1396, for example.[18] The crusading forces orchestrated a head-on charge against the Ottoman infantry, or Janissaries, which then opened its lines and moved to the flanks. Whether a planned manoeuvre or an accidental stroke of good fortune, it exposed the European force's flanks to attack. After fierce fighting, the crusaders' vanguard was decimated and the battle won by the Ottomans.

Manoeuvring in this way mid-battle could be successful, but it was risky. More simply, an army might line up for a flank attack from the start. Concentrating significant forces on both flanks was an option, but it required a heavy numerical advantage to ensure that both flanking forces outmatched the enemy. Another possibility was to use an oblique order formation, massing forces on one flank to overwhelm the enemy while the rest of the army pinned their main body in place. This oblique order, or declined flank, has the advantage of keeping the army concentrated and allowing smaller forces to gain local superiority in a single zone of the battlefield, but it can lack the element of surprise, is dependent on the manoeuvrability of the attacking army, and can be upset by a rapid redeployment from the enemy. A declined flank was attempted by an allied army at the Battle of Rossbach (1757) against the defending Prussian left. Although outnumbered, the Prussian forces counterattacked with an oblique order of their own on the allied right. Using an effective combination of infantry and artillery fire to the front to keep the allies immobile, the Prussian cavalry destroyed the allied right and effectively routed their army.

When successful, a flanking manoeuvre can develop into an envelopment, where an attacking force breaks through the flank into the enemy's rear. This has several advantages: it allows defending units to be attacked from behind; it creates panic in the defenders' minds; it can force them to deploy reserves away from other important areas on the battlefront; and it can cut lines of supply, communication and retreat. Its intention is generally to compel the enemy army to withdraw in disorder or, if developed into a full encirclement, to ensure the destruction of the opposition force. An envelopment usually requires an attack to pin the enemy centre while significant forces work around the flank to create an opening that can be exploited. Variations on the theme include a single envelopment, where only one flank is turned, a double envelopment where both flanks are turned, or an airborne envelopment where troops are moved over rather than around the enemy army. The blitzkrieg campaign of 1940 relied heavily on a series of envelopment manoeuvres against increasingly disoriented and fragmented Allied forces, and saw the successful use of paratroopers as well as mobile armoured vehicles in turning enemy defences inside out.

Both envelopment and more limited flanking manoeuvres can be aided by indirect approaches, when one army commits a portion of its force to engage the enemy, while the rest of the force advances from a hidden area and attacks the enemy in the rear or flank. Such a manoeuvre was seen at Chancellorsville (1863), when 'Stonewall' Jackson led his corps undetected around the Union right while General Lee held their front in check. The surprise attack from the right and rear of the Union forces caused havoc and went some way to securing Lee's victory. The willingness – and command ability – to split forces in this manner is risky but effective if the enemy is held long enough to allow time to manoeuvre.

Subterfuge, hidden manoeuvres and setting traps for the enemy are key parts of grand tactics, and the ability to surprise an enemy's unprepared flank can potentially win a battle. A weakened flank can put a whole army in jeopardy, but it can also be a carrot dangled to draw the enemy to commit to a manoeuvre that can be counterattacked, as Napoleon did to devastating effect at Austerlitz in 1805. More widely, the adoption of echelon formations – essentially aligning the army's units in an arrowhead shape – can be used to encourage the enemy to attempt to attack the flanks of the apparently exposed front unit, only to offer their own flanks for counterattack by the echeloned forces either side of them. Individual units are best protected against flank attack when formed in a square or rectangular formation. The mass pike squares of the fifteenth to seventeenth centuries were largely invulnerable to direct assault from any direction, while the hollow infantry squares of the eighteenth and early nineteenth centuries provided musket- and riflemen significant protection against cavalry or blade-armed infantry.

The importance of avoiding being outflanked would often be a factor in where a general chooses to fight, as the landscape might be used to shield or fortify a force's exposed extremities. An army might seek to anchor its flanks against features of terrain impassable to its enemies, effectively limiting them to a frontal attack. Difficult or impassable terrain may be a body of water, such as the northern flank of the Western Front trench systems after the 1914 'race to the sea'; it may be a difficult or impassable cliff, gorge, or raised ground, as Union forces managed at Gettysburg (1863), helping them to repel a Confederate flanking attack at Little Round Top; or it may simply be a forest or marshy ground, such as the two woodlands at Agincourt against which Henry V anchored his forces. If features are not particularly imposing or are lacking entirely, fortifications might be used to bolster the flank. At Waterloo, the Chateau of Hougoumont proved an invaluable bastion on Wellington's right flank. The important thing from any anchoring position was that an enemy must be encouraged to choose an easier frontal assault rather than a potentially slow and more costly excursion around the flank, thus limiting and controlling their movements. Of course, if the terrain is not as impassable as hoped, disaster can still strike – as when the German army suddenly debouched from the supposedly untraversable Ardennes to the north-west of the Maginot Line in May 1940.

Should open flanking manoeuvres or frontal assaults be undesirable, an army might fall back on the tactic of ambush. Used perhaps more frequently in skirmishes and guerrilla combat than in traditional full-scale battle, ambushes rely on the attacking forces concealing themselves in order to draw the enemy closer, and then attacking with speed and surprise. Although hard to conduct on a large scale, the ambush is an effective tool against a larger or better equipped enemy. The Mujahadeen in the Soviet War in Afghanistan frequently used the tactic to trap and attack Soviet forces, while combatants on both sides used ambush to entrap the enemy during the Vietnam War; the 1st Australian Tank Force used ambushes on 1,077 occasions against the Viet Cong and People's Army of Vietnam.[19]

Although ambushers retain the tactical initiative, the tactic is often used as part of a wider defensive approach. Defensive tactics are those that, through action or indeed inaction, allow the defending army to play a protective role – protecting perhaps a strategic location, a target, command base, or covering a retreat. A tactical defensive can be useful for armies that are outnumbered or less manoeuvrable, or that simply wish to keep an enemy in check long enough for developments elsewhere, such as the arrival of reinforcements. The need to take a tactical defensive position often stems from the wider strategic situation – if a campaign is based on stopping an enemy advance, it can make sense to sit tactically on the defensive – but by no means always. Napoleon was always aggressive on the battlefield, for example, whatever the strategic position, as he believed in keeping the enemy on the back foot. Yet where maintaining the initiative or mobility is not so important, generals on the strategic defensive have usually found it easiest to hold firm on the battlefield and await attack.

An army remaining on the tactical defensive can boost its chances by occupying a position that offers some physical advantage: perhaps an elevated height to allow better view and greater effectiveness of weapons; or a natural shelter to afford some level of physical protection. When a natural shelter cannot be found, armies may create their own obstacles. These may be very rudimentary, designed simply to slow an enemy sufficiently to confer some advantage on a defending force. A simple abatis, for example, usually formed of felled trees, would disorder attacking ranks and keep their troops in the defenders' field of fire for longer, forcing an attacker to accept casualties and lose cohesion before any hand-to-hand clash. Other defensive barriers can be more elaborate, involving the creation of protective shielding behind which a defending force may take shelter. These manmade battle fortifications might involve earthworks, but could be very mobile and quick to create. The English use of wagons at Crécy allowed for the protection of the English infantry during the Genoese crossbow attack and subsequent French cavalry charge. Their position on a natural rise in the landscape, affording them a better view of the approaching French forces and forcing the French to attack uphill, added to the defensibility of the site. Of course, in the First World War battlefield fortifications were carried to extremes, with complex networks of frontline and supply trenches running for hundreds of miles, allowing troops of all sides the cover and protection afforded by defensive positions.

Adopting a defensive position, however, does not preclude attacking manoeuvre. This could include a bombardment to provoke an enemy attack, such as at Towton or Agincourt. Attacking from a defensive position is a useful tactic to catch an opponent unaware, and the best battlefield defensive positions allow for movement as well as protection. The Battle of Muret in 1213 saw Simon de Montfort and a 1,000-strong crusading force abandon their defended position in the fortified town of Muret to strike unexpectedly at an allied force from Aragon and Toulouse. The surprise and speed of the attack, combined with de Montfort's cavalry mobility, meant that the crusading forces were able to defeat a force numbering perhaps twice their own.[20]

Another variation on this approach is the counterattack, which works best when an army is able to transfer quickly from holding ground to assaulting the enemy; the quicker this transition occurs, the more the enemy will be caught by surprise and off balance. In the age of black powder, counterattacks might loom out of the billowing smoke only yards away, creating panic in the enemy ranks. Timing is vital in a counterattack: too soon and the enemy has time to set himself to receive the attack; too late and the battle may already be lost. A counterattack generally works because the original attacking force is not set for defence; it may not be in a position to deploy its firepower to best effect, it may be out of supporting range of artillery, and it almost certainly will not be on prepared or even suitable ground. Often attackers will also have lost momentum, cohesion, and possibly even morale from their initial attack. Counterattacking is so widespread in warfare that some armies develop specific units skilled at pulling them off, such as the Germans' development of *Eingreifdivisions* from 1917.

Withdrawal or retreat – whether feigned or genuine – can also be a valuable tactic in battle. Although it might be presumed that retreat essentially signified defeat, tactical withdrawal may be used to realign defensive positions while maintaining contact with the enemy. It may be intended to delay another offensive and regroup, to consolidate forces, or to relocate a battle to ground more favourable to the withdrawing party. Deliberate, tactical withdrawal partway through a battle often forms part of a wider strategy, as summarised succinctly by Major General Oliver Smith during the Battle of Chosin Reservoir in November 1950, during the Korean War: 'Gentlemen, we are not retreating. We are merely advancing in another direction.'[21] Smith in fact embarked on a gruelling seventy-eight-mile fighting withdrawal; his combined forces reached the evacuation point at the seaport of Hungnam two weeks later having lost 17,000 men, compared to a staggering 60,000 Chinese casualties.

A tactical withdrawal can be a difficult manoeuvre, requiring much of the army to march with their back to the enemy while leaving only a small covering force to engage or prevent further attack. An army withdrawing in the face of the enemy is vulnerable, and whatever a general's motives, retreat almost always affects morale. With the correct application of pressure an orderly withdrawal can quickly become a rout; it is therefore an opportunity for the best generals to exploit. On the flip side, a withdrawal or feigned retreat can be used to lure an impetuous enemy into an ambush or to place themselves in a position where they can be counterattacked, having perhaps lost cohesion in their rush to follow up apparent victory. A series of feigned retreats was most likely used by the Normans at Hastings, perhaps following a tactical withdrawal down the hill on which the Anglo-Saxon army was positioned. Giving chase to the apparently fleeing Normans, the Anglo-Saxons were lured from their superior position and picked off by a sudden Norman about-turn on the lower slopes. Such a feigned manoeuvre is not confined to a small cockpit of combat like Hastings, however: during the Battle of Kasserine Pass in 1943, the German 21st Panzer Division appeared to flee in the face of US 1st Armoured Division tanks. Giving chase, the American forces drove into a barrage of anti-tank guns, the outcome described by artilleryman Edwin Westrate:

> It was murder. They rolled right into the muzzles of the concealed eighty-eights and all I could do was stand by and watch tank after tank blown to bits or burst into flames or just stop, wrecked. Those in the rear tried to turn back but the eighty-eights seemed to be everywhere.[22]

Feigned retreat is just one of many deceptive tactics that may be employed to try to outfox the enemy. Deceptive tactics are hugely varied, but at their core they attempt to mislead an opponent into making a tactical mistake that can be exploited. Camouflage is a basic form of deception, concealing soldiers and equipment so that their numbers or movements cannot be detected. Soldiers may use uniform, skin paint, or more modern, high-technology stealth measures to disguise their presence from an enemy. Controlling observability, stealth technology is becoming increasingly common on the battlefield, from drones to soldiers' own equipment. American battlefield operations in Operation Desert Storm in January 1991 featured the F-117 aircraft with stealth technology that allowed it to elude radar and infiltrate Iraq's border and aerial defences in preparation for bombing strategic targets. This evasion of air defences was described poetically in a subsequent USAF report as similar to the way 'a commuter might step around pools of water on the way to work'.[23] The effectiveness of stealth technology in the Gulf was certainly clear: although stealth aircraft flew only 2 per cent of combat sorties throughout the air war, they were responsible for attacking 40 per cent of strategic targets.[24]

Conversely, deception may involve ostentatious displays to distract the enemy from a larger or more dangerous threat. As Bevin Alexander summarised, a commander 'must make his opponent believe he's aiming at a point different from his actual target ... [as] Stonewall Jackson put into words in 1862: to "mystify, mislead, and surprise" the enemy'.[25] Diversionary tactics are especially popular on the large-scale battlefield, and can be effective if the enemy is mistakenly convinced that an opponent's diversion is actually the extent of their activities. At Nashville (1864), for example, Unionist Major General Thomas was able to distract Lieutenant General Hood's Confederate army with an attack on their right across the Nashville and Chattanooga Railroad, while directing his main assault on the redoubts of the Confederate left. Although the diversionary action only drew Hood's attention briefly, it bought Thomas sufficient time to outflank the Confederate left. However, diversionary tactics can prove an Achilles' heel if they begin to consume too many resources. Such was the case at Waterloo, when a diversionary attack was attempted by Napoleon's rash youngest brother, Jérôme, on the chateau of Hougoumont. Jérôme's determination to carry the position saw him commit more and more men to the fray, until a move intended to distract Wellington cost Napoleon a key part of his reserves.

No Hope of Safety Except in Victory:[26] Agincourt (1415)

The Battle of Agincourt has become synonymous, perhaps, with Shakespeare's rousing speech from *Henry V* recounting the exploits of that 'band of brothers' that fought and won against a French army significantly larger in size, and more impressive in chivalric spectacle. It has also become seemingly inextricably linked to the dominance of the English archer and longbow, a coupling of soldier and weapon that has been repeatedly credited with winning the day for the English. The battle, however, was perhaps more nuanced than is sometimes acknowledged. Far from being killing machines directly responsible for thousands of French dead, the longbow has more recently been highlighted as a tool of English tactics, allowing Henry V and his commanders to channel the French army into positions on the battlefield that most suited Henry's strategy.[27] It is therefore the success of English tactics, and the failure of French, that are responsible for the outcome of Agincourt.

The battle was fought on 25 October 1415, near the villages of Agincourt and Tramecourt in northern France. After a campaign of several weeks, a desultory, dysentery-ridden English army made a last-ditch attempt to escape capture and return to friendly territory. For the French, it was an opportunity to drive the English from their land and win renown in the ongoing conflict between the two countries.

A recent study has estimated the English force at Agincourt at approximately 9,000, less than a quarter of whom were men-at-arms, the remainder being archers. The French, on the other hand, were certainly numerically superior, although almost certainly not as overwhelming as some contemporary chroniclers would have us imagine. The same recent study has estimated French numbers at 12,000 – of whom two-thirds were men-at-arms.[28]

When deciding on their strategy and tactical plans for the battle, both French and English commanders would have known something of the army that they faced. The French had been tracking the English for some time, perhaps even since they left Harfleur.[29] It is likely that they therefore would have known the approximate size of Henry's forces, but perhaps only have vague information on the proportion of men-at-arms and archers.

Henry, meanwhile, had reconnoitred the battlefield the day before, and used the terrain and conditions to inform the deployment of his forces. He positioned at least some of his archers on the flanks using scrub and the edges of the woodland to cover them, which also served to disguise the numbers of bowmen he had at his disposal. Other smaller groups of archers were probably placed between and even in front of the men-at-arms, able to move quickly from their position if the men-at-arms advanced.[30]

The English adopted a defensive position, utilising a slight rise in the landscape to afford them an elevated view of the field of battle. Both the right and left flanks were anchored on woodlands. The trees afforded the archers, stationed on the flanks, some protection from attack from behind. Not only would the woodland prove difficult terrain through which to attack, obstructing commanders' views of their own forces and rendering command almost impossible, but it would prove slow for the French to mount any attack through them, giving the English sufficient time to respond if such a flanking move was attempted.

By choosing this position, the English also determined that the French would be funnelled towards them between the woodlands of Agincourt and Tramecourt.[31] Henry would have been worried about an attack on the rear; behind him lay salvation and escape to England. If the French were able to manoeuvre around him and block his escape, his campaign would be lost and he himself would risk capture, humiliation, and probable financial ruin for England in ransoming him back. Therefore, to control the field of battle, Henry ensured that the French were incentivised away from flanking or encirclement manoeuvres by presenting them with an easy, frontal assault. This suited French tactics, which were dependent on an initial cavalry charge. Henry would have known the French preference for this tactic, and thus presented them with the perfect opportunity to use it.

Just as Henry hoped, the French commanders, aware of their superior numbers, planned on a frontal cavalry-led attack that would overwhelm the English, placing their heavy cavalry – the knights – in their front ranks and sending archers and crossbowmen further back, 'so all the men of lower ranks, who were enough to have beaten the English, were pushed to the rear'.[32] The monk of Saint-Denys, somewhat more suspicious of the French commanders' motives, claims that this strategy was due to each 'claiming for himself the honour of leading the vanguard' in the hope that 'the sight of so many princes would strike terror into the enemy'.[33]

Both English and French armies were divided for battle into three sections, or battles. The French drew up their three battles in parallel lines, the vanguard nearest to the English and the other two lines behind. The vanguard was crammed with a large number of men-at-arms alongside many nobles including the French marshal Jean le Maingre, and constable Charles d'Albret; it seems that the French wanted to crush the English with one massive initial strike featuring the van and cavalry. The imbalanced size of the vanguard may also have been a consequence of late arrivals to the battle, including the Duke of Orléans, who only arrived on the morning of the battle itself, and the Dukes of Brabant and Brittany, who were expected but had not yet appeared.

The English army was also divided into three battles, each led by a commander with military experience. Lord Camoys led the left and rearguard, Edward of York the right and vanguard, and King Henry himself commanded the central battle, a position of honour from where he would have been most able to command the entire army. It is likely that the three battles positioned level with one another rather than slightly stacked, due to the small English numbers. Contemporary sources provide little information on the position of the archers in relation to the men-to-arms, although the *Gesta Henrici Quinti* provides some clue by describing that Henry placed his archers either to each flank, as well as between the three battles, or embedded his archers within each battle. Other near-contemporary accounts describe the archers on the flanks of the English forces, which would explain how the men-at-arms evaded the archers' protective stakes deployed in a scattered formation to prevent cavalry attack, and would also account for the funnelling effect of the archers on the French troops. Whichever position the archers adopted, each battle would therefore have been protected by archers in close proximity to them, offering the most effective coverage of the ground in front of each force.

After a long stand-off from dawn to mid-morning, the English advanced towards the French. English archers, who had carried stakes with them through days of marching across northern France, now hammered those stakes into the ground around their positions to protect them from French cavalry attack. They then shot initial volleys with their longbows, 'whose shots, as dense as a hailstorm, obscured the sky and wounded a great number of their opponents'.[34] In response, the French vanguard charged the English lines just as they had planned, and as Henry had hoped. The archers kept shooting from the flanks of the English men-at-arms, onto the flanks of the French vanguard. This pushed the French flanks inwards as men-at-arms tried to escape the arrows falling on them; their press into the middle effectively channelled them towards the three English battles of Camoys, Henry, and Edward. An anonymous English chronicler describes the devastating combined impact of the arrows and stakes:

> Our archers shot no arrows off target; all caused death and brought to the ground both men and horses ... Our stakes made them fall over, each on top of the other so that they lay in heaps two spears' length in height.[35]

After their opening offensive move, the English followed a more defensive strategy, waiting for the masses of the French vanguard to attack and responding in kind. That the English were quickly able to shift from advance to static defence is testament to their organisation and discipline; this was no dispirited, broken English army, despite the long campaign march and illness that affected the troops. To make matters worse for the French, as their vanguard attacked, their archers and crossbowmen could not support by bombarding the English from distance; their range was less than that of the English longbowmen, thus the French sacrificed any advantage gained by having crossbowmen present on the battlefield at all.[36]

Meanwhile, the English archers were running low on arrows. When they could shoot no more, and with the French vanguard stalled by the English men-at-arms, they threw down their bows and assaulted the French men-at-arms directly, with small groups attacking French infantrymen who had become scattered or disorientated after the first French infantry charge.[37] The archers perhaps used the very mallets with which they had hammered their stakes into the ground before battle commenced; one contemporary chronicler describes the English weapons as 'great lead-covered mallets from which one single blow on the head could kill a man or knock him senseless to the ground'.[38] This further enveloping attack allowed the English to harry the disorganised troops on the flanks, where many of the French – seeing the carnage at the front and the English archers now bearing down on them – may well have begun to flee towards the rear. There, they were met with further ranks of French soldiers pressing forwards; the confusion and carnage was described in the near-contemporary *Gesta Henrici Quinti*:

> For when some of them, killed when battle was first joined, fell at the front, so great was the undisciplined violence and pressure of the mass of men behind that the living fell on top of the dead, and others falling on top of the living were killed as well.[39]

At this point in the battle, word reached Henry that a group of French cavalry had attacked the English baggage train, which was also where the captured French prisoners were being held. In reality, this 'attack' seems to have been a raid by French peasantry from the nearby villages, led by the Lord of Agincourt. Henry, however, thinking that the French were at best trying to free the hundreds of prisoners, and at worst attempting to envelop him, then noted apparent preparations for a second charge by the French cavalry in the distance. These two events coinciding led to the infamous massacre of those Frenchmen captured for ransom: 'the prisoners, save for the dukes of Orléans and Bourbon ... and a very few others, were killed by the swords either of their captors or of others following after, lest they should involve us in utter disaster in the fighting that would ensue.'[40]

Seeing the mounting dead and the disorganisation of the French, the English then mounted an incursion into the French ranks, again marking a swift turn from defensive to offensive manoeuvres. Soon after midday, Henry's forces were in 'possession of the field', that is, they had taken the ground where the French had drawn up before the battle was joined. The English had taken hundreds of French prisoners, including the marshal Jean le Maingre; meanwhile, thousands of Frenchmen lay dead on the field including the constable Charles d'Albret, three dukes and nine counts.

The English longbow was therefore only one facet of Henry's victory at Agincourt. A larger part of that victory was the tactical acumen that the English forces demonstrated, and the lack of tactical flexibility and adaptation displayed by the French forces. By aiming their longbows towards French flanks, English archers narrowed and funnelled the French attack onto their men-at-arms and confused enemy forces. The tactical deployment of the weapon was therefore the true reason for English victory.

Attack them Head-on: Panjwai (2006)

The Second Battle of Panjwai, 1–17 September 2006, was one of the largest conventional clashes between Taliban and coalition forces during the war in Afghanistan. Since the US-led invasion of 2001, the Taliban had used recognisable insurgency tactics: small groups of fighters launching ambushes, attacking patrols and outposts, and using improvised explosive devices (IEDs) to attack communications and transport routes. But in mid-2006, just as NATO began to assume operational responsibility from US forces, coalition commanders in the southern province of Kandahar noted a distinct change in the Taliban approach: larger forces were massing around the Panjwai district, roughly twenty miles from Kandahar city.

This change was driven by a new operational strategy, in which the Taliban hoped to provoke an attritional battle to defeat coalition forces with heavy casualties, inflicting huge political damage on the occupation. As more NATO intelligence was gathered, a picture emerged of a determined enemy setting up a heavily entrenched encampment. Canadian Brigadier General David Fraser, NATO commander in southern Afghanistan, understood the situation: 'they wanted me to attack them head on, à la World War I, at enormous cost in soldiers, both Afghan and coalition.'[41]

That the Taliban were moving to more conventional tactics came as a mild surprise given their inferiority in firepower, mobility, equipment and training, yet their fighters were confident. They had amassed some of their most experienced men for the coming battle, and coalition forces had already seen their effectiveness in action during recent operations in southern Uruzgan and northern Helmand. A report for US Congress stated ominously that 'the Taliban exhibited a high degree of coordination in their combat operations'.[42] Troops on the ground concurred. Canadian Sergeant Patrick Towers, who fought the Taliban in Panjwai in August, admitted:

> I underestimated them because I figured them to be just a bunch of farmers that pick up AK47s but they employ tactics, they have training and what blew me away was later, when we swept their ambush positions, they had depth to their positions, cut offs with machine guns, anti-tank positions – all dug in ... they were well trained and they can employ tactics ... they're certainly not just a bunch of dirt farmers.[43]

Taliban tactics certainly had a huge influence on the battle. The coalition battlegroup – Lieutenant Colonel Omer Lavoie's 1st Battalion, Royal Canadian Regiment, with attached American and Afghan National Army (ANA) support – would be drawn into a conventional stand-up fight instead of anticipated counterinsurgency ('find, fix, destroy') operations.

The Taliban adopted an almost classic defensive posture. Massing their forces in Panjwai, they largely cleared the area of civilians, and set about fortifying the position. They anchored themselves on ground good for defence: agricultural land, broken by canals, irrigation channels, and mud-walled hamlets that provided plenty of cover and protected firing positions. They supplemented this with an elaborate system of trenches, arms caches, strongpoints, and fall-back positions for defence in depth. There were enfilading positions and interlocking fields of fire covering a killing zone to the south of their position.

Clearly the Taliban aimed to draw the Canadian forces into this formidable position in order to inflict mass casualties. Yet by relying on fixed defences, the Taliban handed the operational initiative to the Canadians, who were able to control the timing and tempo of the action. Taliban fighters did continue to launch small-scale attacks, with almost daily ambushes of the roving Canadian cordon, and in early August a major Taliban force attacked to drive a Canadian company from the Ma'Sum Ghar heights, to the south of the defensive area. The main action, however, would rely on waiting for the Canadians to come to them.

Lavoie and Fraser were aware of this, and planned to turn the Taliban's advantages against them. The defensive zone would be a death trap to an attacker, but it could also prove a trap to the Taliban. Their plan for Operation Medusa was therefore to envelop the position with blockading forces from north (B Company) and south (A and C companies), and use their superior firepower of airstrikes and four 155mm howitzers to pummel the defences. Feint attacks would be made by the blockading companies in their light armoured vehicles (LAVs) to draw the Taliban into the open where they could be targeted and destroyed. Forward operating officers were embedded with the infantry to coordinate the combined arms of ground troops, artillery, close air support, and tactical strike aircraft. The tactical approach was therefore to use long-range bombardment to nullify the Taliban's defensive position and deny them their main aim of engaging coalition troops in a bloody close-quarters firefight. If this was to be a battle of attrition, they planned to use firepower to wear the Taliban down physically and psychologically. As Fraser stated: 'I was going to draw out the fight with the long-range fires as long as I could and go after their minds.'[44]

The battle began well for the Canadians. The blockading forces moved smoothly into position on 1 September, C Company retaking Ma'Sum Ghar unopposed. NATO forces to east and west completed a loose cordon, trapping the Taliban into a battlefield of only a few square kilometres. From the heights the Canadians were able to direct artillery and airstrikes onto Taliban positions, supplemented with fire from their LAVs' 25mm cannons. The plan was to bombard for three days, destroying Taliban materiel and morale. Yet it soon became apparent that it was impossible to assess whether the bombardment was actually effective, as most Taliban fighters remained hidden. Fraser therefore decided to adapt his plan and on 3 September ordered C Company to conduct a feint across the Arghandab river against the southern Taliban position to draw out the enemy.

The tactical use of a feint had a profound impact on the course of the battle. To provoke an enemy response, the company had to advance into effective range of enemy weapons – into their kill zone. The Taliban showed enormous fire discipline to allow the LAVs to come within fifty yards of their position before opening up with small-arms, RPG and 82mm recoilless-rifle fire. The strength of the defensive positions showed; C Company was hit from three sides, with hidden emplacements enfilading their position. LAV cannon and machine guns gave a firm mobile fire base, but the company took losses of vehicles – and men. They were almost immediately pinned down. Although assisted by close air support and fire from across the river, it took several hours of heavy fighting for the company to extricate itself. Four Canadians died in the operation, and eight were wounded.

At this stage, Taliban tactics were working. They had taken more punishment than they would have liked from artillery and airstrikes, but the repulse of C Company raised morale and led to more fighters being funnelled into the battlespace. Moreover, the casualties inflicted had caused significant disquiet in Canadian high command.[45] Despite the losses, Fraser saw some value in having exposed the Taliban positions, and ordered another feint the next morning; tragically, before it could begin, an American A-10 providing air support accidentally strafed C Company's position, killing one and wounding over thirty men, including most of company command. The incident ended the planned feint, and indeed saw the scrapping of much of the Canadian plan.

The coalition shelling and airstrikes continued, but Lavoie knew that the infantry would need to go back in to win the battle decisively:

> we dropped thousands of tons of munitions on them ... But in the end, as we relearned, you just cannot rely on it because until you actually get in there and muck out those fortified defensive positions you just can't be sure [that the enemy are gone][46]

Yet their early losses prompted a change of tack. Firstly, the cordon around the Taliban positions was tightened. On 4 September an American special forces and ANA battlegroup, TF-31, assaulted and captured the imposing 3,000ft feature of Sperwan Ghar, which dominated the landscape to the south-west and had been used as a Taliban command post.[47] Heavy Taliban counterattacks, which mostly revolved around unsophisticated fire-and-manoeuvre frontal assaults, were defeated with accurate small-arms fire and close air support, especially from AC-130 gunships. Superior American tactics (and firepower) were decisive in this clash. Next, the Canadians realigned the axis of their advance. C Company and some support units – designated TF Grizzly – were left on Ma'Sum Ghar as a show of force to pin enemy attention while A Company and a company of US 10th Mountain Division moved to join B Company in the north.

Trapped north of the river and unable to outflank the Canadians to the south, the Taliban defensive lines were undermined by this axis shift; by far the strongest positions faced south. B Company began to advance on 6 September, with dismounted infantry moving slowly down irrigation canals, and LAVs providing support on the flanks. Heavy preliminary artillery bombardment and airstrikes smashed any likely Taliban strongpoints. Resistance was minimal. On 8 September the other two companies reached the front line, and the three advanced in coordinated moves, effectively leapfrogging one another behind a tremendous barrage of firepower. The skill of coordinating the infantry assaults with artillery and air cover, alongside nightly reconnaissance of targets and objectives, allowed coalition troops to advance slowly but surely, grinding down the enemy as they went while taking minimal casualties of their own. Lavoie explained:

We used air to hit deep and close artillery at 300 yards or less. Dismounted infantry rushed in before the smoke cleared and seized the objective. Engineers cleared a route with bulldozers and dealt with IEDs. We pushed LAVs up to support infantry to the next objective and to the next bound.[48]

The evacuation of civilians prior to the battle helped with assaulting built-up areas; anything could be a legitimate target, and rooms could be cleared with grenades and small-arms fire without exposing infantry or non-combatants to unnecessary risks. The Taliban, unable to engage or even move without being hit by airbursts, hellfire missiles, or cannon fire, began to fall back on ambushes and IEDs rather than conventional defence. To keep up the pressure, and prevent fighters escaping the onslaught, on 11 September TF Grizzly crossed the Arghandab river in the teeth of 'medium resistance' and moved to flank the Taliban positions to the east. This further undermined their crumbling lines; resistance began to fade, and by the time A Company linked up with TF Grizzly on 14 September, the fighting was virtually over.

Operation Medusa's success owed much to firepower and technological advantage, but tactics heavily shaped the course and outcome of the combat. In a grand tactical sense, the Taliban defensive approach was undermined by the Canadian envelopment and refusal – except in a miscarried feint – to enter pre-prepared kill zones. The realignment to the north and capture of Sperwan Ghar further disoriented the defenders. The minor tactical approach of the northern companies allowed them to maximise their advantages while minimising those of the Taliban – whose losses were estimated at over 500 fighters killed, compared to thirteen coalition soldiers.[49] The tactics of the combatants played no small role in that outcome.

Chapter 6

Logistics

'The war has been variously termed a war of production and a war of machines. Whatever else it is ... it is a war of logistics'
Ernest King[1]

Against a backdrop of battles, logistical provision for fighting units can appear somewhat mundane. On the contrary, however, as this quote from Admiral Ernest King suggests, logistics directly determine whether an army has the tools to fight, and can influence battlefield victory or defeat. In the simplest sense, logistics encompasses the provision of the requirements of life for an army during a campaign and a battle; it aims to guarantee that an army will be able to sustain combat preparedness while in enemy territory, that soldiers arrive at a battle in a state in which they are able to fight, and that they are able to sustain combat over hours or even days. As such, logistics are of central importance to the management of a battle; the defence of supply lines or baggage often dictates events on the battlefield, as they must be protected. Logistical provisions can include food and drink, weapons and ammunition, clothing, shelter, medical supplies, and technical support, alongside other more personal items to bolster soldiers' morale and, most basically, the soldiers themselves. Logistical support therefore involves the methods of moving materiel from one place to another, a feat managed for much of history on horseback at the pace of walking beasts.

The logistical requirements of armies have changed dramatically in scale over the past millennium, as has the ability of support personnel to supply and resupply deployed forces in the field. In the context of campaigns, this is particularly evident: a two-month *chevauchée* in the fourteenth century would certainly require fewer consumable provisions than a modern multi-year campaign. However, change is also obvious in battle. The resupply required and available in medieval battles, which usually lasted only a few hours, would be very different to those required during a month-long battle in the First World War, and the complexity of arranging those logistical needs would of course differ greatly.

Despite this variance, all armies need to transport supplies into battle. These may be loosely grouped into three categories: the apparatus of battle itself, including weapons, ammunition and any necessary technical military support; food, medical supplies and those items necessary to sustain soldiers' lives while fighting; and additional items whose function is to boost morale by providing for the entertainment, distraction or enjoyment of soldiers. Into this latter category fit everything from card games and bathing supplies to musical instruments; incredibly, British officers of the Boer War took with them champagne, portable baths, gramophones and pianos.[2]

There remain several basic avenues open to commanders in the procurement of supplies which have remained more or less common since the medieval period, although of course the terminology and exact natures of these sources have changed. The first method of supply is the provision of all necessary stores centrally, by the state or army leadership. In the medieval period, this was usually the king or his representative; in the modern era, this duty is the purview of governmental departments and logistics corps. Weaponry, in particular, has been commonly provided in this way. Since the early modern period firearms and ammunition have almost always been issued from central arsenals, but there was also some issuing of weaponry to medieval fighters. In England, bows, bowstrings and arrows were ordered from producers across the country and then stored, ready for use, in the Tower of London.[3] These could then be distributed to troops on the occasion of campaign or conflict.

Echoing the centralised system for weapon distribution, armies throughout the last millennium have often provided food and drink for soldiers from centralised stockpiles. Although there is sometimes a tendency to attribute this kind of systematised supply to the early modern period, medieval systems of provision were often advanced in their logistical organisation. The English medieval Pipe Rolls, for example, are replete with references to supplies gathered for military expeditions and some of the quantities required were significant indeed. A medieval army of 30,000 men is estimated to have needed around 800 tons of grain each week, with an additional 300 tons of grain weekly for a modest 5,000 horses. For Henry II's expedition to Ireland in 1171, nearly 1,400 tons of wheat and 230 tons of oats were provided from the English counties.[4]

The collection of weapons and food supplies was often the responsibility of the sheriffs in each county, who would receive demands from the king and his officials for supplies. Before the mid-fourteenth century, prise or purveyance were common; these were demands for food, transportation and other necessities for military campaigns at little or no cost, in order to provision the king's wars, and were highly unpopular among the populations of Europe. After food had been sourced, it was gathered in a central storage site – or loaded onto ships if destined for a foreign front – overseen by the receiver of victuals.

Similarly, outrage was directed towards suspicions that not all supplies would then be provisioned to the men in the front lines. There is evidence of corrupt practices in getting provisions to fighting men during the medieval period, with numerous records of officials being tried for theft of food and alcohol in particular. This was also rife in later centuries: in the Thirty Years' War, for example, each tier of the logistical organisation of the armies involved would remove a layer of supplies, leaving the general soldiery with very little when the supply finally reached them.[5]

Merchants could also supply armies, with food in particular, either through central purchases or directly to soldiers. This practice of private supply was particularly common for food in the pre-modern era, after the requisitioning of food through prise or purveyance eventually became so wildly unpopular that medieval kings were forced to curtail the practice. As in a modern army, a single merchant provider might be preferred for certain goods, or to provision a certain campaign. For Edward III's Poitiers campaign in 1356, for example, the sheriff of Lincoln sourced most of the oats he had been ordered to procure from a single merchant – perhaps as many as 70 tons.[6]

While food was therefore often gathered en masse in advance of a campaign, the weapons that soldiers fought with in the medieval period were usually sourced privately. Knights and medieval fighting elites would provide not only weapons for their retinues, but also have their own sets of weapons and armour that they would use in battle. Genoese crossbowmen also provided their own crossbows, while in England, retinues and arrayed combatants would often be expected to provide their own weapons. Private provision continued with the mercenary armies of the early modern period, with the vast majority of such combatants in the Thirty Years' War providing their own food, clothing and equipment from the wages that they were paid to fight.

In addition to centrally provisioned food, soldiers could 'forage' or survive through subsistence – from the medieval period to the twentieth century. With horse-drawn transport limited in what it could carry, military commanders utilised wherever possible the resources offered from the land they marched across. As well as gaining supplies, this had the added benefit of undermining the enemy's morale, control and access to supplies themselves. Soldiers gathering their own food was often deliberately incorporated into plans for a campaign. During the Spanish War of the two Peters (1356–79), the forces of Castile destroyed grain, olive trees and vineyards in the Kingdom of Valencia in a series of *cavalgada* until nothing remained to be harvested. In the Hundred Years' War, the battles of Crécy, Poitiers and Agincourt were all preceded by *chevauchées* in which English armies not only provisioned themselves from French land, but pillaged what they needed and burned the rest in a form of logistical warfare. The use of French resources was specifically incorporated into strategic planning, and the reality for most English fighters was that they had been eating French food, cooked over French fuel, and washed down with French wine, for weeks before battle was joined.

Most of these provisions were seized directly from civilian populations, with soldiers spending significant time on their plundering missions, although sometimes finding supplies locally could be organised by the army's command structure. Medieval sources abound with references to provisions taken from towns captured during campaigns. During the siege of Caen in the midst of the Crécy campaign, for example, the English spent four days gathering provisions from the local French population and yet were still low on supplies when battle was joined. Even Henry V's victorious campaign culminating in the Battle of Agincourt in 1415 required Henry to consider how 'detachments might be sent out to obtain food for men and horses for the sustenance of the army'.[7]

Until the seventeenth century, European armies were usually small enough that 'living off the land' during campaigns could be supported by the regions they occupied, albeit only by inflicting grievous harm on local populations and economies. As armies grew significantly larger from the seventeenth century, so their impact on local environs obviously increased. To support themselves, these larger armies began to use systematic magazines, or stores, for weapons, food and other supplies that they could manoeuvre between in order to resupply on campaign. Reliance on this system meant that armies rarely ventured too far from the nearest magazines, leading to some operational inflexibility. However, magazines could be used to great effect in keeping troops supplied and in battle preparedness. The baggage trains required to move stores from magazine to fighting troops grew alongside the armies. These engorged auxiliary units were famously slow and cumbersome, contributing to the ponderousness of eighteenth-century manoeuvre typified by Marlborough's slow and deliberate movements in the War of Spanish Succession (1701–14).

With the arrival of the mass armies of the French Revolution, however, the advantages of living off the land once more became evident. Armies could be fed from central supplies while in cantonments, but on campaign sourcing food locally negated the need for long, slow baggage trains following the main army – a factor that Napoleon famously used to his advantage to march at incredible speeds across early nineteenth-century Europe. For his Ulm campaign into Bavaria in 1805, for example, he marched more than 200,000 soldiers a distance of over 200 miles in thirteen days.[8] Such a blistering pace caused one French soldier to remark that 'our emperor makes war not with our arms but with our legs'.[9] Yet even Napoleon was not immune to the difficulties of large numbers of soldiers stripping the land bare, and had to march his army corps along separate routes to not exhaust the land for those following as they passed through. Moreover, when his troops fought in less fertile areas like Spain or Russia, or when they campaigned in barren winter months, food was often in disastrously short supply, impacting the fighting efficiency of his troops.

Regardless of how any army sources its food, it will still need to transport weapons, munitions, shelter, technological or medical supplies with it towards battle, or to its forward troops. For most of the last millennium, the fastest speed of land transport was the pace that a horse was able to travel – that is, a maximum of twenty miles a day, but in reality, often significantly less. Even well into the modern era, horses have been used to transport ammunition and supplies in combat zones thanks to their relative cheapness, wide availability, and the relative ease with which they can traverse otherwise challenging terrain. In the First World War, ammunition mules were a common sight along the trenches of Northern Europe, while even in the Second World War almost every participant nation used horses for transportation. Perhaps surprisingly, Germany utilised 2.75 million horses and mules alongside modern motorised transportation. The USSR, however, won the horse race with an enormous 3.5 million beasts used.[10] The major drawback to horses in the logistic sense is that they have their own needs that increase the complexity of supporting an army even further. In the Red Army, horses required twelve pounds of fodder daily, which had to be supplied alongside the soldiers' other provisions.[11] This is in addition to the obvious challenges of moving horses – whether transport or cavalry – to the battlefront. For the Hastings campaign, for example, William of Normandy transported perhaps 2–3,000 horses in a fleet of boats across the English Channel; this significant logistical endeavour took months to prepare, but was fundamental to his fighting style reliant on Norman cavalry.[12]

From the nineteenth century, mechanised transportation gradually came into use to supply and resupply troops in conflict zones. The use of railways to transport supplies – and of course troops themselves – meant that resupply could happen quickly, depending on the railway line's location, upkeep, and the absence of enemy interference. Railways could also resupply relatively quickly, especially when measured against the alternative overland transport methods in the early twentieth century. In 1914, it took 117 trains only nine days to carry a corps over 600 miles, although the loading and unloading times required at both ends of the route made it too lengthy to consider for journeys below 100 miles.[13] Railways are therefore not without their own limitations. They are also a fundamentally inflexible means of transportation, the route and destination necessarily set beforehand, and an army dependent on them for logistical support cannot venture far beyond their locale without risking the enemy cutting them off.

In the twentieth century, railway logistics were supplemented by motor vehicles. The USA used almost 2.5 million trucks in the Second World War, and Germany, still dependent on horsepower at the beginning of the conflict, was unprepared for the speed with which Allied forces could move troops and supplies. Though they attempted to quickly assemble mechanised transports (from 1935 to 1944, more than 130,000 Opel Blitz trucks and chassis were produced in German factories), they often ran out of fuel – an additional logistical consideration with the advent of this new military resource – which left German troops open to Allied attacks.

Waterborne transport can also be a useful – or necessary – way of moving supplies. From the Norman use of a fleet of hundreds of ships to cross the Channel in 1066, to the use of freighters to transport over a million tons of goods to Saudi Arabia for the First Gulf War, shipping has provided a relatively quick and cost-effective means of transporting large amounts of materiel and equipment. However, similarly to railway technology, shipping is limited by the inflexibility of ports of disembarkation. River systems do allow for some greater flexibility inland; at the turn of the seventeenth century, Maurice of Nassau used river networks to manoeuvre his troops and surprise Spanish land-based forces, for instance at the Battle of Jülich in 1610 when the river Rhine eased the movement of troops and guns. Even with inland waterways there remains the need for materiel to be transported from the landing site to battlefield or magazine. In the First Gulf War, goods were landed at Dahrain and then loaded onto truck convoys to be moved to the front line – at their peak, one truck passed a certain point on the supply line route every three seconds.[14]

Air logistics are often the fastest way of resupplying troops in the field, especially in areas that are difficult to reach or hazardous to a ground-based supply route. Again, however, air transport is limited in many respects to designated landing points – such as runways – that themselves require significant logistical commitment. Helicopters have much greater deployment flexibility, being able to land virtually anywhere, but their cargo capacity is limited in comparison with the largest plane carriers; a Chinook can carry less than 10 per cent of the payload of a C-5 Galaxy, for example.

With the recent advent of remote-operated technology, resupply of smaller forces can be organised, overseen, and initiated at a significant distance. One of the earliest unmanned systems appeared during the First World War, with the 'electric dog' – a three-wheeled vehicle potentially intended to carry supplies to the trenches. Unmanned logistical systems have developed significantly since. The appearance of Unmanned Aerial Vehicles (UAVs), commonly referred to as drones, is perhaps the biggest change. Drones of course have their own logistical 'tail', requiring not only pilots trained to operate them, but also teams of trained engineers, technicians and support crew. They are also expensive: a single MQ-9 Reaper drone, commonly used for intelligence collection alongside targeting, cost the US Air Force around $32 million in 2020.[15]

The benefits of drone logistics, however – in safety for personnel, speed of transportation, and accessibility of hard-to-reach areas – is certainly worth the investment for many nations. The Chinese army has used drones to provide logistical support for troops stationed at an elevated location of more than 4,500 meters.[16] The civilian sector is also making inroads into the use of unmanned systems in logistics management, for instance with robotics deployment in factories and automatic resupply ordering. The shortcomings of this form of just-in-time logistics, however, have been noted by operational troops. In the Second Gulf War, some American soldiers felt that they lacked sufficient supplies and reported running so low on water that they had to purchase it from Iraqi street vendors.[17]

The importance of remote or drone-enabled supply mitigates one of the most significant limitations on logistical provision: the quality and effectiveness of communication lines. Throughout the last millennium, poor-quality roads, lack of railway infrastructure, or limitations of docking at small ports have all limited armies' abilities to supply or resupply before or in the midst of battle. At times armies have attempted to circumvent poor logistical transport by building it – but even this approach can fail if logistical supply for these engineering projects is inadequate. During the Second Lebanon War, for example, the IDF troops on the ground in Lebanon in July 2006 advanced more quickly than the rate at which logistics routes breached for them were laid. Although airdrops were able to resupply the troops who had moved ahead, some of these supplies then fell into Hezbollah's hands.

In addition to routes of communication and supply, there are any number of factors that, from medieval times to the modern age, influence the ease, speed and scale of logistics. Some of these factors impact on both sides in a conflict; weather, for instance, can hamper both armies equally. Other factors are more specific, however, and can help to give one side a significant advantage in battle. Poor lines of communication or transport links endured by one army may not be experienced by the other and can severely hinder operational and logistical functioning.

Weather conditions and terrain partly dictate what supplies an army will need, and influence how easily they can be procured, from increased need for food and winter uniforms in cold climates, to the increased demand for water in desert environs. Failing to tailor needs to the prevailing climate can have a crucial impact on battles. Often the problems of meeting specific logistical needs, and the challenges of transporting necessary supplies over significant distances, are compounded by the failure of military command to prepare properly. The battles of the Crusades, for example, are marked from the Franks' perspective by a repeated inability both to estimate correctly the water needed by their forces, and then to deliver this when required. The sieges of Jerusalem (1099) and Damascus (1148) were marked by crusader armies without adequate water convoys setting up camps in dry, arid landscapes, while their defeat at the Battle of Hattin (1187) was precipitated by King Guy of Jerusalem's repeated inability to guarantee water supplies for his vast army in the height of an Outremer summer.

Weather also impacts the ease of transporting supplies over distance, meaning that conditions far from the site of combat can still influence its outcome. Poor roads that become quagmires with rainfall or dustbowls in dry spells would hinder the movement of horse-drawn baggage wagons as much – if not more – than they would hinder the soldiers marching in front of them. Such problems are not limited to the muddy roads of pre-modern warfare. During twenty-first-century counterinsurgency engagements in Afghanistan, inclement weather risked reducing the availability of air transport and forcing the increased use of ground transportation, which could itself be slowed by worsening conditions on roads or terrain.[18]

Long distances covered by conflict can further exacerbate the challenges posed by terrain. The need to cross expansive deserts, oceans or mountain ranges can delay or even cripple logistical supply to an army on campaign. During the American Civil War, for example, supply routes could cover significant distances: the Union army wintering at Murfreesboro, Tennessee, 1862/3, used the Louisville–Nashville and Nashville–Chattanooga railroads for logistical support across long distances back to the Ohio river. In the Crimean War the distance to the Russian front line meant that ammunition could take up to three months to resupply the imperial army, compared to a relatively quick three weeks for resupply for the British and French by sea. The distance involved in fighting across its vast territory is a familiar issue in Russian military history; in the twentieth century, the 4,000-mile distance to the front line during the Russo-Japanese War (1904–5) meant that Russian supplies could take months to be delivered. The challenges of provisioning an army on the move over long distances are arguably even more complex. Rommel's German army in North Africa struggled to supply itself across the vast desert distances, even with resupply via coastal ports and motorised transport, and their dependence on fuel was a further barrier to logistical support.[19]

Difficulties in resupplying armies in the field are compounded by lack of foresight. One of the greatest challenges for logisticians – especially in the pre-modern era – is to plan for circumstances that they know very little about. That ignorance is particularly notable in times of significant and rapid changes in warfare when logisticians without the benefit of foresight are unable to predict the demands of their troops. During the First World War, for example, despite careful preparation, the British army's logistical requirements soon outstripped supply. On average, ammunition was consumed at ten times pre-war estimates. The ensuing shortage of weaponry caused the 'shell scandal' of 1915, particularly following Neuve Chapelle, and underlined a British failure in planning and preparation for campaigning on the Continent. The sheer scale of the global conflict, encompassing as it did battles in so many theatres of war, seemed to catch some commanders unprepared. The Allied attack on Gallipoli is a clear example of this: logistical preparations were uncoordinated between the three different branches of the Mediterranean Expeditionary Force (MEF), and areas of logistical support for the attack were apparently planned in isolation. Medical requirements were largely overlooked, with casualty projections a fraction of the actual number, and many basic logistical requirements were unplanned – even the provision and accessibility of water were marginal to Allied plans.[20] In fact, the commander of the MEF, Ian Hamilton, was appointed with the condition that he did not ask for additional resources.[21] Of course, in the context of a larger conflict, an individual battle or even campaign must be planned alongside others. Such was the case at Gallipoli, with the Western Front remaining the Allied strategic priority.

Conversely, careful planning can often help to support an army and ensure morale and fighting ability continue unimpeded. Despite the problems faced by crusaders in the Holy Land in the eleventh and twelfth centuries, the Third Crusade led by Richard I of England demonstrated superior logistical planning and management. Not only did Richard's commanders keep in contact with the fleet off the coast, calling up supplies when necessary, but commanders manoeuvred marches between water sources and even had laundry organisation to keep clothes clean and help morale and health.[22]

Richard I's washerwomen notwithstanding, logistical supply can often be complicated further by the scale of technology required to resupply an army in combat. As military hardware has become more sophisticated, so have the requirements for specialist support and resupply grown. While medieval siege towers required wood, manpower, and time to build, modern military weapons require extensive research, development, and production time in order to resupply, as discovered by the USAF in Yugoslavia in 1999, when they started to run out of cruise missiles.[23] The complexities of technological resupply are further compounded by the growing internationalism of technology industries, in which it is possible that necessary resupply provisions may be manufactured by a country on the opposite side of the conflict. North Korea found itself in such circumstances during the Korean War (1950–3) when, although it controlled the bulk of Korea's railway network, engines and railway cars, it did not have access to replacement parts which were manufactured in Japan. That is not to say that conflict will always prevent supplies, however; Napoleon continued to import British boots for his French armies despite the two nations being at war.

It is of course possible for the best-equipped, most carefully planned logistical operation to be stymied by enemy action. Encirclement that cuts off an enemy's supply line can be a potent battlefield tactic. This was evident at Stalingrad in November 1942, when a Soviet double encirclement cut German lines of communication, enabling them to effectively choke the Sixth Army. Enemy logistics can also be undermined by disrupting communications routes rather than encirclement. Shortly before the Battle of Carcano (1160), Frederick Barbarossa blockaded Milanese lines of communication – a single mountainous road – with felled trees in order to prevent any messages or support from getting through.²⁴ Of course, unknown third parties are always an additional risk factor to supply lines, as Edward II discovered during his Scottish expedition of 1322. The army was forced to return to England when, arriving at the Forth, it found that Flemish pirates had prevented their ships from bringing necessary food supplies up the East Coast.

More direct action is also possible to destroy an army's supplies during battle, thus hampering their ability to fight. Munitions provide a particularly tempting target, and examples abound of weapons caches being targeted by enemy fire. At Marengo (1800), an exploding Austrian ammunition wagon not only denied them supplies, but spread panic in nearby units. In the Vietnam War, munitions attacks were a common occurrence on US bases. Long Binh was home to a major ammunition depot and was attacked each year from 1966 to 1969. On 4 February 1967, for example, the National Liberation Front attacked the depot and destroyed an estimated 15,000 155mm artillery shells.²⁵ Such attacks underscore the vulnerability of ammunition supplies – without which, even a well-fed and otherwise adequately supplied army will struggle to ready itself for battle.

The Heat of War: Hattin (1187)

Few battles have been decided by such an utter lack of logistical support as Hattin, fought in arid heat near Lake Tiberias (the Sea of Galilee) on 4 July 1187. Saladin's forces did not simply beat the Frankish army of Guy de Lusignan, king of Jerusalem, they annihilated the crusaders' defence of Jerusalem and momentarily destroyed the Franks' military ambitions in Outremer. While the uncertain leadership of King Guy, Saladin's own military strategy, and battlefield tactics all contributed to the eventual outcome of the battle, it was the inaccessibility of water for the crusaders – and the complete lack of logistical support – that left them, in the sweltering heat of summer, defeated.

Saladin led his massive army into the Frankish lordship of Oultrejordain in April 1187, summoning forces from across the twelfth-century Muslim world to drive the European-originating crusaders, the Franks, from Jerusalem and the crusader states that they had established along the Mediterranean coast. Saladin was an experienced military commander, and this previous experience almost certainly highlighted to him the importance of undermining the enemy's logistical support – the availability of supplies, predominantly food and water. It was to this end that, almost as soon as his armies had crossed into the Kingdom of Jerusalem, Saladin ordered them to destroy crops and raze the land as they progressed. They prosecuted raids on Kerak and Montréal, burning food supplies and laying waste to crops. Of course, this approach could be a double-edged sword; although the lack of food available to the Franks may impact on their own ability to fight, Saladin was banking on those same shortages of food not impacting on his own forces, which he kept moving ever-westwards.

On 27 June, Saladin's forces – comprising approximately 12,000 professional cavalry and upwards of 30,000 volunteers – finally crossed the river Jordan, just south of Lake Tiberias. Such a large force would undoubtedly have put pressure on the land that it marched through, particularly given the need to waste crops in order to undermine the Franks' rule. To ease the logistical burden, Saladin therefore divided his forces up into three main contingents. Each was capable of operating semi-independently from the others, albeit with close communication between them. By marching separately, however, Saladin was able to limit the troops' demand on the land they marched over, reducing the risk of overdependence on one locale's resources. Saladin himself commanded the centre of his army, while the flanks were given to two trusted subordinates: the right flank under the command of his own nephew, Taqī al-Dīn, and the left flank under the leadership of Gökböri, the ruler of Erbil.

When he received word that the Muslim forces had crossed the Jordan, King Guy left Acre and immediately began to summon his own forces to defend the Kingdom of Jerusalem. Guy even put out a general call to arms – an unusual step since it required every man capable of fighting to report for military service at the Franks' traditional mustering site of Sepphoris, thus leaving the kingdom's fortresses, settlements, and even the great city of Jerusalem itself exposed and virtually undefended. As the Frankish forces began to muster, the scale of Guy's army became clear: it was perhaps the largest crusader force to be mustered in Outremer. Knights and cavalrymen, those retained by the lords of the realm, and of course multitudes of local foot fighters arrived. Still not satisfied with the numbers flocking to his summons, Guy used money from King Henry II of England – provided by Henry in lieu of crusading himself – to pay for mercenaries. Eventually, there gathered somewhere in the region of 1,200 knights and as many as 4,000 lighter cavalry sergeants and Turcopoles (locally recruited mounted archers and light cavalry), supplemented by 15–18,000 infantry comprising a range of experience and military ability. Such a massive army would undoubtedly require immense efforts to equip and supply it; the Franks' baggage train was substantial, and included both supplies and tents for Guy and his knights.

The Frankish mustering point at Sepphoris was well-supplied with natural fresh-water springs and directly by the Frankish army, who brought supplies with them from Jerusalem. The Frankish policy was to remain there and threaten the Muslims' more exposed positions, effectively relying on the enemy's weak or disorganised logistical support to force them to retire. Indeed, the Franks were able to sustain themselves indefinitely at Sepphoris, with the supplies of water able to quench the thirst of men and horses, and regular supplies from Jerusalem meaning that they could rely on logistical support to hold their position.

Saladin knew it would take a lot to lure the Franks from such a well-supplied and supported position. He therefore attacked Tiberias, before camping his main army by the springs at Cafarsset (Kafr Sabt), midway between Tiberias and the enemy's position at Sepphoris. By doing so, Saladin hoped to lure the Franks into a battle on the high, dry plateau between Sepphoris and Tiberias without access to water. The attack on Tiberias caused immediate fractures in the Frankish camp. Some lords, including Raymond Count of Tripoli, whose wife was in Tiberias, counselled Guy against going to Tiberias – the army, they pointed out, would suffer acute thirst on a road that lacked adequate water sources and crossed a 'desert' – by which Raymond probably meant they would find no fodder for their horses. Better to lose a wife and a city, he stated, than a kingdom. Guy, however, was mindful of his failure to confront a Muslim army four years earlier, and his pride demanded action.

At dawn on 3 July, the Franks broke camp to march to relieve Tiberias. Certainly, Guy's ego played a part in this decision to leave his logistical support and water supplies, but he may also have presumed that the Muslim army would remove itself in the face of a Frankish army coming to confront them. The Frankish army marched along the old Roman road from Sepphoris to Lake Tiberias, demonstrating that for all of his mistakes, Guy was still conscious of the need to use existing routes of communication to make the logistics of travel easier. The march was long – twenty-six kilometres of almost-waterless plateau – but Guy may have presumed it could be accomplished with the personal water supplies that the Franks carried with them. However, here Guy was outplayed by Saladin, who ordered water points along the Franks' route be closed up and wells to be filled in – and then waited. The harsh midsummer sun of the Holy Land did the rest.

As the Franks' march continued, extreme thirst set in. Guy had little choice but to press on, his army now being harried by the Muslim forces. By late morning, the beleaguered Franks reached Turran, the only major springs between Sepphoris and Hattin, but Guy's army did not stop to rest or take on water. The size of the army, combined with Guy's haste, precluded many from slaking their thirst. Even most horses were denied a chance to drink. Saladin himself was to later remark on the Franks' mistake of passing straight by Turran: although 'the hawks of the Frankish infantry and the eagles of their cavalry [were] hovering around the water', he wrote in a letter, 'the devil seduced him into doing the opposite of what he had in mind'.[26] The vast majority of the Frankish army marched past the springs without relief – which doubtless had a terrible effect on morale as well as soldiers' and horses' physical health.

Meanwhile, the Muslim forces continued to harry the Franks with arrows. One Muslim narrator, Imād al-Dīn, described the heat on the march across the dry, arid land between the Sepphoris springs and Tiberias. 'The day was hot,' he wrote, 'the [Franks] were on fire, the midday sun shone with an incessant strength. The troops had drunk the contents of their water bottles and had nothing more.'[27] Guy and his commanders realised that their priority could no longer be reaching Tiberias; instead, they had to reach water. It was at this point in their march that the Franks instigated a major change of plan and turned towards a series of springs at Hattin, only six kilometres away. There they could rest, and set out the next day to reach Tiberias once they had taken on water.

Once again, however, Saladin was one step ahead of the Franks. Seeing what they were trying to do, he sent Taqī al-Dīn's division to block the way to Hattin. Unable to reach water and with the perishingly hot sun giving way to darkness, Guy ordered the army to camp for the night. The

Franks were finally able to rest, although they remained without water and must, at this point, have been suffering greatly. With Muslim troops behind them and the forces of Taqī al-Dīn ahead, the crusaders must have realised that supplies would not reach them, even if a message was able to be dispatched to Sepphoris. Saladin, however, had ensured that his army continued to access logistical support. The Muslims got water via camels from Lake Tiberias, which was then emptied into makeshift reservoirs. More camels arrived with resupplies of arrows, some of which were packed on camelback in case they were needed the following day.

The next morning, Saladin's forces were rested and hydrated. They allowed the Frankish troops to march on, still aiming for the springs at Hattin, now only five kilometres away – again, the heat of the sun eroding their strength without Saladin's forces needing to intervene. Perhaps unsurprisingly, members of the Frankish army began to desert. William of Tyre recounts how 'some foot sergeants surrendered to the Saracens with their necks bared, such was their suffering through thirst'.[28] Others died from heat and thirst before they could surrender, their bodies lying beside the track as the Franks marched on. The soldiers were not the only ones to suffer, however. The Franks' horses would undoubtedly now have been parched and desperate for water as well, in particular, the warhorses who wore protective apparel themselves. A 1,000lb horse needs around forty-five litres of water a day to remain hydrated, and could lose up to twenty litres per hour during exertion in high temperatures.[29] With no water for a day and a half, it is likely that those soldiers dying at the roadside would have been joined by horses expiring in the heat.

By now, the Franks may have been able to glimpse the waters of Lake Tiberias tantalisingly shimmering in the distance, but still the Muslim armies followed them, shepherding them away from any route to water. 'At every way out, they were barred', wrote one contemporary chronicler, 'and tormented by the heat of war without being able to rest.'[30] By this point in the day, the weight and heat of the knights' armour was surely unbearable. They had no option but to keep wearing it as Muslim arrows prevented them from shedding its protection. To make the Franks' plight worse, Saladin's forces lit brushwood fires, the flames and smoke adding to the heat and thirst of the crusader army as it continued at a snail's pace.

Finally, in the noon heat, Saladin ordered his archers to increase their attack. Having waited until Guy's forces were exhausted from their march

The eleventh-century Bayeux Tapestry shows Norman horsemen stumbling as they charge over rough ground at the Battle of Hastings in 1066. The Anglo-Saxons made good use of terrain – but still lost the battle. (*Courtesy of jorisvo/shutterstock.com*)

View of the Sea of Galilee from the Horns of Hattin. In 1187 the army of the Kingdom of Jerusalem was destroyed when Saladin's forces came between it and sources of fresh water. (*Courtesy of RnDmS/shutterstock.com*)

The Wallace monument today marks the site of the Scottish command post at the Battle of Stirling Bridge in 1297. Wallace's leadership was crucial to the victory. (*Courtesy of Craig Duncanson/shutterstock.com*)

A mid-fourteenth-century cannon of the same type that may have been used at Crécy in 1346. This example was discovered in Sweden in 1861. (*Courtesy of Historiska Museet, Stockholm*)

Painting of the Battle of Crécy, 1346. The wide range of weapons and armour used at the battle is visible. The figure in the left foreground struggles to reload his crossbow – a significant problem for the Genoese at the battle. The English cannon are not depicted, however. (*Courtesy of Everett Collection/shutterstock.com*)

Early sixteenth-century woodcut depicting troops armed with pikes and staff weapons. Pikes would dominate the European battlefield throughout the following century. (*Courtesy of Everett Collection/shutterstock.com*)

Portrait after van Dyck of Prince Rupert, Charles I's loyal commander in the Civil War. His obedience to the king's grand strategy led to the Battle of Marston Moor in 1644. (*Courtesy of Everett Collection/shutterstock.com*)

Napoleon Bonaparte at his desk. Napoleon was a hugely inspirational leader, but also devoted himself to the minutiae of army command. (*Courtesy of Everett Collection/shutterstock.com*)

British medal issued to commemorate the Battle of Salamanca, 1812. The right-hand image commemorates the central role that Wellington was seen to have played as commander of the allied forces, while the left-hand image shows the importance of junior leadership in the battle. (*Courtesy of Yaroslaff/shutterstock.com*)

Jan Willem Pieneman's 1824 painting of the Battle of Waterloo, fought on 18 June 1815. The artist has highlighted the range of different troops involved on the relatively compact battlefield. (*Courtesy of Everett Collection/shutterstock.com*)

Mid-nineteenth-century illustration of a French soldier showing his appreciation to a cantinière – women who played a vital role in keeping troops supplied with food and drink. (*Courtesy of Marzolino/shutterstock.com*)

Timothy H. O'Sullivan's famous image of Federal casualties at Gettysburg. Early war photography allowed the horrors of battle to be brought to a wider audience. (*Courtesy of Everett Collection/shutterstock.com*)

African-American soldiers at Camp Meade in May 1899. Many African-Americans volunteered in the hope that military service would help to improve their civil rights. (*Courtesy of Everett Collection/shutterstock.com*)

A mule-drawn ammunition wagon is stuck in the mud on the Western Front in the First World War. Use of horses and mules was common alongside motorised transport in the first half of the twentieth century. (*Courtesy of Everett Collection/shutterstock.com*)

A gun crew covering an advance through ruined trees at Belleau Wood in June 1918. As much as landscape shapes battle, so can battle have an enormous impact on the landscape. (*Courtesy of Everett Collection/shutterstock.com*)

American troops advancing through a captured town during the Second Battle of the Marne, 1918. The broken landscape shows the destructive power of modern munitions. (*Courtesy of Everett Collection/shutterstock.com*)

German artillery on the Eastern Front in the Second World War. Requiring a crew of several soldiers, these guns had enormous destructive power. (*Courtesy of Everett Collection/shutterstock.com*)

These abandoned tracks were used to move shells between the clifftop magazine and a gun emplacement on the south coast of England during the Second World War. The size of shells for high-calibre artillery made mechanical transport a necessity. (*Courtesy of the authors*)

The ruins of Stalingrad in November 1942. Soviet victory in this battle marked a turning point in the Second World War. (*Courtesy of Everett Collection/shutterstock.com*)

A Sherman Tank salvaged from the English Channel serves as a memorial to Operation Tiger at Slapton Sands, Devon. As the operation showed, training for battle could be as deadly as combat. (*Courtesy of the authors*)

US Air Force aircraft patrol over the oilfields of Iraq in the First Gulf War, 1991. The Coalition's use of airpower was a decisive factor in its victory. (*Courtesy of Everett Collection/shutterstock.com*)

A military convoy in Helmand, 2009. Coalition forces' technological superiority was crucial to their tactics of counterinsurgency. (*Courtesy of Jonathan Park/shutterstock.com*)

through the morning sun, Saladin guessed that the Franks would be sluggish to respond to the renewed attack – a gamble that paid off. Only a handful of Guy's battle tents were erected, despite the effort it had taken to cart them from Sepphoris the previous day. Members of the infantry panicked and ran for the high ground at the Horns of Hattin, crying to Guy and his commanders that they were dying of thirst and refused to fight. Raymond of Tripoli, perhaps trying to escape in order to lead the defence of Jerusalem, or perhaps in a desperate attempt to open a route to water, broke through the Muslim lines only for them to close behind him, effectively separating a sizeable portion of the Frankish cavalry – their elite troops – from the rest of their forces.

That final desperate bid for water was to seal the Franks' fate. Eventually, only a handful of soldiers remained, fighting around the royal tent of King Guy until that, too, collapsed and the king of Jerusalem was forced to admit defeat. In truth, the fate of the Frankish army had been sealed when they abandoned a well-supplied logistical hub at Sepphoris, for a march through barren, dry territory without infrastructural support or provisions. With the defeat at Hattin, almost a century of Frankish rule in the Holy Land was brought to an arid end; whereas the logistical superiority of Saladin's army proved the foundation for their success.

The End of the Line: Stalingrad (1942–3)

Stalingrad was the high-water mark of the German advance into the USSR in the Second World War. The tale of the battle is one of immense courage, fortitude and suffering for the men and women involved, and one of stubbornness and horrendous callousness from commanders on both sides. It is also the tale of desperate attempts to feed, clothe, supply and fuel enormous fighting forces under the most trying of circumstances.

War came to Stalingrad in summer 1942 because of Hitler's decision to push south towards the oilfields of the Caucuses. General Paulus's Sixth Army and General Hoth's Fourth Panzer Army were detailed to cut the river Volga – the major waterborne artery from the Caspian Sea to central Russia – at Stalingrad. Initially there was no intention to fight a battle through the city itself.

Simply getting towards Stalingrad proved a major logistical challenge. As the German army had found the previous year, movement in the

USSR was difficult. Railways on a different gauge to their own had to be relaid so that German wagons could be used to bring up supplies.[31] Roads were often poor quality and became quagmires in the rains of spring and autumn; in winter, the frozen landscape and deep snows made not only movement but basic survival enormously difficult. Getting fuel to forward units was a constant headache. Almost all air transport was redirected to the crucial task of refuelling mobile ground units, taking priority over even the evacuation of the wounded. The forward momentum of the panzers towards the Don and Volga rivers was nevertheless maintained through July 1942, albeit with frequent and frustrating pauses for fuel and ammunition, and high rates of attrition due to lack of spare parts.[32] Such was the success of the advance that Hitler considered the Red Army incapable of much further resistance; instead of just cutting off Soviet supplies along the Volga, Paulus was now ordered to take Stalingrad itself.

If getting fuel and spare parts to the front was difficult, feeding the troops proved a little easier in the fertile countryside during the summer months. Rations were still brought forward by train, and taken from railheads by truck or horse cart to where they were needed. The transport available was barely adequate for the task, but the troops were able to supplement their diet by stripping the countryside of food. In some cases, local people with no love for the communist regime bartered with the invaders; in others, victuals were simply plundered.

The Soviet forces, although falling back on their supply lines, also had difficulty in bringing up fuel and ammunition to sustain their defensive efforts. Soviet industry was at this stage easily outproducing that of Germany, but poor organisation and lack of transport meant that resources were not always finding their way to where they were needed. By August, units in the 62nd and 64th armies falling back on Stalingrad were so low on munitions that they had to scavenge on battlefields or use weapons taken from enemy dead. When fighting reached Stalingrad, Soviet artillery ammunition was in such short supply that many of the defenders had never even fired a shot in training. Food was also scarce and often had to be acquired locally, generally amounting to little more than boiled wheat.[33] The Soviet authorities nevertheless stripped the countryside and city of all food, stockpiling it over the Volga for the use of the Red Army.

Assaults on Stalingrad began in late August, preceded by a massive aerial bombardment that destroyed much of the water system, telephones and electricity, and reduced large parts of the city to rubble. At this stage, the Germans were in a generally good position; supplies were adequate, some luxuries remained, and posts from home tended to get through.[34] Although over 2,000 miles from their own frontier, the rear transport system of railways was able to bring up hundreds of tons of supplies each day, using rolling stock commandeered from across Europe. As the Germans moved into Stalingrad, two railheads were established a few miles outside the city, at Gumrak in the north and Tungita to the south. Trains could come straight through on the more circuitous southern route from Rostov, but the bridge across the Don had been destroyed on the northern branch, so all goods had to be laboriously trucked or carted to Kalach, taken across the river, and reloaded onto trains for the final stretch. The single-track lines could cope – just – with the demands of the Sixth and Fourth Panzer armies, although as the intensity of combat increased and winter approached, they would struggle to deliver necessary supplies.

The assault on Stalingrad, which intensified through September and October, was enormously costly in both men and supplies. Almost incessant artillery and aircraft bombardments expended an enormous weight of ordnance, and placed a huge strain on fuel and maintenance resources. The infantry used over 25 million rounds of small-arms ammunition and tens of thousands of grenades and mortar shells in September alone.[35] Food was almost impossible to forage in the city and had to be supplied as rations; Soviet snipers became adept at killing food carriers, denying frontline troops much-needed sustenance. Water was even more precious, as bombing had destroyed the mains supplies. Thirst was a constant enemy. Fuel was still needed for assaulting panzers and transport units, and spare parts were continually in demand. The Sixth Army extemporised, improvised, and cannibalised equipment where it could, but the inadequacy of food and fresh water increased men's exhaustion and vulnerability to disease, contributing in no small part to the difficulties of the advance.

Things were no better on the Soviet side. Food and water were universally lacking, and few units had ammunition for more than a day or two of combat. The 13th Guards Division arrived at the battle with one in ten men lacking even a weapon.[36] The nature of fighting in the shattered streets and buildings meant that small Soviet 'garrisons' often became cut off, sometimes for days at a time, rendering resupply impossible. Such was their valour – or fear of execution for cowardice – that these units often fought to the last man or woman. Their utterly inadequate supply chain hastened the end of many units, adding to the enormous human toll of the battle.

The problems of Soviet supply were more complex than those of the Germans. Although fighting on home territory, with easier access to reserves, Stalingrad was cut off from the rest of the USSR by the German army and Volga river. Everything that General Chuikov's 62nd Army needed to defend the city had to be brought over by boat, and German aircraft and artillery constantly targeted the vessels to try to cut off the defenders entirely.[37] A small footbridge built from Zaitsevsky Island to the west bank helped to alleviate supply problems, but they remained critical.[38] The Soviets used the cover of darkness to ferry over ammunition, reinforcements and food, but it was never quite enough, and casualties among boatmen were high. One minor advantage was that Chuikov had stationed all of his heavy artillery on the Volga's eastern bank, making it much easier to supply. Chuikov's tactics of keeping his defenders pushed right up against the German lines also meant that Soviet artillery concentrated on disrupting German lines of communication, rather than firing at the front where they might hit their own troops.

The logistical priorities of each side also differed. Both prioritised ammunition – a battle could not be fought without it – but the Soviets gave less prominence to food and medical supplies. Despite the increasing cold, soldiers at the front were sent no replacement clothing, being expected to take what they needed from the dead, although at least in the city of shattered beams and furniture, material could be found to burn. The Soviets equally gave little thought to the wounded who were no longer useful to the battle. Supplies of all kinds were lacking and medical evacuation was slapdash, despite the incredible heroism of orderlies – mostly women, mostly untrained – who rescued thousands of men under fire.[39]

By 1 November, exhaustion, heavy casualties and a lack of ammunition forced a temporary halt in German offensive operations, bringing some relief to the defenders. But on 10 November, the Volga began to freeze over, further limiting the operation of supply boats. In 138th Rifle Division, soldiers were reduced to thirty rounds of ammunition and fifty grams of bread per day.[40] On neither side could supplies be brought up rapidly or regularly enough to sustain fighting troops at any level of efficiency. Renewed attacks in Stalingrad in mid-November brought some German gains, but with diminishing returns for their expenditure of manpower and materials. Outside the city, German covering forces were by now having to begin digging in for winter. There was little shelter on the steppe, and relatively few trees for firewood. Limited transport capacity meant that there were nowhere near enough building materials. The plentiful food of the summer had now gone, and the nearly 1 million German, Hungarian, Romanian and Italian soldiers had to be fed by rations brought up by train. The army also boasted 150,000 transport horses, many for artillery. The creaking supply system simply could not provide the forage required for such an equine host, so in late October the horses were ordered withdrawn over a hundred miles to the rear, reducing the army's mobility enormously.

The decision of the battle ultimately came not in Stalingrad itself, but from a massive Soviet counteroffensive – Operation Uranus – begun on 19 November. It was conceived on a grand scale to encircle the German forces at Stalingrad, and to cut Sixth Army off from its supplies. Soviet high command concentrated almost 1 million troops and launched a vast operation on the railways to supply sufficient ammunition, fuel and food. Some 100,000 civilians were drafted to repair roads, bridges and infrastructure ahead of the advance. Supply problems led to an initial ten-day delay, and even then some soldiers still lacked winter clothing or even adequate arms, but overall the provision of these counterattacking forces was a logistical triumph. The initial advance was largely successful but struggled to maintain momentum. To the south, the 64th Army had to ferry all supplies across the Volga, and was forced to repurpose all motorised transport – including ambulances – to deliver ammunition. Food immediately ran short, and without trucks the infantry struggled to keep up with the armoured breakthrough.

For the Germans, however, the situation was more critical. Recognising the threat to his supply lines, Paulus suspended offensive operations in Stalingrad and moved to reinforce his lines of communication. Yet without pre-planning, the realignment of his armoured divisions was extremely difficult. Fuel supplies were catastrophically low, and many tanks were out of action awaiting repair or spare parts. Little assistance could be given to beleaguered screening forces, who were forced to abandon or burn huge quantities of materiel as they retreated. Almost no trucks and few horses were available to move stores away from the advancing Soviets. All artillery and heavy equipment had to be abandoned.

Within days, the Red Army had brushed aside the covering forces and cut off the crucial railway lines supplying Paulus's army. Encircled, Paulus requested permission to attempt a breakout, but was refused. Hitler planned to supply the encircled forces by air, as had been accomplished for over two months for a force of 100,000 at Demyansk the previous year.[41] Yet the Luftwaffe simply did not have the lifting capacity for such an operation. Paulus estimated his army's daily needs at over 700 tons of supplies; in the event, hampered by the weather and lacking planes, aircrew, fuel, forward controllers, groundcrew and runways, the Luftwaffe averaged only 117.6 tons per day – although it did manage to evacuate almost 30,000 wounded men.[42]

A German counteroffensive in December to relieve Stalingrad petered out without linking up with the Sixth Army, which remained immobile from lack of fuel and Paulus's refusal to disobey orders not to abandon Stalingrad. With Paulus's command cut off, and with air resupply inadequate, the outcome was inevitable. Food, ammunition and fuel stocks dwindled, and with them the army's morale and health. Fuel for heating was almost non-existent, and the lice-ridden, raggedly uniformed men were constantly cold. Many perished from frostbite or exposure. Daily rations were reduced to 200 grams of bread, occasionally supplemented by horse soup, although even these meagre amounts could not be guaranteed.

Even where supplies were available, transport from magazines to the troops was wholly inadequate, with a few horse-drawn sledges the best that could be mustered. On 24 January, Paulus bluntly told Berlin: 'Fortress can be held for only a few days longer. Troops exhausted and weapons immobilised as a result of non-arrival of supplies.'[43] By the last week of January, the airstrips were overrun or put out of action, cutting off any remaining hope of holding out. Many Soviet troops were little better off, but supplies and even luxuries like alcohol and cigarettes tended to be more readily available. Moreover, morale was much higher than in the German pocket. The final Soviet victory with the capitulation of the remaining German forces on 2 February 1943 can be attributed to many factors – command decisions, strategy, tactics, the sheer heroic tenacity of Stalingrad's defenders – but the vital role of logistics cannot be overlooked.

Chapter 7

Weapons and Armour

'These are the devil's devices to make us kill each other'
Blaise de Montluc[1]

So wrote Blaise de Montluc, Marshal of France, in 1523 about the new handguns appearing on the battlefields of Western Europe. However, de Montluc could have been writing about myriad weaponry developments from the medieval period to the present day; each generation has its 'devil's device' that has changed the way that battles could be planned and fought. Soldiers going into battle will usually be armed with at least a rudimentary weapon. These weapons may be highly specialised and personalised to the country, region, army, or even individuals using them. While generalities do exist – particularly perhaps in the modern period with mass production of standard-issue weaponry – there is also significant diversity in the range of weapons created and adapted for battle.

Even the weapon arguably most synonymous with warriors, the sword, comes in an enormous number of variations. The weapon of martial identity for millennia, by the eleventh century swords were carried into battle by the military elite and featured a bewildering variety of designs, from short stabbing daggers such as the misericorde, designed to penetrate between plates of armour, to enormous broadswords such as the German Zweihänder or Scottish claymore, which could cut the legs from under a horse during battle. Still today, they are a symbolic representation of military power and prowess.

The primary role of weapons in battle is to confer advantage on one side at the expense of the other. This advantage may be through sheer destructive power, in killing, maiming, overcoming equipment, intimidating, terrifying, or otherwise removing the enemy's ability to fight. It may be an advantage of morale, manoeuvrability, or tactical options. On the opposite side, armour has been adopted throughout history to nullify or reduce the effectiveness of enemy weapons. In the most basic sense armour simply acts as a barrier to deflect enemy weaponry, and allows fighters to move within striking distance of their opponents – whether they intend to strike with projectile or blade – while remaining impervious to enemy shots or blows. For most of the past millennium it has been confined to personal protection, although armoured wagons occasionally appeared on the later medieval battlefield, and armoured vehicles were introduced in the early twentieth century, opening up the possibility of mobile weapons systems that were far less vulnerable to the enemy.

The ability to inflict physical injury, damage or death has historically been the primary purpose of weapons on the battlefield. Traditionally, this was accomplished either through penetrative weaponry designed to pierce armour into flesh, or impact weaponry meant to injure by the force of a blunted but forceful blow. Some weapons developed to combine these two attacking styles, with both penetrative and impact effectiveness. Axes, for example, were often a favoured alternative to swords on the medieval battlefield as they offered both cutting and blunted impact. The one-handed axe offered the same manoeuvrability as the sword but focused the power of a blow into a smaller area – especially when wielded from horseback. Even weapons traditionally associated with blunt-force trauma, such as maces, were often adapted to also lead to penetrative injuries.[2] Injuries inflicted by a hearty blow from such weapons would generally be sufficient to incapacitate an opponent; weapons that took two or three strikes to achieve the same effect would put their wielder at a significant disadvantage.

Projectile weapons were also at their most effective when able to incapacitate opponents with a single strike. This can be seen in medieval broad-headed arrows; with barbs designed to rip flesh, they could cause not only death but also grievous injury if they pierced a limb, preventing anyone who was struck by one from fighting on. Despite their limitations, early gunpowder weapons offered similar advantages in stopping power. The earliest firearms were handgonnes, effectively barrels of metal down which were poured powder and a projectile before heat was applied. The projectiles themselves – usually stones, but later metal balls – had to be round to fit in the barrel. A single piece of ammunition is still called a round. Early firearms were notoriously inaccurate and the rounded projectiles quickly lost energy due to air resistance, but at close range the projected ball delivered a massive impact, crashing through armour or flesh to inflict devastating and often deadly trauma on the target.

The same principle applies to most modern firearms. The simple early barrels on sticks were later replaced by the arquebus, which employed a shape followed by smoothbore muskets and later modern rifles. The calibre and velocity of modern munitions mean that they are able to incapacitate combatants even without a fatal head or torso shot; neat, minor flesh wounds from direct impacts are relatively rare. Projectiles also have the advantage of striking an enemy with greater force than hand-held weapons, giving a greater chance of piercing armour. With some modern heavy weapons, the detonation of the high-explosive payload can cause massive concussive injuries to those nearby, killing or wounding without any apparent external injury.

Human ingenuity has devised plenty of other technologies with different techniques for maiming combatants. Nuclear, biological and chemical weapons can incapacitate enemies either by vaporising them entirely or causing the failure of their internal organs or central nervous system. Although most such weapons are now banned, they have seen sometimes extensive historical use, from rudimentary biological weapons of medieval or early modern warfare (chucking diseased or rotten animal corpses into a besieged city was a favourite technique, for example) to the poison gas of the First World War. Tactical nuclear weapons have never been deployed but the issue has been given serious thought. In 1967, with American troops at Khe Sahn under threat from overwhelming force, General Westmoreland instructed aides to look at the feasibility of using tactical nuclear weapons – until Washington banned any such talk.[3]

Of course, an enemy does not need to be physically injured in order to be removed from battle. Weapons can also have an impact on the enemy's psychology, in particular by intimidating and instilling fear. Intimidation can come from previously unknown technologies, deployed as weapons in war for the first time. The terrifying sound of English cannon fire at Crécy intimidated the Genoese crossbowmen in the French vanguard; the near-contemporary Giovanni Villani described how the Genoese turned and fled from the noise, 'being constantly ... blasted by the bombards'.[4] Several other writers noted the fear caused by English artillery, as well as the effect that the noise had on French horses.[5]

Artillery's role as a psychological weapon was by no means confined to its earliest appearances. Facing the massed batteries of Napoleonic artillery was a horrifying ordeal, while the later development of high-explosive shells fired by far-distant guns made the battlefield appear even more terrifying than before. Lieutenant Sidney Rogerson recalled at the Somme (1916) that German Minenwerfer mortars:

> had a more demoralising effect than any other single form of enemy action ... The very leisureliness of their descent was demoralising. The uncertainty as to where they would pitch was demoralising. The immense clamour of their explosion was demoralising. But most demoralising was the damage they could do. Men do not easily or soon throw off the shock of seeing all that could be found of four of their comrades carried down for burial in one ground sheet.[6]

Demoralising these giant mortars may have been, but more immediately terrifying was Rogerson's experience of an intense bombardment:

> there was a whoosh of metal overhead, down came the barrage! Explosions whirled, stamped and pounded the tortured ground; the splitting hiss and bang of the field guns screaming above the deep, earth-shaking thud! thud! of the heavies until they blended into one steady pandemonium of drumfire. The trenches rocked and trembled, while their garrisons, blinded by the flashes, choked by the acrid fumes, pressed themselves tight to the sodden walls as the avalanche of metal roared above and around them.[7]

The words eloquently communicate the sheer violence and terror of shelling by heavy artillery. Soldiers have naturally noted the advantages of terrifying the enemy with noise and potential death, and some weapons were designed with features intended to instil fear. The German Stuka dive-bomber aircraft of the Second World War, for example, emitted a deeply unnerving, ear-piercing shriek as they swooped to attack. Lord Gort, the British commander in France in 1940, stated that this was 'a new experience for British troops. Even those who had grown accustomed to heavy shellfire in France during 1914–18 found that this form of attack, when first encountered, placed a strain on morale.'[8] With such intimidation, weapons can change the course of a battle regardless of their effectiveness in causing casualties.

While the psychological impact is important, weapons still tend to be judged on their ability to do damage. Whether weapons have actually become more effective at causing casualties is an issue of debate. Weapons have clearly achieved far greater destructive power – a bomb blast can self-evidently do more damage than a sword swing – but this has not necessarily translated to greater deadliness. For all the ferocity and terror of the bombardment related by Rogerson, not a single man of his command was killed or wounded in that particular incident. Indeed, in raw statistics, it is hard to maintain that weapons have become more deadly. Average casualty rates as a percentage of forces engaged in battle have tended to decrease since the seventeenth century, despite the obvious advances in military technology.[9] Despite improvements in the range, accuracy, and explosive payload of artillery, there has actually been an increase in the amount of ordnance fired per casualty. At Waterloo, a good proportion of the 20,000 French casualties would have been caused by cannon fire, despite British gunners (who made up just over half of the allied artillery) firing only 10,400 shells.[10] In the First World War, on the other hand, the German army on the British sector of the Western Front suffered an estimated 1,680,396 casualties, but the British Expeditionary Force (BEF) fired just over 170 million shells during the war – or just over 100 shells for every casualty inflicted.[11]

A large part of the explanation for this apparent anomaly is tactical. The propensity of men to take shelter rather than standing in the open to receive fire, combined with bombardments concentrating on infrastructure and interdiction as much as directly targeting personnel, meant that each shell in the First World War was less deadly than those of Napoleonic artillery batteries. Yet these tactics were themselves a direct result of the increased capabilities of weapons; as John Keegan said of the First World War, 'It was as if arms manufacturers had succeeded in introducing a new element into the atmosphere, compounded of fire and steel, whose presence rendered battlefields uninhabitable.'[12]

Attempts have been made to quantify the deadly potential of weapons in order to compare their effectiveness. Trevor Dupuy, for example, proposed a Theoretical Lethality Index, measuring rates of fire, the number of targets that each shot could strike, range, accuracy, and reliability to come up with a score that allowed comparison of different weapons through history.[13] According to Dupuy's index, the longbow had the same effectiveness as an early nineteenth-century rifle, but was almost a hundred times less lethal than a First World War machine gun.

The theoretical approach demonstrated the growing destructive potential of weapons, but not their actual battlefield killing power. For that, Dupuy included the tactical dispersal of soldiers, dividing the theoretical scores depending on the era of conflict and average concentration of troops on the battlefield. The resulting Operational Lethality Index showed that the actual deadliness of small arms in action has, with a few exceptions, tended to decrease rather than increase, although modern artillery, machine guns and aircraft remained far more destructive than previous weapons. Again, the suggestion is that tactical approaches have negated advances in firepower. Indeed, the great slaughter caused by some of these weapons, such as the machine gun on the first day of the Somme, was only possible due to blunders and wholly inappropriate tactics of the attacking forces.[14] These calculations remain theoretical and do not take into account issues such as availability of munitions, specific operational employment of equipment, or competence of operators, but they do hint at an explanation of why average battle-casualty rates have not increased despite the introduction of ever more destructive weapons.

A further issue that muddies the waters of weapon lethality is the widespread use of armour. Armour comes in many forms, from the full plate of medieval knights to the reinforced hulls of modern tanks, and from simple leather jerkins to the steel helmets of the world wars. Armour will rarely stop all weapons; the perennial calculation for armour is protection against movement, as heavier armour generally provides more protection, but at the cost of speed, manoeuvrability, and sometimes visibility. Excessively heavy armour will exhaust the individual or put undue mechanical strain on armoured vehicles, severely reducing battlefield effectiveness. The very best medieval armour was usable only in tournaments, because its sheer weight made it impractical for battle.

Yet armour can serve to make some weapons virtually useless in battle. There is still some debate about the lethality of longbows against armour, for example, with suggestions that good-quality plate was invulnerable to arrows at anything other than point-blank range. In this thesis, the longbow's primary use at Agincourt (1415) was to funnel French knights towards the English men-at-arms, rather than committing mass slaughter. The developing strength of personal armour by the fifteenth century certainly afforded increasing protection against traditional weapons, helping to fuel the rise of pike and shot – two weapons with the striking power to continue to penetrate the new reinforced plates. The ingenious development of ever more effective armour is matched only by the development of ever more effective ways of getting through it, but there is no denying armour's success in reducing lethality for those who benefit from it on the battlefield.

Reliability is another key factor in limiting the effectiveness of weapons, and sometimes armour. This can affect all weapons, with brittle blades failing against well-forged steel, muskets misfiring due to fouling or poor powder, or stoppages caused by unreliable moving parts on repeating rifles and machine guns. Reliability issues can indeed be a great equaliser, diminishing technological advantage, or can give significant benefit when weapons systems are otherwise equal in range, striking power and so on. Reliability issues have plagued armoured vehicles, for example, perhaps preventing them from achieving their full potential as battle-winning weapons. The earliest tanks were notoriously unreliable, with far more lost to mechanical breakdown than to enemy action. In the Second World War, the early versions of the German Panther tank were atrocious, breaking down with remarkable rapidity and regularity. The Panther easily outmatched equivalent enemy hardware in armour and firepower, but remained a poor battlefield weapon, never achieving more than 'average automotive reliability'.[15] Even very modern armoured vehicles are not immune to failure. In Iraq in 2003, for example, 'according to the US Army, of the sixteen tanks lost, only two were actually destroyed and most losses were due to mechanical failure'.[16]

Despite any questions over decreasing lethality, battles fought where there is a serious discrepancy in technology show that possessing weapons of greater range, rate of fire, accuracy, or explosive power does confer enormous advantages. Technological superiority does not guarantee victory, but it offers an army the opportunity to inflict greater casualties while avoiding losses of its own. The very different fates of the British and Italian invasions of Abyssinia in 1867–8 and 1895–6 provide an illustrative example. At Aroge (1868), a British army of 13,000 using rapid-firing breech-loading rifles, modern artillery and rockets routed an Abyssinian host armed mostly with traditional bladed weapons or muzzle-loading guns. Nearly thirty years later, an Italian army of similar size came up against an Abyssinian force now boasting modern weaponry, and were destroyed in a single day of fighting at Adowa. While other factors played their part, the weapons differential – or lack of it – was clearly important.

The Zulu War, on the other hand, offers an example of the limits of technological advantage. At Isandlwana (1879), a British force possessing breech-loading rifles was wiped out by a Zulu army largely armed with traditional blades, shields and a few firearms. Tactics and numbers in this instance trumped technology. Later the same day, a portion of this force attacked a British outpost at Rorke's Drift. The Zulu force not only outnumbered the British garrison approximately thirty-five to one, but also outgunned them twenty to one. The Zulus had both muskets and Martini-Henry rifles taken from the dead at Isandlwana. However, the Zulu forces were neither proficient in operating the rifles, nor had sufficient time to train in their effective tactical employment. The British defenders therefore retained the effective technological edge, which contributed greatly to their ultimate victory.

The role of weapons in shaping a battle stretch far beyond their destructive impact, however. Weapons can have an effect on the nature of the battlefield itself: the location, size and scale of the theatre of combat. This influence is particularly evident when an individual commander or army can decide the site of a battle, as sensible generalship would choose a location that negates the enemy's advantage in weaponry while providing the best conditions for one's own. Since the Romans' use of chariots dictated that battles would be best fought on flat and level terrain, the use of specific weapons and military technology has dictated the site of battle. When the British selected Cambrai as the location for a mass tank engagement in 1917, they chose a location partly based on geology, as the large, chalky plain was ideally suited for the slow-moving machines.

In other cases the simple need to access weapons directly influences where a battle takes place. Commanders might be reluctant to fight beyond the range of supporting artillery or airpower, limiting where they can engage; more simply, they might require proximity to stores of weapons or ammunition to be able to fight. The Battle of Fallujah (2004) was oriented around fortified underground bunkers that stored weapons caches that Iraqi insurgents were using to support their conflict with

American forces in the city. While Iraqi insurgent forces were unable to move far from their weapons caches for ammunition and even anti-aircraft weapons, American forces were keen to remove the improvised arsenals from enemy hands.

Advancing weapon technology has also been a key factor in the growing size of battlefields over the last millennium: from a central field site in the medieval period, to an area of potentially thousands of square miles in the twentieth and twenty-first centuries. As well as contributing to a lengthening of battlefronts, weapon technology has caused a significant deepening of combat zones, as the range of projectile weapons has increased dramatically from line-of-sight to indirect fire over several miles' distance. Airpower, cruise missiles, and recently drones have added an altogether new dimension to this expansion of the battlespace, with operators now able to strike targets thousands of miles away.

At the same time, more complex weapons systems require more soldiers to operate them, and have therefore increased the cooperation and coordination necessary on the battlefield. In the earlier medieval period, most weapons were wielded in isolation by single individuals. While some siege weapons required a team of combatants to operate, the majority of weapons used on the open battlefield – from swords and axes to bows and slings – needed only one soldier. With the advent of gunpowder technology, however, artillery in particular began to be crewed by groups of combatants working together to operate a single weapon. By the eighteenth century, for example, gunners formed crews of six to eight men, each with a specialised, pre-designated role – laying, loading powder, inserting shot, ramming and so forth – to fire a single weapon.

As technology has grown more sophisticated, so the nature of the battlefield has changed. The tail upon which soldiers at the front depend has become longer, and the number of places a battle can be decided (beyond the immediate point of contact) has grown. Fewer combatants are required to produce the same level of force, or to dominate the same area of battlespace. In many modern clashes the bulk of the mechanised weaponry is operated by a handful of soldiers, some of whom may be many miles from the site of battle itself. The advent of non-linear battlefields, in which combatants seek to employ conventional and irregular military forces in conjunction with psychological, economic, political and cyber assaults, has effectively expanded the combat zone to a global outreach with the advent of new forms of weaponry and consequent new arenas of battle – hence battlespace rather than battlefield.[17]

Alongside the location, spread and nature of the battlefield, weaponry can have a direct impact on how battles are approached and fought. In a very basic sense this includes whether the army fights as a mobile or static force, whether it relies on remote firepower or close combat, and whether it has cover from air, water, or any of the other dimensions of the battlespace. Major discrepancies in technology can even cause some combatants faced by more sophisticated weaponry to drop conventional tactics altogether, as was the case at times in the Vietnam War.

Weapons or equipment can dictate the speed with which battle is joined and proceeds. Weapons that are quick to deploy, or technology that gives greater speed of movement than an opponent, will allow an army to concentrate and enter action more rapidly. This offers greater scope for retaining initiative, affords greater tactical flexibility, and potentially avoids being drawn into a costly battle of attrition. It was the speed with which weapons could be deployed that – alongside logistics – provided for American 'shock and awe' and 'rapid dominance' tactics during Operation Iraqi Freedom in 2003.[18] Even increasing the manoeuvrability of weapons can speed up an army's ability to respond to an opponent. Early firearms, for example, were cumbersome weapons that militated against rapid deployment, and so to increase their mobility without compromising on size (and therefore firepower) they were sometimes mounted on wagons.

The fifteenth-century Hussite campaigns offer an example of both speed of movement and increasing manoeuvrability of weapons. The Hussites created defensive formations in battle with wagons chained together to give handgunners a good position from which to use their weapons. Because they could form the *tabor* (wagon-laager) so quickly, the Hussite army could manoeuvre aggressively in front of the enemy. Neighbours soon copied the tactic: Matthias Corvinus of Hungary hired a Hussite wagon force to provide a core to his army. He used it against the Ottomans at Varna (1444), a battle where both sides employed artillery, although the numbers given in contemporary sources are probably hugely inflated.[19] In Western Europe, artillery also began to be mounted on moveable wagons in the mid-fifteenth century. French military developments were led by artillery commanders Jean and Gaspard Bureau and evidenced in particular at the Battle of Castillon in 1453, where Jean's command of the French army and extensive use of artillery camps – entrenchments of guns – proved brutally effective against the English.[20]

The technological limitations of early cannon nevertheless affected how far commanders were able to rely on defensive firepower on the battlefield. With a relatively short range and the difficulty of moving or slewing weapons to aim them, early cannons were of limited use in open battle. Lighter, large guns were occasionally more useful in the field, firing cannonballs or grapeshot, and could be effective defending a position. Ribauds or multi-barrelled 'organ guns' – featuring several light cannon or handguns mounted on a cart or platform and discharged in a single volley – were used effectively by the English at Crécy when defending their elevated position. It was the development of lighter but increasingly more powerful field artillery that allowed cannon to become a constant feature of seventeenth-century battle, a vital component of any eighteenth-century army, and a weapon to dominate the nineteenth-century battlefield.

The ability to rely on bombardment as a key tactic came with further refinements that focused on increasing guns' speed and manoeuvrability without sacrificing range or accuracy. In France, for example, the Gribeauval system of the mid-1760s lightened guns and carriages and made their artillery arguably the finest in Europe going into the Revolutionary and Napoleonic wars. The introduction of horse artillery – lighter pieces that could be moved at speed by mounted crews – further increased the tactical potential of artillery. By the twentieth century, breech-loading rifled pieces, epitomised by the French 75mm, were able to fire considerably faster, at greater range, and deliver a considerably deadlier payload. The perfection of predicted fire, sound ranging, and long-range artillery observers during the First World War made indirect-firing artillery the undoubted kings of the battlefield, both in defence and in support of offensive operations – although perhaps ironically, their sheer range and effectiveness rendered the once-great advantages of manoeuvrability and speed of deployment less important. By the Second World War, aircraft had begun to take up the mantle of rapid, manoeuvrable artillery platforms. The ability to call on air support has become an enormous advantage on the modern battlefield, as seen at the Battle of Ia Drang (1965) during the Vietnam War, where intensive supporting airstrikes allowed an American battalion to hold out against and eventually defeat a far larger force of North Vietnamese troops.

Beyond issues of manoeuvrability or an ability to strike from distance, weapons, armour and equipment can have a key influence on how soldiers enter battle – whether on foot, on horseback, in vehicles, or even from the air. The first significant decision to be made amongst Western European medieval armies, for example, was whether to fight on horseback or on foot, which would be informed by the weapons that combatants in that army preferred to use or were able to employ. The most successful and widespread weapons were therefore those that could be easily adapted to use either on foot or horseback. Pole weapons proved relatively simple to mass-produce and adapt to different armies' needs and fighting styles. They could be couched underarm during cavalry charges, or used to jab both over- and underarm when fighting on foot. They could also be thrown as range weapons, although use in these circumstances was rare as, once thrown, a lance obviously becomes unusable – except perhaps to the enemy. At Hastings (1066), the lance was used in various ways as depicted in the Bayeux Tapestry, which shows combatants using them on horseback and on foot, both over- and underarm, reflecting their versatility.

Later in the medieval period, the basic spear shape was adapted to further specialise the weapon, although this largely restricted it to infantry use. The pike, for example, was an elongated spear up to five metres long that was used on foot and could be braced against the ground for maximum force against a mounted opponent. Alternatively, the front ranks of a pike unit could carry their weapons level while braced by those behind them. These attacking squares could be devastating against other foot soldiers who were unable to group and attack such a reinforced formation. At the Battle of Nancy (1477), Swiss pikemen demonstrated the success of this tactic in a devastating charge against Burgundian infantry. The Swiss at Nancy were also successful against cavalry, although other pike units were not always so effective. The Scots at Neville's Cross in 1346, for instance, failed to use defensive pikes effectively against their mounted English opponents despite forming tightly packed schiltrons. From the late fifteenth to early seventeenth century, the pike enjoyed great importance on the European battlefield, especially in the Spanish tercios or German Landsknechts, but the increasing effectiveness of firearms and the tempting target provided by massed pike squares eventually saw the weapon fall from fashion.

Other staff weapons were adapted with a specific tactic – if not a specific tactical system – in mind: halberds, for example, developed in southern Germany and Switzerland in the thirteenth century, although earlier examples existed in China.[21] They featured an axe head on a wooden shaft with a spearpoint protruding from the top, thus creating both stabbing and cutting blades, with a primary function of disabling a knight's horse by targeting the weakly protected body and legs. It was used to such effect at Arbedo in 1422, when Swiss halberdiers attacked the Milanese horses before killing the dismounted knights.[22]

Although many weapons in their most general form could be used by both mounted men or foot soldiers, the majority had adaptations allowing them to be used to greatest effect by either a man on foot or horseback. The most common requirement of a weapon for mounted combat was a long reach, as the soldier wielding it would need to extend to engage an opponent who may be on the ground. Similarly, weapons for foot combat would often be shorter and lighter, allowing greater speed and precision. Throughout the medieval period there were men who specialised in one form of combat over another, but from the sixteenth century the standardisation of weaponry within units, and therefore the standardisation of their tactical role on the battlefield, became more common.

Of course, individual armies or regions often had a preferred fighting style and often the weapons they used simply reflected this broader approach. The Seljuk Turks, for example, developed their fighting style and the weapons that they used as nomadic tribes on the open steppes before advancing into Anatolia and the Byzantine Empire in the mid-eleventh century. They therefore needed weapons that were light and could be operated from horseback while providing maximum manoeuvrability; as a consequence, their bows were shorter and had a longer range than European counterparts. Their mastery of this shortened bow, combined with proficiency in operating it against Byzantine opponents, was demonstrated in a skirmish preceding the Battle of Manzikert (1071), where a force of Byzantine soldiers was routed by a smaller group of Seljuk horse archers.[23]

Projectile weapons in general have tended to influence the tactics of their users. Rates of fire can set significant limitations on projectile-armed infantry units. This generally hinged around the speed with which a weapon might be reloaded, and was important even before the widespread use of gunpowder. The crossbow, for example, had a complex system of loading in which the string was pulled back by either a foot-operated stirrup, or with a handle windlass mechanism. Both techniques required the crossbowman to stop, the former also requiring him to balance on one leg as the other was placed into the stirrup. Such a manoeuvre was slow and difficult to perform in the midst of battle, robbing crossbowmen of speed of movement as well as resulting in a relatively slow rate of shot of perhaps one bolt a minute. Problems of reloading contributed to the annihilation of the Genoese crossbowmen at Crécy, despite their greater power and more direct aim, as the English archers' simpler reloading procedure allowed them to achieve a rate of six to ten shots a minute with ease. Such differentials of rates of fire generally narrowed on early modern battlefields as most armies wielded broadly similar firearms, although breech-loading and later magazine-fed rifles gave significant advantages over muzzle-loading or single shot weapons.

Weapon capabilities can also heavily influence battlefield formations. Projectile weaponry, which requires space to prepare and launch, can require different formations to manual arms which rely on proximity – both to the enemy, and to fellow soldiers for protection. Most line-of-sight heavy projectile weapons, whether black-powder cannon or heavy machine guns, required room around them for gun crews to operate; one weapon was therefore allocated up to several metres of battlefield ground from which to fire. Space could also be needed for small arms. Archers tended to stand in loose open order, both because bows require space to draw, and because a tighter formation afforded no real defensive advantages for that particular weapon. Bows were intended to bombard the enemy from a distance; they were of virtually no use in a mêlée, and so their wielders tended to remain distant from enemy formations. If attacked at close quarters by a formed enemy, archers either fought with hand weapons or simply ran away.

Troops wielding hand-held bladed or blunt-trauma weapons would benefit from a far tighter formation, however. Standing closer to other combatants afforded a level of protection and could make the weapon more effective. One of the most basic hand weapons, for example, the sword, required little room to swing and were therefore frequently employed in close-quarters fighting, particularly in combat where both sides were on foot. As already noted, pikes were especially effective in tightly packed formations or pike squares that presented a wall of weaponry to an enemy.[24]

Unlike bowmen, the musket-armed soldiers from the later seventeenth to nineteenth centuries did tend to use close-order formations. In part this was because muskets required less room to operate, but mostly it was because of their slow rate of fire, relative inaccuracy, the need for mass bayonet formations to protect against cavalry, and a perceived need for close control and discipline. Again unlike bowmen, musketmen were expected to shoot from a distance, but also to close with the enemy and fight hand-to-hand if necessary. Tipping muskets with removable bayonets facilitated this, turning the firearm into a short pike – the versatility of the weapon in this case giving musketmen a rather different role to archers on the battlefield. Once the limitations of rate of fire and accuracy faded – which in European conflicts meant that enemy fire also became faster and more deadly – firearm-wielding infantrymen once again moved towards open-order formations.

Weapons and armour are therefore crucial to the way that battles are fought. At a fundamental level, weapons determine the deadly potential of an army, and the ways in which it can do damage to an enemy. Through this they can affect the very nature of combat: the location and nature of the battlefield; the formations and tactics employed by armies; the injuries inflicted on combatants; and ultimately, the outcome of conflict.

Diabolical Machines: Crécy (1346)

Crécy has been described as one of the greatest victories of Western history.[25] It certainly marked a military shift in that France, hitherto viewed as the unassailable military might of Europe, was beaten by an English army only half its size. It was the means of that triumph, however, that was truly noteworthy: the use of longbows and, to a lesser extent, gunpowder artillery by the English led to their crushing victory and would inform Western European battles for the following century. This victory was all the more astonishing for contemporary writers and subsequent commentators because of the comparative size of the armies involved. The English, having already conducted a *chevauchée* across northern France, numbered perhaps 13,000. Around 8,000 of this English force were infantrymen, including maybe 5,000 archers. The remainder comprised 2,800 men-at-arms – including the king and his commanders – and a similar number of mounted archers and hobelars who would dismount to fight.[26]

The French host, on the other hand, likely comprised a number similar to that previously taken into Flanders in 1340: 22,500 men-at-arms, 2,500 infantry, and 200 crossbowmen. Given that the French forces at Crécy also included contingents from Genoa and Bohemia, it is likely that the French army may have numbered 26,000 fighting men.[27] Despite the smaller size of the English force, they travelled at half the speed of the French, averaging 1.3km/h while the French managed 2.6km/h.[28] Perhaps, alongside the unfamiliar territory, the need for food, and avoiding the French, this was in part due to the heavy cannon that Edward's men carried with them. Their slower pace eventually forced the English to turn and fight.

There is some debate surrounding the location of the battle site. All agree that the English positioned themselves on a ridgeline, with an area of lower ground in front of them, in front of or alongside the Forest of Crécy. One of the most recent interpretations, proposed by Livingston and DeVries in 2015, suggests convincingly that the battlefield was an area today known as the Herse and the Jardin de Genève, some five miles south of the previously accepted position.[29] This position maximised the effectiveness of the English weapons whilst partially nullifying that of the French weapons.

In part, the continued uncertainty over the battle's location stems from the lack of clarity or consistency in the contemporary sources – and these sources are also confused about battle tactics. The positioning of the English archers, for example, has led to heated debate concerning whether they were located in front of the English lines, or in blocks to either side. The location of the English gunpowder artillery is also unknown, although several commentators have presumed that they were grouped with the archers.[30] The English seem to have orientated their main forces on a wagonburg, or a formation of wagons that provided cover for soldiers – although again, contemporary sources are unclear about whether this formation was a circle or a horseshoe shape, so any attempt to reconstruct the battlefield position of the English is clouded in uncertainty.

A tactic that is widely accepted, on the other hand, but one that remains confusing, is the placement of the Genoese crossbowmen who fought with the French. There were perhaps 2,000 Genoese crossbowmen at Crécy, led by Carlo Grimaldi and Aitone Doria. While each crossbowman would be expected to provide his own crossbow, both contracts – Doria's from 1337 and Grimaldi's from 1338 – required them to provide crossbow bolts, helmets (bascinets), mail to cover the shoulders (iron gorgets) and pavises – large shields to cover the rest of the body – among other weaponry.[31]

The military value of the Genoese crossbow was already well known by 1346. Even before Anna Comnena, the Byzantine princess, had described crossbows as 'a truly diabolical machine' in the twelfth century, their impact in conflict was well established.[32] However, Philip VI's use of them at Crécy was novel and was to be disastrous for his battle plan. Near-contemporary writer Jean Froissart described how Philip had initially positioned the crossbowmen 'on both sides' of the French army as it marched after the English, perhaps to protect the army's flanks.[33] However, in the immediate prelude to Crécy, Philip repositioned these men in the vanguard of his army. Historians have variously blamed Philip's military incompetence and his desire to get at the English as quickly as possible as potential explanations for this novel use of the weapon. However, it also seems reasonable that if Philip knew the English had such a large longbow contingent, as his spies would have undoubtedly informed him, it made sense that he would pit his own projectile weapons against them. He had not personally faced the English longbow before – indeed, very few of his commanders had – and it is possible that he grossly underestimated its range and effectiveness sufficiently to believe that his crossbowmen would incapacitate them before the French cavalry charged, which was a much more regular French battle tactic that had served Philip in the Battle of Cassel eighteen years previously.

Whatever his reasoning, Philip ordered the crossbowmen to advance towards the English position. Shooting uphill and towards the setting sun, the crossbowmen were further hampered by the slowness of the reloading mechanism on their weapons. A crossbowman could shoot perhaps one bolt a minute, needing to reload in a cumbersome process that required him to balance on one leg while stepping on the bowstring with his other foot in order to draw it back. In the case of Crécy, rain directly preceding the battle would have made this delicate balancing act even more difficult. The traditional interpretation – that the crossbow strings had become saturated in the wet, and thus stretched, lacking the tension to project the bolts – has been demonstrated to be false. The Genoese used a bowstring protected by a leather wrap, sheltering the strings from the rain. Instead, the rain and mud meant that the Genoese were unable to step into the stirrup required to reload their crossbows, leaving them unable to shoot at the English.[34]

The English longbow was not a novel weapon at Crécy, although it had not before been used against the French in quite the numbers seen at this battle. Edward III himself had previously used them to good effect against the Scots at Halidon Hill in 1333. It is unclear whether the longbow was capable of piercing armour (as argued by Clifford Rogers) or was used as a more psychological weapon in the English battle plan (as supported by Kelly DeVries). English longbows were not routinely carried strung, as the constant tension weakened the stave, and stringing required experience and accomplished technique. Once strung, however, arrows could be loaded and shot with relative ease and rapidity – dependent on upper-body strength. The power needed to draw these weapons was enormous: skeletons have been found from tenth-century Hungary to fifteenth-century Yorkshire that suggest that archers' musculature developed in a specific manner thanks to the physical stresses of using bows regularly.[35]

The English archers at Crécy were armed with supplies brought with them from England, including 6,518 bows, 32,126 bowstrings and 13,206 sheaves of arrows (each containing twenty-four arrows) from the Tower of London armoury.[36] From their position on top of the hill, the English rained these arrows down upon the unprotected Genoese – with their longer range and faster reloading time, the English archers proved decisive. A trained English archer could shoot ten arrows a minute, but presumably in battle this rate would be reduced, perhaps to six shots per minute. The English archers could therefore have shot over 46,000 arrows a minute as a conservative estimate – but the entirety of the Tower supply would then be gone in less than seven minutes! The fact that Philip was hit in the face by an arrow later in the battle suggests that their use extended past a series of first volleys against the Genoese.

These Genoese were virtually defenceless; not only were they within range of the longbows without being able to retaliate with their own weapons – with both a smaller range in this case, and a much slower rate of shot – but the Genoese were without their protective pavises to shelter behind while they aimed or reloaded.[37] These had been left in the French baggage train, the crossbowmen – or their commanders – too eager to engage the English to wait for them. Defenceless and against weapons with a greater range and faster shooting rate, the Genoese were massacred.

Perhaps seeing their Genoese soldiers annihilated, or perhaps completely unaware of the massacre of their vanguard, the French now collected into a mass cavalry charge. This tactic had served them well for centuries, and used not only the men-at-arms but also their horses as massed weapons that crashed straight into – and often through – enemy lines, breaking up defensive formations so that the horsemen's weapons could be used to greatest effect. Riding straight through and over their now-retreating Genoese allies, who by this point had had enough of the English longbows, the French horsemen charged the English lines.

Again, however, the French were to find the English defences limited their impact. In addition to the wagonburg surrounding their position, the English had dug a deep ditch to funnel the French cavalry into a small section of the English vanguard, led by Edward of Woodstock, Prince of Wales, accompanied by various other experienced English commanders. Once again, the English army had managed to nullify the enemy's weapons through their choice of defensive position and preparation for battle.

An additional weapon that the Genoese and French had to deal with, for the first time on a Western European battlefield, was gunpowder artillery. Crécy saw the first recoded use of firearms by the English in pitched battle. Gunpowder artillery of the mid-fourteenth century was small and crude, firing metal bolts and rounded stones rather than large projectiles. Edward III's military preparations for the Crécy campaign had included the organisation of one hundred ribauds, bound gun barrels designed to fire metal bolts. Cannonballs found on the battlefield may also have come from Edward's other cannon at the clash.

The English gunpowder weapons at Crécy were not in themselves effective at killing the enemy; while they may have supplemented the archery attack on the Genoese, it was predominantly as a weapon of intimidation that they were employed – and contemporary accounts would suggest that they were effective in terrifying horses and adding an additional layer of confusion to the mêlée.[38] As weapons of intimidation, they even perhaps contributed to the Genoese flight from the English onslaught.

Due to superior positioning and use of weapons by the English at Crécy, French losses were staggering. More than 1,500 French men-at-arms were killed, including the Duke of Lorraine and the counts of Alençon, Auxerre, Blois, Flanders, Harcourt, and Sancerre. Jean le Bel wrote that no one could remember so many great princes dying in a single encounter.[39] Nobody counted the archers and infantrymen who died, although their number must have been in the thousands. By comparison, English losses were minimal; the official tally of knights and esquires was 300, but this apparently also included men-at-arms who died during the subsequent siege of Calais.[40]

Weaponry therefore both won and lost Crécy. It was the incorporation of projectile weapons into a wider battle strategy that really won the battle for Edward, and marked a significant shift in English tactics that was to dominate their approach for the next century. Tactically and technologically the battle hinted at a military revolution, a triumph of firepower over armour that was to pave the way for the dominance of powder weapons in the centuries ahead.

Seeking an End to Stalemate: Cambrai (1917)

Battle in the First World War was very much shaped by the weapons and equipment deployed. By the time of the first Battle of Cambrai in late 1917, three years of warfare had honed the deadly capacity of armies; the lethal but relatively limited repertoire of weapons envisaged by pre-war planners had been supplemented by an array of munitions and machines designed to make the battlefield intolerably inhospitable for enemy troops. Cambrai saw many of those weapons, old and new, brought together on the battlefield, with tactics that were beginning to ensure the weaponry's effective use. For both the British and German armies, the battle was a demonstration of what their arms could achieve when correctly handled.

The very appearance of First World War battlefields was shaped primarily by the weaponry in use. Unlike battles of the Napoleonic or Crimean wars in the previous century, the armies at Cambrai did not line up to face each other in the open. The range, accuracy and sheer concentration of firepower meant that men spent most of their time huddled in dugouts or trenches, protected from direct fire. Artillery dominated the battlefield but remained thousands of yards to the rear of the front lines, employing indirect fire guided by observers rather than shooting on lines-of-sight. For the infantry, high explosive, shrapnel, machine guns, and magazine-fed rifles had rendered close-order formations obsolete, and when soldiers ventured out of their subterranean shelters during battle it was in open order, either to advance on a particular objective or to flee a particularly objectionable enemy.

The Germans at Cambrai were entrenched in well-prepared positions that formed part of the wider Hindenburg Line. There were three main defensive lines, defended by deep dugouts and thick barbed-wire fences. British commander Douglas Haig was keen to break through these defences and to end 1917 with a battlefield victory, especially after the relatively marginal gains of the costly Third Battle of Ypres. He therefore approved plans by General Byng, commander of Third Army, to attack the previously quiet sector of the front around Cambrai, making use of innovative weaponry in the shape of the Tank Corps, improved artillery shells and targeting, and greater cooperation between air and ground forces to achieve a breakthrough with limited casualties.

The main thrust of the initial offensive was to come from a mass of 476 tanks – 378 fighting and 98 support vehicles – supported by infantry of III and IV corps. The terrain around Cambrai was largely flat, chalky, and little damaged by artillery bombardments, making it perfect for mechanised units. The tanks were intended to soak up much of the German small-arms fire and to destroy the wire in front of the German positions, allowing the infantry to pass. In order to prepare the way for them there would be a very short, sharp artillery bombardment, with a focus on destroying German guns that might fire on the advancing tanks. Overhead, the Royal Flying Corps (RFC) was tasked not only with air superiority, but with a ground-attack role that would further discomfort German defences.

The opening of the battle on 20 November, for once, seemed to go right for the British. The tanks moved up overnight to their start positions 150 yards behind the line with relief drivers to keep their crews fresh for combat, the noise of their movement covered by demonstrations from the RFC.[41] Approximately ten minutes before zero hour, just over 1,000 guns that had been concentrated for the offensive opened up on German positions. Unlike the Somme the previous year, or Third Ypres only weeks earlier, there was no prolonged preliminary shelling. That they were able to launch such a short and sudden bombardment was down to the new and more effective fuses for high-explosive shells, and the very recent adoption of the technique of 'predicted fire', which allowed for the fall of shot to be precisely calculated without the need for 'registration' or ranging shots to alert the enemy.[42] Careful reconnaissance, including aerial observation and sound ranging, had identified enemy batteries and strongpoints, which had then been equally carefully targeted. The new instantaneous 'No.106 Fuze' made high-explosive shells much more effective against enemy wire and allowed the German front lines to be targeted without cratering the ground badly enough to impede the attacking units – a major benefit for the tanks.

The advantage of the sudden bombardment was that their targets would have little time to move (in the case of enemy batteries, at least), and enemy high command would have no time to bring up reinforcements to respond to the initial advance. In some places, the shelling began only as the first attacking units reached the enemy wire.[43] Although short, the bombardment by experienced men with quick-firing guns put down a huge weight of fire on the German positions. Artilleryman Major Richard Foot of 62nd Division reckoned that a six-gun battery could land thirty aimed shots on a target in as many seconds.[44] Even at a far slower rate of fire, tens of thousands of shells would have flown across no man's land in just a few minutes at the opening of the battle.

When the advance began at approximately 6.30 am, the German wire and defensive lines remained mostly intact. As at the Somme, where attacks against prepared positions on the first day had been an unmitigated disaster, the defenders sported well-positioned heavy machine guns, rifles, and enjoyed artillery support, albeit that some of the 150 German guns on the sector had been hit by the initial British bombardment. Yet there was no repeat of the disasters of July 1916. Smoke shells dropped on the German front lines confused the defenders, some of whom were in any case poor-quality reservists, and the advancing tanks quickly spread terror down the line.[45] German Lieutenant Miles Reinke recalled later that 'when the first tanks passed the first line, we thought we would be compelled to retreat towards Berlin', so terrifying did they appear.[46] The thick barbed-wire barriers that were impassable for infantry proved easily surmountable for tanks, which used steel anchors to drag whole sections out of the way of the foot soldiers. Captain Douglas Wimberley of the Machine Gun Corps recollected:

> The wire at Cambrai was about four foot high and fifteen yards wide, but the tanks that had gone in front of us had ploughed through it like a ship in the sea, and we had no difficulty at all in following their tracks.[47]

Casualties in this initial assault were relatively light. Many defenders either withdrew in disorder or simply surrendered, while the few strongpoints that held out were quickly suppressed by tank fire and infantry assault. The combination of the Mark IV tank's half-inch armour and its firepower – the 'male' version boasted two six-pounders and three Lewis machine guns, and the 'female' five Lewis Guns – rendered it a formidable opponent against infantry and lightly fortified emplacements. By the time of Cambrai the British infantry had also developed somewhat more effective tactics for assaulting enemy strongpoints. Each platoon now had four sections of twelve men based around a primary weapon: bombers, rifle grenadiers, Lewis gunners, and riflemen.[48] This diverse array of weaponry gave each platoon a solid base of fire, the ability to hit targets beyond grenade range with explosives, and a core of assault troops, yet it did not overburden them with excessively cumbersome kit. The weaponry in use allowed flexible assault tactics without compromising the infantry's mobility.

The artillery bombardment, smoke, apparent invulnerability of the tanks, and the firepower of the assaulting troops gave the British a decisive advantage in the opening attack. They were even able to mitigate against the problem of getting their heavy tanks across the German trenches to continue the assault:

> To cross [the Hindenburg Line] with tanks was quite impossible, as it was enormously wide and deep, but the ingenuity of our headquarters staff produced the answer. Enormous bundles of fascines (in other words brushwood) were provided … As the tank came to the trench, this bundle was released and fell into the bottom of the trench. This enabled the tank to nose down, rest on it and crawl up over the other side[49]

Although not everything went perfectly, the first day of the Cambrai offensive was nevertheless a general success, with almost unprecedented gains of four or five miles across much of the front. That these gains were not exploited should not detract from the achievement. Despite the mythologising of the tank at Cambrai, the initial successes were down to the effective combination of weapons systems and tactics that maximised their advantages. Artillery played a crucial role – perhaps the most crucial role, according to Brian Bond – in softening the defensive lines, blunting the Germans' immediate ability to respond, and maintaining the element of surprise.[50] The infantry's array of small arms allowed them to overrun strongpoints that withstood the bombardment and tank onslaught, while the RFC provided valuable assistance in a ground-attack role. The tanks themselves might have had the greatest psychological effect on the defenders, but their frailties as weapons were already being demonstrated as dusk fell on the first day of the offensive.

Aside from tanks knocked out by artillery fire, several were disabled when German infantry 'discovered they could stop the tanks by throwing a hand grenade into the manhole on the top'.[51] More simply suffered mechanical failure. By the end of the first day only 297 were still operational, with crews at the end of their physical endurance.[52] The tanks had helped to carve a hole in the German lines, but they could do little to turn it into a wider breakthrough. As the battle wore on failures became more prevalent: under 40 per cent of tank losses came from enemy action, with the rest attributable to breakdown or ditching.[53] The tanks' struggles were echoed elsewhere. The artillery continued to pound at the German lines – over a million high-explosive shells were fired by the BEF in the final week of November, and half a million of shrapnel – but the battle degenerated into another attritional struggle.[54] Infantry ground their way forward with rifle, grenade and mortar; even cavalry armed with lances and swords made an important contribution to combined-arms operations at Gauche Wood and Villers-Guislain.[55]

Although innovative British weapons systems had made headway, the German counterattack from 30 November showed that new weaponry had by no means revolutionised the battlefield. Twenty German divisions attacked using stormtrooper tactics that would serve them so well in battles the following year: sudden, intense shelling of the enemy front line and gas bombardment of enemy batteries was followed by small group attacks, centred on light machine guns and mortars, which penetrated enemy lines quickly and in depth. Strongpoints were ignored and left for second-wave attackers. In just over a week, they recaptured almost all of the ground lost in the first ten days of the battle. The weapons used were largely those that had existed throughout the war. As Paddy Griffith argued, 'without the benefit of any revolutionary new weapon, [the Germans] showed the potential power of deep infiltration and surprise … At Cambrai the combination of stormtroopers and well-orchestrated artillery proved to be as much of an answer to the problems of modern battle as the tank itself.'[56] Yet it was still the weaponry that allowed this tactic to be successful: not only the high-explosive, shrapnel and gas shells of the artillery that allowed them to open up the enemy line, but the magazine rifles, grenades, portable mortars and light machine guns that allowed the infantry *gruppe* to pack a considerable punch with small numbers.

If new and innovative weaponry did not dictate the outcome of Cambrai, weaponry certainly shaped its course. The sheer deadliness of weaponry kept face-to-face confrontations between troops to a minimum, leaving most combat conducted at a distance. Innovations such as mass tank attacks, air support and predicted bombardment were all successful to a greater or lesser extent, but so were more traditional approaches of infantry attacks supported by rifle, grenade, machine gun and mortar.

Chapter 8

Armies, Personnel and Training

'I have got an infamous army, very weak and ill-equipped, and a very inexperienced staff'
Arthur Wellesley, Duke of Wellington[1]

Such was the Duke of Wellington's unflattering assessment of his command in 1815, shortly before the Battle of Waterloo. The duke was unimpressed by the multinational nature of his army, and by its relative lack of experience. He complained that many of the Dutch and Hanoverians were either half trained or recently embodied militia, while the British troops were far from the quality of the regiments with which he had won the Peninsular War the previous year.[2] Perhaps he was merely getting his excuses in early lest Napoleon proved too tough an adversary, but Wellington's *bon mot* also highlights a vital issue in the outcome of battle: the quality of the armies matters. But what makes an army strong or weak as it faces its enemy across the field of battle? As the duke hinted, size, coherence, organisation, training, equipment and experience are all important factors in an army's strength, and to that list we might add issues such as doctrine, discipline and structures of command. These factors fundamentally underpin the quality of personnel arrayed for combat.

The first measure of strength of any army is generally its size. Other factors being equal (which of course they rarely are), it stands to reason that a larger army possesses a greater mass of attack, density of defence, and a deeper pool of reserves. It can conduct simultaneous operations that the enemy cannot match without spreading themselves too thinly. In modern armies, it allows a heavier weight and concentration of fire to be brought to bear on enemy positions. In a battle of pure attrition, weight of numbers gives the best chance of outlasting the enemy. Bringing the greatest mass together at the crucial moment therefore theoretically gives an army the best chance of success.

Attempts have even been made to quantify the importance of numbers in battle. In the early twentieth century, British engineer and mathematician Frederick Lanchester devised a series of formulae to explain the relationship of army size to casualties inflicted (and therefore, he assumed, victory obtained). Initially stimulated by his interest in the new field of aerial combat, Lanchester's work has also been applied to land and naval warfare, and eventually incorporated putative factors of military effectiveness.[3] These models, and adaptations that have followed, unsurprisingly hinted that a bigger army was likely to win if it forced a general engagement on equal terms, but that a smaller force could win if it possessed significantly more effective firepower, or if it was able to divide the enemy army and engage in detail.

Such conclusions may strike even the casual student of military history as astoundingly obvious, but the Lanchester formulae do possess the advantage of demonstrating the theoretical effect of numbers, firepower and concentration with simple mathematical elegance. Moreover, they provoke the student of military history to reflect more closely on *why* a simple mathematical calculation is insufficient to decide who will win a battle.[4] Bigger armies do frequently win battles, but just as often (or so it seems) they lose them.

The first thing to acknowledge is that raw numbers can hide huge disparities within a force. Besides issues of morale, weapons or leadership that are dealt with in other chapters, or training which is discussed below, an analysis must take into account whether an army has a balance of all arms, whether it contains mobile, mechanised or air units, the ratio of combatants to support personnel, and the number of soldiers actually physically able to fight. The ratio of support staff to combatants has risen significantly in more modern warfare, meaning that headline figures of personnel can bear little relation to fighting strength. The homogeneity of an army can also be a factor. Composite international forces have been a feature of battlefields throughout the past millennium, and at times the differences in quality between contingents can be stark. Foreign mercenaries have often been used to strengthen armies, but unwilling auxiliary contingents might equally prove a weakness. Differences of language or culture can make cooperation within multinational armies difficult, rendering numbers less effective.

Moreover, an army's fighting strength on paper does not always translate to numbers engaged in combat. Aside from troops unable to reach the battlefield in time, operational issues such as the need to screen enemy forces elsewhere or guard lines of communication may prevent units on the battlefield from actually engaging the enemy. Those present may also be unable to come into action through exhaustion, poor staff work, the element of surprise, or even uncertainty about whether they intend to fight. The latter issue is rare, but can be vitally important. On the morning of Bosworth (1485), for example, Richard III would have been confident of significantly outnumbering Henry Tudor, but the blunt refusal of Lord Stanley to join Richard's attack greatly shortened the odds. Similarly, at Leipzig in 1813, Napoleon's numerical disadvantage grew as several of his German contingents crossed the battlefield to join their fellows in the coalition forces. Nominal strength is therefore less important than the concentration of effective force on the battlefield.

The question of effective concentration can be more a matter of a commander's operational skill, but is often linked to the army's structure and organisation. Advantage in numbers can be quickly negated if there is no system to make sure that men turn up in the right place, at the right time, in the right formation, and with the right weapons. Staff work is a rather modern concept, but armies throughout history have benefited or suffered from their system for marshalling and moving troops. Chronicler Jean Froissart remarked of Crécy (1346) that 'It must be stressed that the French lords – kings, dukes, counts and barons – did not reach the spot together, but arrived one after another, in no kind of order.'[5] The lack of central control contributed significantly to their defeat.

The structures and command-and-control of any army are crucial to its effectiveness. Medieval armies tended to be smaller, and could be 'commanded' by line of sight. Armies in combat would be split into a small number of temporary sub-formations, known as 'battles', commanded by noblemen or sometimes professional soldiers. Often (but by no means always) there would be three such sub-units; either a left, right and centre, or a van-, middle- and rearguard. Each unit would function as a block, their strength lying in their weight and cohesion. Tactics tended to be rudimentary once combat was joined, requiring less in the way of manoeuvre. Battle plans were often decided in a council of war before the action, and relatively few orders had to be given once the enemy was engaged. As such, army structure and communication were of less importance in giving a decisive advantage on the battlefield. Disorganisation, lack of coordination, or sheer ill-discipline could certainly help to negate any advantage in numbers, as happened to the larger French armies at Crécy, Poitiers (1356), or Agincourt (1415).[6]

As the advent of pike and gunpowder weaponry led to more complex tactics, the ability of battlefield commanders to coordinate and communicate with their troops became more important. Armies were not always noticeably larger than their medieval counterparts, but had more moving parts that required careful management. The sixteenth-century Spanish tercios, for example, were divided into ten companies and combined pikemen and arquebusiers, requiring coordination not just between tercios but within them. The tercios were permanent, professional formations, and developed clear lines of command, with a commandant and companies led by captains supported by a sergeant and several corporals. A quartermaster and a sergeant major oversaw supplies and discipline. As professional organisations, they tended to possess more veterans and experienced campaigners. They became the exemplar of a well-organised and well-led force. The success of their combined-arms tactical system was at least partially due to the units' organisation, which gave them experienced soldiers, flexible formations, firm leadership, and a degree of self-sufficiency on and off the battlefield. This style of organisation allowed them to deploy both firepower and pike more effectively than traditional Swiss or German Landsknecht pike units, which had proved so effective in ending the reign of the medieval man-at-arms. The tercios certainly proved their worth in over a century of fighting in Europe and the Americas, from Mühlberg (1547) to Valenciennes (1656), but by the end of the Thirty Years' War the preponderance of musketmen on the battlefield was rendering the traditional tercio obsolete.

The increasing dominance of gunpowder was accompanied by a related evolution in military organisation that was felt both on and off the battlefield. Early modern political centralisation was accompanied by a de facto centralisation of the use of military force. The sheer expense of raising, training and equipping firearms-based forces meant that it became largely a royal prerogative; where individual noblemen raised their own units, they now did so as part of a centrally controlled army. The eventual upshot of this for the battlefield was that units were formalised into regiments and battalions (squadrons, for cavalry), while companies or half companies (or cavalry troops) often became the basic tactical unit. The creation of permanent armies was accompanied by a more sophisticated rank structure, assigning command of each body of men to a responsible officer within a clear hierarchy. Permanent units gave armies a further advantage of a stronger esprit de corps, and a greater opportunity for officers to know the capabilities of their men. Although confusion in the heat of battle was ubiquitous, the standardisation of units and command structures gave the trained armies of later seventeenth- and eighteenth-century states an enormous advantage over less-organised opponents. At Tsaritsyn in 1774, for example, a heavily outnumbered Russian army under General Michelsohnen gained a shattering victory over Pugachev's poorly organised rebels, destroying an army of 10,000 for the loss of fewer than a hundred men.

By the later seventeenth century, armies were generally larger than those of the medieval period. While medieval chronicles sometimes describe vast hosts assembling for battle, confrontations before 1500 rarely involved forces of more than the low tens of thousands. Agincourt saw perhaps 20,000 men all told engaged in combat, while at Towton (1461), reputedly the bloodiest battle on English soil, the total may have been double that. At the Battle of Fleurus (1690) during the Nine Years' War, on the other hand, over 70,000 men took part, and the War of Spanish Succession (1701–14) regularly saw over 100,000 soldiers on the battlefield. Nor were these by any means the largest battles. At Vienna in 1683, perhaps as many as 200,000 men were present for the clash between the Ottoman army and the Germano-Polish forces of John Sobieski.

The sheer size of the armies meant that intermediary levels of command were necessary to ensure effective command-and-control. Armies in the field therefore began to introduce a system of brigades, in which two or more regiments might be grouped, and later divisions, which would contain two or more brigades. This system allowed for greater tactical flexibility without overburdening a single army commander, and without leaving individual regimental or battalion commanders lacking orders. Even so, generals could struggle to keep control of their growing forces in combat. Frederick the Great believed the maximum force that could be practically wielded was around 50,000; his fielding of an army of 65,000 at Prague (1757) led to a loosely controlled battle with heavy casualties.[7]

The development of army corps in the wars of the French Revolution and Napoleon went some way to addressing this problem. Comprised of multiple infantry divisions, with attached cavalry, artillery and support units, each was in effect an army in miniature, and could operate independently in a way that single divisions generally could not. Napoleon used the system to great effect on an operational and tactical level. At Friedland (1807), for example, Marshal Lannes's apparently isolated V Corps was able to pin Russian General Bennigsen's army in place for several hours, allowing Napoleon to bring up significant reinforcements to crush them. At Jena-Auerstädt the previous year, the corps system had even helped to turn a miscalculation into a stunning victory, as Marshal Davout's III Corps routed the main Prussian army while Napoleon mistakenly committed the rest of his forces against a smaller Prussian detachment. The system was eventually copied by Napoleon's opponents – a clear sign that they had felt at an organisational disadvantage. These army structures, with suitable tweaks to take into account new fighting methods, remained largely in place throughout the nineteenth and twentieth centuries, with the addition of layers such as the army group or 'front' to accommodate the massive numerical expansion of armies.

Structural advantage could therefore be attained on the battlefield at a grand tactical level, although it could rarely be enjoyed without effective communications and staff work. From the early modern period, this was the role of a general officer's aides-de-camp, who tended to be socially well-connected officers chosen on a campaign-by-campaign basis, without either training or even designated roles. Such a casual approach worked adequately with armies of limited size, especially where a general was able to retain a high level of personal control. Yet as army sizes grew, so too did the need for a more professional staff. Early experiments with a trained central body of officers in France and Austria focused mostly on army administration, but the experience of the Napoleonic Wars led to Prussia creating the first dedicated general staff. These men were trained not only to administer the army off the battlefield, but to ensure its smooth operation on it. Staff officers were appointed to army, corps, and divisional command, ensuring a theoretical consistency of approach to operational planning and execution. The eventual results, in the Austro-Prussian War of 1866 and the Franco-Prussian War of 1870–1, highlighted the advantages of a dedicated staff, which was eventually adopted by all Western powers.

Advantage in communications could also be gained by the use of technology. Signal flags, drums, horns and bugles were all used in pre-modern battle to convey messages to troops in line-of-sight or line-of-hearing, with some instruments and whistles lasting well into the twentieth century. Armies organised enough to use such methods enjoyed a clear advantage in speed of communication, albeit of very simple instructions, and over short distances. In the age of gunpowder, the thundering of guns and rolling clouds of powder smoke rendered visual and aural signals useless for overall command of a battle, although they retained some utility at a local level. Cavalry attacks especially were coordinated by bugle calls rather than shouted orders or hand signals.

By the twentieth century, telephone and later wireless communications could give armies a distinct advantage, although the effective deployment of technology took time. One of the major problems facing First World War generals was ensuring rapid communications with advancing troops; telephone lines that linked the trenches to headquarters were nigh-on impossible to extend over no man's land, meaning that general staffs struggled to coordinate reserves and artillery with advancing infantry. No wholly practical solution was identified by the end of the war. Britain's Committee on the Lessons of the Great War stated in 1932 that the difficulties of communication meant that it was like 'fighting without a brain; or worse still, with a disordered brain which acts regardless of reality'.[8]

It was radio that really revolutionised battlefield communication. In the interwar years, radio sets became compact enough to be useful in field operations, giving technologically developed forces another significant advantage. General headquarters at the rear could now, for the first time since line-of-sight battles had become unfashionable, keep up with action on the battlefront in real time. It also allowed the practice of 'forward control' by enterprising generals like Hans Guderian or Erwin Rommel, who preferred to be nearer the action but also needed to be plugged into their rear headquarters. It was Rommel's belief that 'the commander must be the prime mover of the battle and the troops must always have to reckon with his appearance in personal control' – but personal intervention and overall control of a battle were only possible with the availability of almost instantaneous communications.[9] Radio also allowed different layers of the army to communicate with one another, giving a greater capacity for cooperation and coordination. The technology of course had to be matched by competent operators and useable equipment – one of the many problems of the British Matilda I tank in 1940 was the inability of the commander to access the radio in combat, for example – but the development of increasingly sophisticated and integrated communications networks has been one way of establishing battlefield advantage over the past century. A major disadvantage of course is the risk of remote tactical micromanagement – something difficult to avoid without adequate training and appropriate doctrine throughout the army. More recently, the risk of communications disruption from enemy action has added another dimension to the contemporary battlespace.

While an impression of an army's strength can be gained from its size, organisation, and command-and-control, the quality of troops is another vital consideration. This can include the level of training, whether soldiers are veterans or relative *ingenus*, and their specialist roles. Pure numbers in medieval armies meant little, as trained men-at-arms or archers were generally worth far more than levies, and well-organised forces were far harder to break than uncoordinated hosts. In early modern armies the balance between horse, foot and artillery was important, as was the proportion of firearms to pikemen, but most of all the coordination of all arms gave crucial advantage. By the wars of Napoleon the range of specialisms had grown further, with light and line infantry, grenadiers, light and heavy cavalry, dragoons, and horse and foot artillery all offering different options on the battlefield, and with units such as Guards regiments of various nations being accorded a more elite status in battle as well as on parade. The trend continued apace throughout the nineteenth and twentieth centuries, as new units and specialisms sprung up across various Western armies: commandos, marines, paratroopers, stormtroopers, armoured units, mounted, motorised or airborne infantry, pilots, aircrew, and dozens more different specialisms came to the fore, each with its own distinct fighting strengths.

As fighting corps multiplied so did doctrines for their employment. The concept of doctrine – in basic terms the principles by which the army conducts its operations – is of relatively modern origin, but historically most armies have been influenced by military traditions or common practices. Although doctrine does not dictate tactics, it certainly influences approaches to battle, from whether an army takes an offensive or defensive posture, to its use of mobile units or heavy weapons or air support, to the formations it uses to engage the enemy. In some armies doctrine imparts a heavily top-down approach to command that gives individual soldiers little scope for initiative; in others, delegation and mission command is practised, giving junior officers and minor tactical formations greater freedom of action. General staffs in the Prussian tradition were largely responsible for drawing up formal Field Service Regulations, but manuals of conduct, informal or official, have existed for centuries. Throughout the medieval period, for example, the Roman Vegetius's *De Re Militari* was an influential formative text for aspiring military commanders.[10]

Armies are less likely to prosper, or are more likely to have to rely on extraneous factors such as terrain, weather, or blind luck, if they lack a doctrine or general practices that allow them to emphasise their own strengths and effectively counter enemy formations or weaponry. English success in the early Hundred Years' War was partly down to apparent French reluctance to move away from their habitual frontal cavalry charge, which proved ineffective against the English system of fighting. Similarly, the heavy British defeats in the early Boer War were largely down to continuing with tactics that played to the strengths of the Mauser-armed Boers. Almost all armies were unprepared for trench warfare in the First World War, and the lack of a suitable doctrine for successfully attacking entrenched positions was in part responsible for spiralling casualties. The overwhelming British numerical advantage at the opening of the Battle of the Somme (1916) was squandered when officers and men were sent into battle with little plan beyond charging (or walking in good order) towards rifle and machine-gun fire.

Doctrine is of limited use, however, without adequate training. Men who do not know how to use weapons proficiently, or how to manoeuvre under fire, or have little concept of what might be required tactically on the battlefield, will be less effective in combat. In medieval battle, it was expected that knights and men-at-arms would be highly proficient in the use of their chosen weapon, having engaged in lengthy training as a necessary component of their social station. Archers or crossbowmen were essentially specialists in their field. These attributes were often trained into men as part of their social function. When called up for war, their skill at arms was taken for granted, and was generally considered sufficient training for battle. The ability to manoeuvre in large formations or to learn fieldcraft was largely unnecessary.

It was the development of the close formations of the later medieval and early modern period that made collective military training a necessity once again. Although there had been examples of little-trained pikemen breaking well-mounted horsemen, such as the Flemish victory over the French at Courtrai (1302) or the Scottish schiltron against the English at Bannockburn (1314), the Swiss pikemen, German Landsknecht, or Spanish tercios of the fifteenth to seventeenth centuries were all significantly more effective when trained to work in unison. A pike square was largely invulnerable to traditional edged weapons if it retained its dressings and if the men inside had the strength and steadiness to hold firm their pikes and to trust in their comrades. This required training and discipline, especially if formations were expected to manoeuvre or work in conjunction with cavalry or firearms. The increasingly widespread use of firearms also necessitated greater training, not only in using the mechanisms of gunpowder weapons (a man could be trained to use a firearm in far less time than it took to master a bow) but in learning the formations and drill required to deploy effectively on the battlefield. The linear formations adopted by musket units were more difficult to learn and to execute than the mass pike squares, and the number of evolutions required to move between the different formations (column of march to line, extended line, square, attack column, and so on) meant that basic training became, by the eighteenth century, a matter more of drill than weapons proficiency.

A degree of weapons training was nevertheless vital for fire control. The inaccuracy of muskets meant that volley fire was more important than aimed shooting, absolving soldiers of the need for marksmanship, but it was important that soldiers had the training and discipline to fire and reload on command. In the tightly packed ranks of early modern musket units, the chance of ill-trained troops accidentally shooting their comrades was high, especially in the smoke-wreathed chaos of battle. Once rifles became more prevalent from the mid-nineteenth century, men required greater training in marksmanship and target acquisition. The latter issue also became increasingly vital for artillery as guns moved from line-of-sight to indirect fire. The advantage of rifle training was demonstrated to great effect at Mons (1914), when the accuracy of rapid British rifle fire inflicted significant casualties on advancing German troops, who became convinced that they faced machine guns.

By the twentieth century, the increasing complexity of weapons systems and equipment meant that permanent armies investing in longer-term training enjoyed a significant advantage in conventional battle over extemporised or partly trained forces. It was a lesson well learned by Lord Gort, commander of the BEF in France in 1940, who reflected shortly after the close of the disastrous campaign:

> The days are past when armies can be hurriedly raised, equipped and placed in the field, for modern war demands the ever-increasing use of complicated material … Modern equipment requires time to design and produce, and once it is produced, further time is required to train troops in its technical and tactical uses. Improvised arrangements, made at short notice, can only lead to the shortage of essential equipment, the production of inferior articles, and the unskilful handling of weapons and vehicles on the battlefield.[11]

Aside from ensuring basic individual proficiency in weapons handling, tactics, and familiarity with doctrine, training is important to creating group cohesion. Training inculcates a stronger esprit de corps and generally helps morale, even if the training itself is despised. Soldiers who feel prepared for combat are more likely to enter it confident of victory, and are more likely to react positively if initial plans go awry – which they almost invariably do. On the other side of the coin, soldiers who feel that they are facing a better-trained and equipped enemy are more likely to lose heart. Private Edward Watson of the King's Royal Rifle Corps, taken prisoner in France in 1940, recalled:

> I remember being very impressed with these German soldiers at the time – how bloody tough they looked. How efficient they seemed, relative to us. They were so business-like and how very smart the officers seemed by comparison. Everything seemed so much better than what we had. They were professionals by comparison to us.[12]

Yet even in the best-prepared forces, there are aspects of combat that cannot be adequately simulated in training, including the fear of mortal peril, the experience of ordnance flying all around, or the seemingly random (to those on the receiving end, at least) effect of artillery fire. The ability to withstand such shocks can come down to morale, leadership, and above all, discipline as much as technical training.

Battlefield discipline covers a variety of sins, from obedience in the face of the enemy to fire control, to adhering to petty regulations of dress or behaviour. Indiscipline can include excessive exuberance as well as reluctance to fight. From the Saxons' downhill charge at Hastings to the French nobility at Crécy or the British heavy cavalry at Waterloo, examples abound of soldiers allowing their enthusiasm to get the better of them, often to their own and their army's detriment. Discipline could also be important in holding men steady in combat, especially in the linear armies of the seventeenth and eighteenth centuries. The element of chance introduced by massed firearms, combined with tactics demanding that men stood tall in the face of the enemy, meant that it took iron will to refrain from either moving or returning the enemy's fire until ordered to do so. Jean-Roch Coignet described his experience at the Battle of Aspern-Essling in 1809:

> fifty guns ... thundered upon us without our being able to advance a step, or fire a shot. Imagine the agony we endured in such a position, for I can never describe it ... The balls fell among our ranks, and cut down our men three at a time ... the brave grenadiers closed up without a frown, saying to one another as they saw the enemy making ready to fire, 'The next one's for me'.[13]

Even when movement was finally ordered, conducting tactical evolutions under fire, or delivering coordinated volleys into an enemy formation, demanded unfailing obedience to command.

Yet this obedience was not necessarily imposed at the end of the rod. While the eighteenth century was notorious for its culture of military discipline that kept men in check with the lash, beatings, running the gauntlet, and occasional executions, many of these savage punishments were for infractions of the military code beyond the battlefield. Most armies maintained the death penalty for desertion in the face of the enemy, but few had to (or could) resort to corporal or capital punishment as the sole means of keeping men in line. Even in forces with supposedly brutal disciplinary regimes, such as the Prussian army of the Seven Years' War, the discipline to stand and execute orders under fire came more from group cohesion, comradeship, experience, morale, or motivation than from fear of hypothetical future punishment.

Veteran troops often enjoyed greater group cohesion and experience, but also had to cope with another enemy: the psychological impact of long exposure to combat. While experience confers many advantages in battle, men pushed too far can lose not only their enthusiasm for fighting but also sometimes their judgement, leading to erratic behaviour or even a refusal to fight. Modern militaries are conscious of the issue and for several decades now have tried (with varying degrees of success) to mitigate against it, but the idea of 'battle fatigue' is of much longer standing. Prussian Carl Daniel Küster, who experienced combat in the Seven Years' War, commented:

> On the subject of this so-called 'cannon-fever' I have often talked with officers of all ranks, as well as with valiant private soldiers. They assure me with one voice that anyone who maintains he has gone through battle, and never experienced this appalling fear, must be accounted a braggart and a liar. But they all talked about something which I have often noted myself, namely that such a sensation is spread in such a way over the early, middle and final stages of the battle that the stronger men bear up the weaker ones, and that a general flight sets in only when this disabling fear affects the morale of the majority of the army.[14]

In many cases, veterans were clearly traumatised by their experiences. In the First World War, men coming out of the line with obvious trauma were treated with a degree of humanity, but those who were thought to have shirked combat could – and on many occasions did – face the firing squad. British Corporal Alan Bray sympathised: 'I knew why these men had deserted … It was the fact that they had probably been in the trenches for two or three months without a break, which could absolutely break your nerve.'[15] Whether executions had the intended impact on the fighting spirit of other men is a debatable point.

The draconian punishment for deserters nevertheless underlines the importance that military authorities attached to the fighting qualities of soldiers. They, like Wellington a century before, were acutely aware of the benefits of well-trained and disciplined troops on the battlefield. Wellington's infamous army did, of course, go on to win at Waterloo, albeit with the vital assistance of Blücher's Prussians, offering a timely reminder that the putative strength of an army does not always dictate the outcome of a battle. Nevertheless, size, organisation, training, doctrine, discipline and cohesiveness can all give armies an edge over their enemies, and can be significant factors in battlefield success.

Prussian Apotheosis: Rossbach (1757)

Victory at Rossbach is traditionally attributed to Frederick the Great's strategic skill, tactical acumen, boldness, and to the poor decisions of his opponents, Prince Saxe-Hildburghausen and Prince Soubise. Fought on 5 November 1757, Rossbach was one of Frederick's greatest triumphs, won in only about ninety minutes and at unusually low cost to his own army. Frederick had arrived in western Saxony with only perhaps 22,000 soldiers to the Franco-Imperial allies' 41,000, but was determined to fight a decisive battle to counter defeats that Prussia had recently suffered on almost all other fronts.

After several days of jockeying, the armies drew up opposite one another in the vicinity of the village of Rossbach. Seeing Soubise attempting a rather foolhardy and ill-executed flanking manoeuvre with the bulk of his army, Frederick ordered a rapid realignment and caught his enemy struggling to deploy from column of march. Prussian artillery pounded the Franco-Imperial troops before Frederick's cavalry under Lieutenant General Seydlitz launched a devastating charge on their opposite numbers. Some French infantry units moved to attack Frederick's lines, but their columns were pushed back by the fire of half a dozen Prussian battalions under Prince Henry, before being scattered by a second cavalry charge. Aside from a few units, the remainder of the Franco-Imperial army broke and fled the field, leaving perhaps 5,000 casualties and the same number of prisoners.[16] Prussian losses were minute by comparison. Writing to the Marquis d'Argens, Frederick claimed, 'we lost one colonel, two other officers and sixty-seven soldiers; 223 were wounded.'[17] Even had his casualties been double, it was a spectacular triumph.

Such is the bald narrative. Tactical skill on the one side and ineptitude on the other certainly played their part in the outcome. But at the level of the ordinary soldier, this was also a victory for organisation, training and discipline, which gave the Prussian troops an advantage over their more numerous and generally well-motivated opponents.

The basic composition of the forces certainly played in Frederick's favour. Although far smaller, his army was a homogenous force of Prussian troops with himself as unchallenged commander, allowing him to practise his maxim that a general 'should act on his own' rather than share command.[18] His opponents, however, were a composite force of a French army, which made up the bulk of the allied troops, and an Imperial army comprised of small contingents from several German states. The French force was commanded by Soubise, whose position owed more to petticoat influence than military skill, and the Imperial troops by Hildburghausen who was, in the words of one historian, 'an old and quarrelsome Saxon, who seldom got up before noon. His main concern was to assert his superiority over Soubise.'[19] The two commanders struggled to agree on a combined stratagem, and when they did march into battle did so for different reasons. Hildburghausen believed that the flanking manoeuvre would lead to the annihilation of Frederick's army, Soubise that it would simply force Frederick to withdraw to protect his communications.

The allies also suffered from a disadvantage in training and experience. Organisation in the French army of the Seven Years' War was a rather ramshackle affair, with recruitment, training and discipline generally left to each individual regiment. As such there was a wide gulf in quality between the best and worst French units. Generals could be stymied by the 'limitless professional ignorance of the French officer corps', which favoured noble birth over military skill.[20] Moreover, by no means all of the French army was actually French. It was common practice to buy in foreign units wholesale, or to raise corps of foreign soldiers, and France had several such units at Rossbach. Some such troops were very good indeed – the Swiss regiments in French service performed well at Rossbach – but others were rather weaker.[21] Daniel O'Conor, an officer in a French Irish regiment, complained in 1756 that much of his corps was recruited from 'robbers and criminals from all parts of the world' rather than native Irishmen, destroying both its cohesion and fighting spirit.[22] The Imperial troops were of even more mixed ability.

At Rossbach, weaknesses in training cost the Franco-Imperial army dear. Soubise's bold flanking manoeuvre required careful coordination between units along the line of march, and good discipline within each corps to make sure that men arrived in good fighting order. They had neither. Men shambled along as much as marched, and several units got in each other's way. The reserve artillery became sandwiched between columns of infantry, leaving it unable to deploy with any speed. When the Prussian forces began to move from their initial positions at about 2.30 pm, the allied commanders assumed that it was a retreat, and did nothing to try to untangle the mess that their march had created. Few allied units were ready to meet the Prussian cavalry attack, allowing the horsemen to gain a significant local victory. When the allied infantry prepared to march against the Prussian foot soldiers, the lack of training, cohesion and adequate doctrine pushed the French regimental commanders to adopt a column formation that took brutal punishment from Prussian artillery and infantry fire.

The Prussian forces, on the other hand, benefited from standardised and thorough training. Prussian infantrymen were trained to manoeuvre rapidly and with precision, retaining their dressings even over difficult ground. Their musket drill taught men to load, fire and reload with rapidity, and to do so while advancing rather than just remaining stationary. Cavalrymen were drilled to change formation at speed, and to ride knee to knee into the charge, giving a significant advantage over enemy formations whose galloping charges were disordered by faster horses pulling ahead of the slower. Prussian cavalrymen were also trained to remain in hand after a charge rather than riding off in pursuit of a beaten foe, as was the wont of most horsemen of the time.

A Prussian soldier's basic training lasted for up to a year. In a typical regiment, recruits would be drilled every morning for five days a week, with afternoons spent cleaning kit or in the myriad non-battle-related tasks required of a soldier.[23] Much of the Prussian army by 1757 was made up of 'cantonists' – sons of the peasantry and craftsmen conscripted for service in their cantonal regiment. Stringent height and health requirements meant that most were relatively fit and strong. Once trained, regular drill and annual peacetime manoeuvres helped to craft unit cohesion, and allowed senior commanders experience of conducting operations with large numbers of troops. Such training was exacting but worthwhile:

> During exercise and manoeuvre periods, drill could start at 2 am and end at 12 pm or 1 pm and could be extremely demanding ... The drill procedures were tiring and demanding but not senseless. The aim was not to produce blind obedience to meaningless or even stupid commands, but rather to result in expert knowledge on the battlefield.[24]

Nor was Prussian training as brutal or sadistic as has sometimes been made out. Discipline on campaign could be savagely enforced, but corporal punishment during training was used in the same spirit as in other educational settings of the day. Excessive brutality was seen as counterproductive. The overall effect of the rigorous training was to produce soldiers with the skills for battle, and with confidence in their officers and fellows: 'standardised drill and training assured every soldier that any comrade next to him was a professional.'[25]

Prussian soldiers' faith in their comrades was strengthened by the army's organisational structures. At regimental level, the cantonal recruiting system meant that men tended to serve with others from their locality, often from the same town or village, creating strong bonds of loyalty within each unit. Within companies, men were grouped into small 'tent comradeships' who ate, slept, marched, and stood in line of battle together, strengthening the sense of cohesion and trust on and off the battlefield.[26] The Prussian army in 1757 was also 'backed by good administration in the form of regular issues of pay, rations and clothing', which went some way to assuring men's physical well-being.[27]

The benefits on the battlefield of this training, preparation and organisation were shown to full effect at Rossbach. Although Frederick was slightly tardy in responding to Soubise's flanking move, his troops had the discipline and skill to strike camp and march within an hour of receiving the order. The cavalry had the discipline and fighting ability not only to rout the Franco-Imperial horsemen, but to rally and reform for a devastating secondary attack on the infantry. The Prussian gunners were able to deploy rapidly and effectively, and did great slaughter against the ponderous French infantry columns. And the Prussian infantry's fast musketry and ability to advance while delivering steady volleys gave them significant superiority over their enemies, allowing only a handful of battalions to thrust back the French advance. The Prussian troops were kept in place by bonds of comradeship, professional soldierly skills, and even belief in their cause, their iron discipline coming from self-belief as much as (and probably more than) threat of punishment. The mass peacetime army exercises also allowed Seydlitz to manoeuvre his cavalry and Prince Henry to advance his infantry en masse with far greater precision and order than their enemies could manage. Rossbach was certainly a great victory for Frederick, but it was a victory founded on the hard work of army organisation, training and doctrinal development.

Fighting far from Home: Darwin-Goose Green (1982)

The Battle of Darwin-Goose Green on 28–29 May 1982 was the first major clash of the Falklands War, and the British army's first pitched battle in a generation. It ended with complete victory for the attacking British forces, even though the Argentine defenders enjoyed parity of numbers, terrain favourable to defence, and time to prepare their positions. Although many in Britain celebrated the victory as a reaffirmation of national strength that had seemed so absent during the pell-mell retreat from empire, the reasons for victory are more prosaic. While the Argentine troops fought hard, they were at a disadvantage in training, experience, command-and-control, logistics, and air and sea support. These factors, translated into action alongside the sheer grit and courage of the men of the 2nd Battalion, Parachute Regiment, handed Britain a much-needed boost in their campaign to reconquer the Falkland Islands.

Having responded to the Argentine invasion of the Falklands on 2 April by dispatching a heavily armed task force to the South Atlantic, by late May, Margaret Thatcher's government was coming under increasing diplomatic pressure to agree a ceasefire. The British landing at San Carlos Water on 21 May had given them a military bargaining chip, but the lack of any notable advance since had made London twitchy.[28] There was pressure for British troops at the beachhead to move inland and show that Britain was winning the war. The settlements of Darwin and Goose Green were the nearest major Argentine positions, sitting on a thin isthmus connecting the northern and southern halves of East Falkland, but they held little strategic significance. The airstrip there was considered too exposed for combat aircraft, and if adequately screened the Argentine garrison could have been safely ignored by forces advancing on

Port Stanley. Nevertheless, instructions were given to prepare an assault on the position.

On the Argentine side, Britain's response to their military incursion into Las Malvinas had been unexpected, but Buenos Aires was determined to make a fight of it. Reinforcements had been rushed to the islands, but the British naval blockade prevented much heavy equipment from joining the troops. Despite enjoying far greater proximity to home bases, supplies were a problem for the Argentine garrison. Since the sinking of the *Belgrano* on 2 May, the Argentine navy had mostly remained at home, and relations between them and the other two services had become strained. Nevertheless, the garrison hoped to hold out against the limited British ground forces, especially with the southern winter fast approaching.

The structures of the two forces shortly to be engaged largely favoured the British. Brigadier Julian Thompson, commander of 3 Commando Brigade to which the Paras were attached, detailed 2 Para, supported by three 105mm guns, to deal with the garrison around Goose Green. This battalion was a coherent fighting unit with clear lines of command, integrated support sections, and clear communications with the attached artillery. The Argentine garrison, on the other hand, was a composite force made up of two companies of 12th Infantry Regiment, one company of 25th Infantry, and a platoon of 8th Infantry. There were also over 200 air force personnel.[29] The garrison was commanded by Lieutenant Colonel Piaggi of 12th Infantry, although the ranking officer in the area was air force Vice Commodore Pedroza.

In terms of combat preparation, there was a clear gulf between the two sides. The Argentine soldiers were, aside from officers and NCOs, all conscripts. They were enlisted for a single year, meaning that their training had to be significantly shortened to ensure useful service. Most were trained for only three months; Piaggi later claimed that 12th Infantry had trained for only forty-five days before the Falklands deployment, and never in cold weather.[30] For men from the subtropical north of Argentina, the cold and wet made the islands an unusually inhospitable environment. They had few adequate winter clothes, and had spent long, cold, wet weeks on garrison duty. Moreover, the battalion's heavy equipment had mostly been left in Argentina, including vehicles, mortars, heavy machine guns, and even radios.

The Paras, on the other hand, were among Britain's elite forces. Britain had abandoned the inefficient expedient of national service two decades earlier, leaving them with an all-volunteer army.[31] The focus on quality of personnel over quantity meant that national-service-era training, which had relied on bull, Blanco and beastings, had been replaced by a more innovative and appropriate regimen. Unlike the Argentine officers, whose time was spent drilling endless streams of conscripts, British officers were able to focus on honing their professional skills. Their men were well trained, with a longstanding esprit de corps, and had greater experience of cold-weather conditions. Furthermore, they were better versed in fieldcraft of keeping dry and clean in an endlessly wet environment.[32] Their supply, too, was better. Each man was issued with forty-eight hours of Arctic rations and additional ammunition, and all wore winter battledress. The artillery was well provisioned, with 320 rounds per gun.[33]

The British attack began in the early hours of 28 May. Lieutenant Colonel 'H' Jones, 2 Para's commander, had devised a complex battle plan that would see his companies leapfrog one another towards Darwin and Goose Green down the flanks of the isthmus, supported by artillery and fire from HMS *Arrow*. He would coordinate affairs by radio with company commanders. Piaggi, on the other hand, had set his men in prepared defensive positions on favourable ground. Here, however, differences in command-and-control favoured the British. Although political intervention pushed the British to engage in battle, tactical command was left to Jones once he had been detailed to lead the attack. Piaggi, however, was in a constant struggle with Pedroza over ultimate command in the area, and was subject to unnecessary tactical interference from HQ in Port Stanley.[34] One such interference was to order a more aggressive stance of patrolling ahead of the prepared positions, and it was these patrols that the Paras first engaged.

The exposed Argentine troops were taken by surprise and quickly pushed back by the assault, which soon took Burnside Hill and advanced towards Coronation Ridge on the left. Going was a little slower to the right, but steady progress was made in the darkness. This was, as Max Hastings and Simon Jenkins observed, a 'section commanders' battle', requiring initiative and courage from well-trained junior NCOs and private soldiers to keep the attack rolling.[35] As the Argentines fell back to their prepared positions, resistance became stiffer, especially with dawn breaking. As the Paras approached Darwin Hill the Argentines put up such a barrage of fire that the attack began to stall. It has been suggested that an Argentine counterattack at this stage might have put the Paras in considerable difficulty.[36] Yet even if his troops were up to the task, Piaggi had little chance of organising such a rapid thrust. With his radios largely still in Argentina, he relied on runners to relay information to many of the forward units.[37] Compared to Jones's ability to communicate with company commanders and artillery support in real time, Piaggi was at a significant disadvantage.

The Argentine defenders nevertheless held the upper hand as the morning of 28 May drifted on. Both left and right prongs of the attack were pinned down, although Jones was able to order 'D' Company in a flanking manoeuvre that would bear fruit on the right. On the left, however, little progress was possible. Jones, in an attempt to break the deadlock, moved forward with his HQ fireteam to add impetus to the assault, and was killed while closing on an Argentine machine-gun position. Major Chris Keeble, his second-in-command, quickly assumed leadership of the battalion, but by now the Paras were beginning to establish the upper hand. With more aimed and controlled fire, 'A' Company was slowly silencing enemy positions, which were running low on ammunition, while judicious use of heavy weapons (and 'D' Company's flanking manoeuvre) prised open Argentine defences on the right.

Keeble's assumption of command led to the general abandonment of Jones's complex six-stage plan of attack. Instead, applying a mission command approach, Keeble gave company commanders licence to achieve their objectives as they saw fit. A dozen years after the conflict, Spencer Fitz-Gibbon argued that this made the subsequent assaults much easier, as Jones had a tendency to overmanage his companies.[38] Whatever the truth of this, the company commanders of 2 Para had the training, professionalism and understanding with their troops to make the best of the situation, despite the loss of their popular CO. With Argentine forces low on ammunition, as cold and wet as their attackers, but hungrier and with worse kit, the defensive line on Darwin Hill disintegrated. Dozens of men surrendered, but others pulled back towards Goose Green. The Paras continued to apply pressure, aided by Harrier airstrikes when the weather overhead finally cleared.

As night fell on 28 May, the Paras were very much in the ascendency. The Argentine position was not hopeless; 132 additional combat troops had arrived during the day, and none of the support troops had yet been repurposed as infantry, including the 200 airmen. They therefore had plenty of manpower. But with their forces now surrounded around Goose Green, threatened by artillery, naval guns, airstrikes, and assault by a force that had already hurled them out of strong defensive lines, there was little appetite to continue. Central command in Port Stanley chose this moment to delegate control entirely to the men on the ground, abdicating responsibility for any surrender to Piaggi and Pedroza. Even now the two men could not agree on who held ultimate command, but both had the same views on the battle. At 10.45 am on 29 May, the remaining Argentine garrison, some 900 men, surrendered.

The will to battle, bravery, and dedication of men and officers on either side at Darwin-Goose Green cannot be questioned. Yet the British forces enjoyed clear advantages in organisation, unit cohesion, training, communications, command-and-control, supply, and inter-service cooperation. When things went wrong, the discipline of individual soldiers and skill of officers throughout the chain of command allowed them to find a way through. Argentine preparations, on the other hand, were hampered by interference from HQ and the failure to equip men properly for the campaign, while the lack of training and unit cohesion, plus poor communications, limited tactical options. Army organisation and training is never the reason for a victory, but at Goose Green it laid the essential platform. The courage of the Paras did the rest.

Chapter 9

Motivation and Morale

'As a rule, men stand up from one motive or another – simple manhood, force of discipline, pride, love, or bond of comradeship'

Joshua Chamberlain[1]

Motivation and morale are closely entwined concepts, but their meanings are subtly different. Motivation can most generally be understood to explain why a soldier fights; the reason for his or her presence on a battlefield. There are various elements that may motivate soldiers to fight: external influences such as command or leadership; internal emotions or instincts of combatants; and incentives or goals that a combatant may be striving for.[2] Many soldiers are compelled to fight, either through obligation or necessity; others are soldiers by profession and fight to make a living. Others may fight for personal reasons: comradeship, societal expectation, personal honour, or other intangible personal rewards. Each of these soldiers, however, must still face a crucial decision at the moment of battle: whether to stay and fight, or flee from possible harm.

Morale refers more specifically to how willing that soldier is to fight, and how satisfied they are in doing so.[3] Once combatants are actually on a battlefield, the threat of combat suddenly becomes visceral. The enemy is within sight, with the intent to harm; battle is imminent. In such a moment, many combatants experience apprehension and dread. The unknown of the impending conflict, or indeed a return to conflict for veterans, can be a point of extreme anxiety for combatants. US veteran David Bellavia describes his emotional state during an ambush in the midst of the Battle of Fallujah in 2004: 'Waves of fear rock me.'[4] Fear and anxiety can naturally elevate combat stress, limiting effectiveness of combatants and preventing them from clear combat decision-making.

In these circumstances, what keeps these soldiers on the battlefield, despite a natural fear of what is ahead? What allows them to continue moving forward, even though they are aware that they face possible harm or even death? One of the most powerful influences on this is morale. If motivations for battle comprise the reasons why soldiers turn up to the battlefield, morale describes the feelings of combatants once they are on the battlefield itself.

The motivation of soldiers to fight is of course a contributory factor to their morale. Combatants with powerful motivations are more inclined to positive morale as they have what they perceive to be a just or worthwhile cause for combat. Even those coerced to fight will be kept on the battlefield by powerful motivations: avoidance of harsh punishment, for example, or the avoidance of death at the enemy's hands may alone be powerful enough to incentivise combatants in the fight.

Low morale, on the other hand, does not necessarily mean that soldiers will refuse to fight; many soldiers are compelled to do so regardless of their personal feelings. However, combat effectiveness is tied to soldiers' morale, as 'unless the individual is reasonably content, he will not willingly contribute to the unit.'[5] Soldiers in a satisfactory condition will usually work harder and have a stronger sense of collective responsibility to the unit or army than those who would otherwise try to remove themselves from the field of combat. Although closely interlinked, therefore, it is valuable to explore the impacts of both motivation and morale on battle, as well as to suggest some likely influences on the reasons why soldiers fight, and how content they are to do so.

Each soldier's reason for fighting will be individual and distinct, but there are a few generalisations that can be made. One of the first distinctions is between coercive and voluntary motivation. Soldiers can be described as subject to coercive motivation if they are required to fight – be that a societal, legal, or financial obligation. Furthermore, there will normally be punitive measures taken against any soldier who refuses to fight in cases of coercive motivation. Voluntary motivation, however, suggests factors that the soldier personally accepts as necessitating combat. This may be born of a desire to protect people, place, or principle; it may stem from personal honour, pride, or intangible benefits for the individual. Despite the distinction between a desire to fight and coercive motivation, often coercion can be covered with the veneer of volunteering to fight in order to reinforce participants' dedication to a cause. Propaganda may play a particularly valuable role in this, dressing coercive recruitment as a voluntary act that appeals to higher ideals.

The obligation to fight, the basis for coercive motivation, is clearly visible in armies of the medieval period. Across Western Europe, and in the Holy Land from the twelfth to the fourteenth century, individuals owed military service to their lords in exchange for land. This system provided medieval rulers with core forces of combatants. In England in the mid-twelfth century, King Henry II could call upon approximately 5,000 knights.[6] Under this obligatory service, combatants were motivated through not only the reward of land and the resulting financial income, but also an elevated role in society as one of the emergent knightly group. Each of these men would, in turn, be expected to produce combatants to swell the ranks of an army. They were increasingly accompanied by retinues of retained men, kept at their lord's expense for the protection of his lands and to serve with him on campaign. For example, in 1369 Sir John Neville agreed to serve John of Gaunt, Duke of Lancaster, in exchange for fifty marks a year. Neville was expected to produce twenty men-at-arms, to include five knights, and twenty mounted archers as part of Gaunt's retinue. In times of war, he would receive 500 marks annually to cover their costs.[7]

In addition, armies' ranks could be swelled by soldiers drawn from the lower levels of rural society, such as the Anglo-Saxon fyrd, who fought for service but also increasingly for monetary reward. Some troops also came from towns and municipal authorities, who often kept small watches during peacetime and then swelled their ranks with additional men drawn from the population for campaign.

While in the earlier medieval period therefore, recruitment to armies centred on municipal authorities and lordly groups, by the thirteenth century this process was being regulated further with the use of array. Introduced for instance by Philip the Fair in France and Edward I in England, combatants were summoned from specific groups within society to serve the king in war. In England, for example, Edward summoned all men with an income between £20 and £40 to serve.[8]

Although soldiers had been paid from the twelfth century or earlier in some territories, by the later Middle Ages, professional, paid soldiery was a common form of military service. These mercenary soldiers were common on the battlefields of Late Medieval and early modern Europe, bringing with them a level of training and professionalism hitherto unseen in the armies of earlier centuries. It was the shift towards standing armies and mercenary forces that eventually precipitated the creation of permanent, professional armies whereby soldiering was a chosen career for combatants.

Although many modern armies operate on a system of voluntary service, conscription – the requirement of categories of civilians to join the military and be prepared to fight – is still used in times of national or international crisis. During the First World War, 53.3 per cent of all British wartime enlistments occurred after the introduction of conscription in January 1916.[9] There are also many states, such as Russia, where national service remains a compulsory component of society.

Financial gain from battle was not restricted, however, to pay or financial recompense. While wider campaigns contributed to the upkeep of a field army through looting or pillage, from the English *chevauchées* in France during the fourteenth and fifteenth centuries to Napoleon's despoiling of Italy in the 1790s, being in enemy territory provided impetus for individual soldiers to plunder or loot money, precious objects, or simple luxuries – both from civilians and from the bodies of fallen combatants. Battles themselves historically presented ideal opportunities for the amassing of loot with the removal of possessions from the beaten party itself. At Marston Moor in 1644, 'Many souldiers … met with much Gold and Silver, and other Commodities of good worth.'[10] The promise of such financial reward was enough of a lure to some combatants that they relished any opportunity to seize it. Such looting often provided a private way of gaining wealth outside the jurisdiction of commanders; looted objects could be small and easily hidden by those who took them. They also presented a tempting way to gather luxuries that soldiers may not have enjoyed for some time; simple things like tobacco or grooming items may be taken from the bodies of fallen men. Furthermore, the consequences of such gains on soldiers' morale were undoubtedly positive, as money gained from looting could then be spent on other luxuries.

A Prussian observer in the wake of the Battle of Beaumont in 1870, in the midst of the Franco-Prussian War, wrote with revulsion at the practice of looting dead bodies after the battle had drawn to a close:

The first man I saw was a French captain who had been shot through the head ... and was completely ransacked; all his pockets and bags were open and personal belongings without value for the looters were scattered all around him. I learnt that as soon as night falls over the battlefield the looting of the dead starts. It appears that it does not matter how many men of the military police are present, this horrific kind of behaviour seems unstoppable and thousands of ordinary soldiers are guilty of this despicable behaviour.[11]

As the above extract makes clear, in searching for pecuniary loot in particular, an army's discipline and order could break down. At Vitoria in 1813, for example, the British commander the Duke of Wellington complained that the plunder of French supplies by his victorious army threatened its fighting capability:

The soldiers of the army have got among them about a million in money ... The night of the battle, instead of being passed in getting rest and food for the pursuit of the following day, was passed by the soldiers in looking for plunder. The consequence was, that they were incapable of marching in pursuit of the enemy.[12]

Financial gain was also possible through the taking of people, as well as money and possessions. The capture of prisoners was a common medieval practice that allowed a captor to claim the ransom for those enemy combatants taken during battle, and this private income was an important motivator for soldiers in combat.[13] One of the most infamous examples of this was at the Battle of Agincourt in 1415, during which 'the king of England and the nobles of his army bought ... the most important of the lords of France so that they could put them to ransom and gain great sums of money.'[14] In fact, Henry V's English army took hundreds of prisoners, including the French marshal, Jean le Maingre. Towards the end of the battle, with a French counterattack apparently in the offing, Henry ordered a massacre of prisoners to prevent them potentially escaping and attacking his rear at a critical moment. The English soldiery, however, apparently initially refused to kill their captives. Far from a burst of moral altruism, this was instead likely a refusal to allow the king to interfere with what was a private settlement between captors and prisoners; ransom money went, in large part, to the soldier responsible for the capture.[15] It is certainly unsurprising that those prisoners guaranteed to fetch the highest ransoms – including the marshal – made it back to England in one piece; the sums that such men could raise were enormous. The ransom taken from prisoners at Poitiers (1356) alone totalled more than £300,000, three times the cost of the English war effort over the past year.[16]

The motivations of many combatants, however, have extended well beyond the tangible acquisition of wealth or the fulfilment of a job. Fighting for comrades, for the soldiers standing alongside one another in battle, has been a common theme throughout centuries of conflict. Although many positive influences on motivation can deteriorate after days or weeks of combat, research has suggested that unit cohesion is amongst the more lasting and meaningful motivating factors.[17] In short, soldiers fight because of the other members of their unit: either fighting to protect or reinforce bonds of loyalty, or the impact of peer pressure and fear of letting others down. Soldiers may therefore fight 'because they realise by fleeing their post and rescuing themselves, they would expose their companions to grave danger'.[18] At the same time, having a sense of belonging and collective identity with comrades can have an important impact on morale.

In the medieval period, this fraternal relationship manifested among knights; in particular, chivalric orders of knighthood were the ultimate expression of this brotherhood. The Order of the Garter in England, created in 1348 by Edward III, sought to unite knights from both England and abroad in a collective brotherhood of knights. These men often fought together in battle as well; many were present at Poitiers including Edward the Black Prince alongside Thomas Beauchamp, Jean de Grailly, and William Montagu. The bonds that these men made at Garter festivities and jousts created unity between them that could only aid their efforts on the battlefield.

In the First World War, this sense of comradeship was used as a recruiting tool by British authorities. The creation of 'Pals battalions' led combatants to join up en masse so they could serve together with men they knew from home, perhaps lived near, or worked or socialised with. While conceived to emphasise the positive impacts on motivation and morale that serving alongside close friends could produce, in some areas almost entire streets were bereaved simultaneously when a battalion went into action. Many of the Pals made their combat debut at the Battle of the Somme in July 1916; in an appalling first day of action, battalions such as the Leeds Pals and Accrington Pals lost over 80 per cent of their men killed, wounded or missing. The devastatingly high casualty rates, combined with the introduction of conscription, eventually led Pals battalions to be phased out.

Comradeship was often expressed through cultural output from soldiers themselves. For example, through communal songs, language or rituals that emphasised cohesion and collective identity, soldiers' morale could be boosted as well as their motivation to fight for one another reaffirmed. German soldiers in the First World War sang parodies about the war to keep spirits up. They developed their own language of humorous names for equipment, just as the British did: while the British had 'tin hats' rather than 'steel helmets', the Germans turned Minenwerfer (mine throwers) to Marmaladeneimer (jam buckets).[19] On a larger scale, this same collective culture can be seen in units' symbols, mottoes and even mascots. These serve to remind their members of the wider team, and inspire them to fight for their fellow soldiers as well as for the success of the company itself.

Alongside comradeship, discipline amongst combat troops is essential to their effectiveness, and can further reinforce motivations to fight. Indeed, discipline and morale have generally gone hand in hand. Even the best trained forces can suffer significant ill-discipline once morale lapses, leading to a breakdown of trust between men and officers, which can have fatal consequences in combat. The mutinies in the French army in 1917 were, in the words of Private Robert Poustis, 'in those [regiments] that had attacked too often, or when there were heavy casualties'.[20] They were solved mostly by addressing the grievances that affected men's morale, backed up by a few executions *pour encourager les autres*. In 2003, an American army detachment in Iraq, left to garrison a former prison without proper supplies or a clear mission, saw their combat efficiency plummet as tempers frayed. One man, in refusing what he saw as a particularly vexatious command, bellowed back at his officer: 'I'm in Iraq, what the fuck are you going to do? You going to shoot me? Go for it. Send me home!'[21]

Punitive measures for ill-discipline often dissuade soldiers from action that could threaten the military effectiveness of the force, from disobeying orders to refusing to fight altogether. Medieval rules about discipline stemmed from Roman law, and several texts list those crimes that warranted punishment. Discipline was the responsibility of the marshals of royal armies in many Western European countries, although captains also took responsibility for controlling combatants. Punishments for cowardice could be especially severe due to the detrimental impact that it could have on the morale of a fighting unit. In 1444, for example, François de Clermont hanged one of his men who had shown cowardice.[22] Military ordinances also attempted to prevent combatants from withdrawing from the field of combat. The Swiss military code allowed men to strike dead any fellow soldier 'fleeing or spreading panic', while English ordinances issued in 1385 noted in their first item that 'all manner of persons ... shall be obedient to our lord the King, to his constable and marshal, under penalty of everything they can forfeit in body or goods', and in the sixth item, 'that everyone be obedient to his captain'.[23] Such regulations are echoed in the twentieth century, and again suggest enforcement in even more brutal terms. Stalin's Order 227, introduced in July 1942 at the height of the Soviet struggle against Germany, forbade Soviet troops to hold back during battle; execution awaited those who did. It is perhaps easy to understand in such circumstances why soldiers would chance the enemy's bullets over those of their comrades.

As well as these attempts to regulate perceived cowardice, societies also develop complex models of shaming for those deemed to not fight confidently. In the fourteenth-century *Livre de Chevalerie*, French knight Geoffroi de Charny advised young men-at-arms to 'dread vile cowardice more than death'.[24] Instead, Charny argues, 'those who put their lives in danger with the deliberate intention of avoiding shame are strong in all things.'[25] This societal expectation was echoed in cases of public shaming and ridicule for combatants who displayed apparent cowardice in battle. Occasionally, reported dishonour also carried very real punishments for commanders seen as responsible for defeat. English knight Sir John Fastolf was unceremoniously thrown out of the exalted Order of the Garter after he had reportedly withdrawn prematurely from the Battle of Patay in 1429. It would take him thirteen years to reclaim his position, demonstrating both the harsh, public punishment for perceived dishonour and the longevity of its association with an individual.

This fear of publicly declared cowardice and resulting shame can also have a direct impact on soldiers' decisions to join conflict in the first place as well as affecting their conduct when on the battlefield. Receiving a white feather, for example, marked you out as a coward in the First World War. British Rifleman Norman Demuth describes how he joined up after 'somebody press[ed] something into my hand and I found it was a woman giving me a white feather'.[26] Social expectation was therefore a powerful motivator for soldiers wishing to avoid shame or dishonour, and propaganda campaigns in many conflicts have played on this public pressure to encourage soldiers to join up, and to fight.

Given the societal and legal ramifications of cowardice or dishonour, the desire to display honourable behaviour, rather than accrue shame, may influence combatants to fight rather than turn and run. The desire to win honour was certainly presented as a motivating factor in the medieval period. Charny described how warfare deserved plaudits and praise:

> love, value, praise, and honour all those whom God by his grace has granted several good days on the battlefield, when they win great credit and renown for their exploits; for it is from good battles that great honours arise and are increased.[27]

This pursuit of honour can therefore motivate soldiers to fight, but may also lead them to take greater risks in battle in order to earn ever greater plaudits. Perhaps following Charny's call for 'great honours', French knights at Agincourt 'came to the rather unfortunate conclusion that they should all place themselves in the front line' as the most dangerous, and thus most honourable, position.[28] The concentration of so many nobles at the front of the charge led to massive casualty rates among the French leadership. A more modern equivalent of the cult of honour would perhaps be the award of medals for gallantry, which stand as recognition of prowess. Napoleon famously proclaimed that soldiers fought for glory and reward, not for abstract notions, insisting that 'it is with baubles that men are led'.[29] The fact that almost all modern armies have adopted the practice of awarding 'baubles' hints that the idea of renown and reputation retains some value.

Alongside a desire to gain honour, soldiers' pursuit of intangible gain is also reflected in their belief in a higher cause. This could include belief in a just cause for conflict, or national pride, or even a political ideology. This may also include religious motivation and a belief in salvation or eternal reward through combat in a deity's name. National pride may be particularly motivating among combatants in wars fought between nations or states. In part, this nationalism is itself often promoted by national leadership in order to maintain unity and positive morale amongst combatants, as well as galvanising and reaffirming soldiers' motivations to fight.

When harnessed, therefore, patriotism and belief in the justness of war can have a crucial impact on motivating soldiers to fight. A swell of patriotic pride swept through both North and South in the weeks after the attack on Fort Sumter at the dawn of the American Civil War. Northern cities and towns erupted into recruiting rallies. In New York, one witness described how:

> Everyone is anxious to do his utmost and determined to raise a force strong enough to go down there and thrash the conceit out of the rascals. The feeling runs mountains high, and thousands of men are offering their services where hundreds only are required.[30]

By the twentieth century across much of Europe, simple patriotism was supplemented by increasing appeals to ideological causes – democracy, fascism and communism being the most prominent – that portrayed military service as not just a service to the state or nation, but to humanity. Just how many people were motivated by nationalistic and ideological impulses is hard to say, as there is plenty of evidence that large numbers of men, above all conscripts, joined up for more traditional reasons such as natural obedience to authority, peer pressure, a desire to defend one's home, or even a sense of excitement.

Arguably the greatest factor behind belief in a just cause in war is religious faith. Nowhere was the power of religion as a motivator more evident than in the Crusades, launched by Europeans from the eleventh to the fifteenth century. Although many crusaders were undoubtedly motivated by material gain, the concept of crusading continued in the face of failure, losses, and enormous costs. That does suggest that material factors were not the sole motivators, but that religious salvation was also to be found in waging war in the East. Religious faith may also have made the prospect of death on the battlefield less terrifying. Pope Urban declared that the First Crusade would lead to 'full remission of sins' – a powerful promise for people well versed in the principle of penitential acts for divine forgiveness.[31] Such a motivation was focused on by crusaders before and during battles themselves, as they believed both that they were doing God's work and that He was supporting them in their labours. Roger of Calabria, desiring in the 1060s to retake Sicily from the Arabs, 'perceived two means by which he would profit, one for his soul and the other for his material benefit'.[32] Reflecting on the promise of religious salvation during the Ikhwan rebellion in 1925, one combatant described how his forces 'had again and again been told of the great reward that would come to us from God for every infidel we slew'.[33]

Beyond emotional or psychological motivations, physical conditions in which soldiers fight can impact particularly on morale, affecting their will or even ability to fight. Physical circumstances can include weather, terrain, combatants' weapons, and available food and drink. The demoralising impact that poor physical conditions may have on combatants are summarised by Lieutenant Douglas St George Rich in 1901, during the Second Boer War: 'It's a case now of hard work and no grub and no mistake, the weather is miserable too, drizzling every day. Today the fog was so thick we couldn't go out which came as a blessing.'[34] Just as shortages or weaknesses can be a hindrance, better quality food or alcohol can boost morale for combatants in battle. The provision of alcohol for troops was common before battle through to the twentieth century. Rather than enjoying a fine vintage, however, this was intended to provide additional morale to soldiers who would enter battle under the effects of alcohol, with their courage boosted.

Armies do try to mitigate against problems in physical conditions adversely affecting their soldiers. For example, in medieval and early modern northern Europe, the annual campaigning season tended to run across the spring and summer months. This was in part to avoid snowy or cold weather. Edward III of England attempted a campaign to Scotland in late 1334 but considerable numbers of his supporters refused to fight because of the weather; having attracted only 5,300 men, Edward was forced to postpone the campaign until the following year.[35]

Support from units elsewhere on the battlefield can also have an important impact on morale. RAF effectiveness at El Alamein in 1942 improved the morale of Allied troops and positively impacted on their fighting due to 'the excellence of our equipment', while simultaneously undermining the negative morale impacts of the German dive-bombers.[36] At Dunkirk in 1940, on the other hand, the lack of air support left men on the boats and beaches exposed to German aerial assault, significantly dampening their enthusiasm for combat.

Finally, securing victory can itself be a considerable morale boost, especially in the context of a wider campaign. If troops hear of wider successes for their forces – on a different front or battlefield, for example – they can be reassured about the competency of leadership and equipment, alongside wishing to emulate this success in their own conflict. The Allied victory at El Alamein boosted morale across North Africa, for instance, alongside bolstering domestic morale, which was credited with contributing to increased production in factories.[37]

Give unto us your Attendance: Bosworth (1485)

The Battle of Bosworth has become one of the most studied battles fought on English soil. Even in the late fifteenth century, however, contemporaries disagreed over their interpretations of the two main protagonists. On the one hand, Richard III was viewed as either a respected and experienced leader with the support of large parts of England and the stable inheritance of the Plantagenet throne, or a usurper who had his own nephews declared illegitimate, murdered, and himself installed as monarch. On the other hand, Henry Tudor, Earl of Richmond, was either a usurper himself, a stranger to England using a foreign army to steal the throne, or a just and fair alternative to Richard's dastardly ways. From our perspective, this debate has considerable implications for the motivations and morale of those fighting for both Richard and Henry on 22 August 1485.

For both Richard III and Henry Tudor, their primary motivation could not have been more important: they both wanted the crown of England, and the power, wealth and authority that would accompany it. To gain that crown, however, both were required to recruit armies. Without any standing armies to seduce to their cause, they would both have to muster their own forces by motivating a sufficient number of men to fight.

Certainly, Richard seems to have been confident preceding the battle. On hearing that Henry had landed at Milford Haven in South Wales, with a considerably smaller force than Richard may have feared, the king was delighted and almost certainly believed that he would soon defeat this upstart. This confidence stemmed from a number of factors. Firstly, Richard was by far the more militarily experienced of the two combatants, having fought at Barnet (April 1471) and Tewskesbury (May 1471), and having led campaigns into Scotland in 1480 and 1482. Even contemporary critics agreed that he was a capable military leader: it was reported to Parliament in 1483 that 'by his manyfold and diligent labours and devoirs', Richard had 'subdued grete part of the west bordures of Scotlande adjoynyng to Englond'.[38] Furthermore, Richard was the crowned king, with legal right to the throne through hereditary succession following Parliament's declaration that the children of his brother, Edward IV, were illegitimate. He therefore may have rallied support not only from his military experience but also his apparently just and legitimate cause. His confidence would have bolstered the morale of his followers – after all, no soldier wants to follow a leader uncertain of victory.

Richard did not, however, rely purely on his own military experience and right to rule to motivate men to fight for him. He issued letters to his commissioners of array in each shire, asking them to use money raised from local communities to assemble arrayed forces and prepare them for imminent action. Soldiers raised from the City of York, for example, were incentivised with pay at 12d a day for a total of ten days to fight for him. Commissioners were also instructed to advise all knights, squires and gentlemen to be ready to fight – threatening that any refusal or delay would result in the loss of that individual's lands, wealth and, eventually, life. The Crowland Chronicler describes how Richard decreed:

> whoever should be found in any part of the kingdom after the victory should have been gained, to have omitted appearing in his presence on the field, was to expect no other fate than the loss of all his goods and possessions, as well as his life.[39]

This 'carrot and stick' approach motivated men by both reward and sanction: serve him and be paid and rewarded for loyalty; fail, and risk losing lands, status, and life.

Alongside these general summonses, Richard and his closest supporters tried to use personal allegiance to call on the nobility and gentry to join them in battle. A letter sent by Richard himself to Henry Vernon, one of the esquires of his body, ordered:

> you in your person with such number as you have promised unto us sufficiently horsed and harnessed, be with us in all haste to you possible, to give unto us your attendance without failing.[40]

There is, however, no evidence that Vernon presented himself to fight for his king, let alone provided a retinue of other combatants. Another letter was sent to Sir John Paston as sheriff of Norfolk and Suffolk, by the Duke of Suffolk on 20 October 1484. In a personal plea – addressed to 'our trusty and well-beloved' John Paston, and signed off 'Your friend' – Suffolk asks that Paston aids Richard 'in defence of the church as of the said nobles and subjects of this realm, against his said enemies and rebels'.[41] The pleasantries were to do Suffolk no good; like Vernon, Paston did not fight at Bosworth, preferring instead to await the outcome of the battle.

Their lack of response highlights a potential problem for Richard: that doubts over his rule lingered. To counter this, Richard issued a General Proclamation on 23 June to attempt to rally the English people against Henry.[42] He firstly identified Henry Tudor as descending from bastard blood on both his mother's and father's sides; as illegitimate, Henry's cause could not be just. Secondly, Richard implied that all England's nobles would lose their lands and wealth if Henry triumphed, claiming that Henry had already promised English estates and titles to his supporters, and appealed to his subjects' desire to protect their personal possessions and families against vague but certainly dire threats from the invading army. Richard extended this to a patriotic appeal for the protection of English lands, calling on the people 'like good and true Englishmen' to unite against 'the king's ancient enemy of France'.[43] Richard was not above casting Henry as a villain to scare the English into uniting against him.

Richard, therefore, as an experienced military commander, had a robust array of motivations to bring men to his cause. Henry, on the other hand, was untested and unproven in battle. Since 1471 he had been considered the only remaining Lancastrian heir, but he had spent the years since then living in exile in Brittany. Bosworth was his first battle and his first time on English soil in fourteen years; it was perhaps for this reason that

Henry, landing in the Tudor homeland of Wales, chose first to recruit from this area before proceeding into England to confront Richard.

Many of those in Henry's army as it arrived in Wales were English exiles who had fallen foul of Richard, or hoped for advancement from Henry. John Cheyne is perhaps a typical example: once a Yorkist, he was attainted by Richard for trying to rescue Edward V from the Tower of London and then leading the failed Buckingham rebellion (1483). Cheyne fled into exile, returning to England as one of Henry's bodyguard. Even some men pardoned by Richard for their part in the rebellion threw in their lot with Henry, such as Sir William Brandon, who was killed bearing Henry's standard at Bosworth. It is easy to surmise that foremost in these men's minds was the desire to reclaim lands, wealth, titles and authority that had been denied to them under the Ricardian regime, and to further themselves under a potential Henrician kingship. Many would also have been motivated by distrust in a ruler they thought responsible for doing mischief to his nephews. The rest of Henry's invasion force was comprised of French soldiers, funded by a grant of 40,000 *livres tournois* from the French king. These were foreign soldiers, without a political angle on the affair, who were motivated to fight to receive payment from the man holding the purse strings.[44]

While self-advancement and pecuniary motivations are therefore evident in Henry's forces, the third group within his army at Bosworth – the Welsh who joined him on his march to the English Midlands – were motivated by potentially more intangible aims. Henry deliberately fanned Welsh resistance to English rule: he used a standard depicting 'a red firye dragon beaten upon white and grene sarcenet' on the march to Bosworth and at the battle itself – a symbol associated with the great Welsh leader Owain Glyndŵr in the earlier fifteenth century and alluding to the Tudor claim to descent from Cadwallader, the first king of Wales.[45] The thousands of Welshmen who joined Henry's forces in the weeks preceding Bosworth may of course have been motivated by personal ambition and financial advantage, but perhaps also held loftier ambitions of national freedom and fulfilling Wales's destiny when they threw their lot in with Henry.

Both royal claimants therefore attempted to encourage support through appeals to financial, political and personal gain, although Richard also relied far more on threat and coercion. On the face of it, Richard was the more successful in motivating men to fight for him. Henry's supporters numbered around 5,000 men, whereas Richard's host was approximately 15,000 strong. However, Henry had managed to possibly double his forces during his march through Wales and the English Midlands, and had gained the support of experienced military commanders such as veteran John de Vere, Earl of Oxford, who compensated for his own military inexperience. For all the size of the royal army, fewer had rallied to Richard than he would have liked. Perhaps only a quarter of the peerage of England turned out for the battle, and some of them appeared on Henry's side.[46]

A disappointing turnout from the nobility should have been balanced by the arrayed troops from the shires, but there is no explicit evidence of these levies being at the battle itself. Some of Richard's commissioners did fight for him at Bosworth – presumably the motivations of both payment and advancement ensured their support. Commissioners Thomas Hampden and Thomas Straunge from Buckinghamshire, for example, fought and were both killed in the battle.[47] Whether they brought with them the arrayed forces from Buckinghamshire is unknown. What is known, however, is that some commissioners – and perhaps even their arrayed men – fought for Henry. This number included John Savage from Cheshire, who not only sided with Henry at Bosworth, but commanded his left flank according to Polydore Vergil, despite having been Richard's commissioner of array in Macclesfield Hundred in December 1484![48]

Richard's royal army met Henry's combined force of Continental mercenaries, Welsh and English fighters, on a marshy plain between the villages of Dadlington, Shenton, Upton, and Stoke Golding on 22 August. A third army also waited on the battlefield: that belonging to the Stanley family, comprising Henry's stepfather, Thomas Lord Stanley, and his brother, Sir William Stanley, who together commanded around 6,000 men. Although theoretically present to support the king, as the day of the battle dawned their loyalties remained uncertain.

The reluctance of many of Richard's men to fight is evident from the opening moves of the battle, with a clash between the two vanguards. Here, Richard's reliance on threats and assumptions of loyalty to motivate his followers began to cost him dearly as at this critical moment, chroniclers describe men already deserting the king. Indeed, so many of Richard's supporters were there because they had been browbeaten into attendance that Polydore Vergil's *Anglica Historia* records how 'they all forbore the fight ... and that verily dyd many with right goodwill, who rather covetyd the king dead than alive, and therefor fowght fayntly'.[49]

Perhaps seeing his men's morale dipping, Richard attempted to rejuvenate their belief through personal example. All accounts of the battle attest to Richard's strength as a soldier. Even John Rous, who otherwise compared Richard to the Antichrist, admitted that 'though small in body and feeble of limb, he bore himself like a gallant knight and acted with distinction as his own champion until his last breath'.[50] Richard himself knocked down the 6-foot 8-inch John Cheyne and other members of his household attempted to emulate their commander's deeds: the royal standard-bearer, Sir Percival Thribald, had both his legs cut out from under him, but managed to keep the king's standard aloft.

Perhaps seeking to continue to inspire his men through his prowess, and certainly seeking to remove the reason for the enemy soldiers to continue fighting, Richard chose to lead a charge personally aimed at Henry and his closest guards, who had become separated from the rest of their forces. It was then that the Stanleys chose to smash their considerable force into the flank of the royal army. Lord Stanley owed loyalty to both men: he was Henry's stepfather, but Richard held his son Lord Strange hostage to guarantee loyal behaviour. Therefore, the Stanleys were motivated to fight for both: the coercive bounds of his son's capture contrasting with the voluntary desire to fight for his stepson and almost certainly gain power and prestige in the process. In the end, sensing perhaps the swing of the battle in Henry's favour, it was his stepson who won his intervention on the battlefield.

Richard was slain in the press resulting from the engagement of the Stanleys, and his body paraded in front of the victorious army before being taken for burial in Leicester. Such a deliberate public desecration of his body can only have been designed to further undermine the morale of any of Richard's supporters who had escaped the battle. Henry, meanwhile, was crowned king of England on the battlefield and began his victorious march to London and to the next century of Tudor rule in England.

Bosworth therefore highlights the importance of ensuring and maintaining the motivation of soldiers during battle: they must be motivated to turn out to fight, and motivated to continue fighting without being tempted to hang back, desert or change sides. As Bosworth showed, coercion and threat can build an army, but do not always lead to an effective fighting force. Henry's more refined approach of mercenary soldiers fighting for their pay, combined with deeply personal and intangible appeals to nationhood and idealism, proved more effective.

All Hell Breaking Loose: Tet Offensive (1968)

On the night of 30/31 January 1968, coinciding with the Vietnamese festival of Tet Nguyen Dan, North Vietnamese forces launched a massive simultaneous assault on dozens of South Vietnamese cities, airfields and American military posts. The sheer scale of the Tet Offensive caught American and South Vietnamese forces off guard and resulted in weeks of ferocious fighting as they struggled to regain control of urban centres or to push North Vietnamese soldiers away from sensitive military targets.

In purely military terms the offensive was ultimately a North Vietnamese defeat, but the battle was never intended as a solely military venture. Its aims were as much to shatter the cohesion of the South Vietnam-American alliance, cause unrest in the Army of the Republic of Vietnam (ARVN), and provoke the people of the South to rise up against Saigon. That the entire offensive was conceived partly for its moral impact added weight to the importance of morale and motivation on the battlefield. For both sides, maintaining the will to combat became an end in itself for the battle, rather than simply a means of maintaining combat efficiency. In this, the offensive sowed the seeds of later North Vietnamese success.

The aims of Tet were based on the assumptions that the ARVN 'would not fight when struck a hard blow', that the Saigon government did not have popular support, and that the Vietnamese people would turn on the Americans if given the chance.[51] As early as 1965, North Vietnamese Communist Party First Secretary Le Duan had suggested: 'We will launch a general insurrection in coordination with a general military offensive aimed straight at the heart of the enemy ... This will shatter the morale of the puppet army.'[52] By mid-1967, his ideas had been accepted as the basis for a plan to deal a potentially war-winning blow. Although sceptical of the prospect of immediate success, veteran Defence Minister Vo Nguyen Giap accepted the need for increased military action:

Armed struggle which becomes more and more vigorous does not make political struggle decrease in intensity but, on the contrary, gives it a stronger impulse; together they pursue the aim of annihilating and dislocating enemy armed forces, striking vigorously where the enemy is basically weak, on the political ground.[53]

The political ground was indeed where Tet found success. The contribution to waning American support for the war was probably its most important legacy.

The leadership on both sides of the battle understood the importance of political motivation. This was especially the case for North Vietnamese forces deployed in irregular roles in the cities, as their dual task was to fight independently of central command and reinforcement, and to encourage uprisings in the local South Vietnamese population. In the run-up to Tet, 'political officers conducted *chin huan*, or reorientation, sessions where they indoctrinated the troops', ensuring that they understood the full political ramifications of their mission.[54] Communist ideology played some role in this, but so did a quasi-nationalist and anti-colonialist desire to see American presence removed from Vietnam. There were few religious qualms about launching an offensive during a sacred festival, although it angered some in the South.[55] On the other side, American troops were reminded of their mission's importance to the cause of the Free World. Robert Simonsen, a Marine corporal whose unit was rushed to Vietnam shortly after the offensive began, recalled 'a few hectic days of reorganisation, receiving indoctrination lectures and getting several shots' before deployment.[56]

A core part of the political motivation for fighters on the ground was not just the abstract cause, but the idea that victory in battle would quickly win the war. North Vietnamese leaders went to great lengths to tell their troops that victory was imminent, and continued to peddle this line even after the major casualties of the first month of the offensive.[57] Desertion rates certainly dropped in the lead-up to Tet as the promise of victory was dangled before the troops.[58] Both sides were quick to publicise triumphs and downplay losses, although the North Vietnamese were able to make better use of negative American reactions to the fighting to persuade their own troops that even defeats were helping the cause. General Tran Van Tra later claimed that 'the Anti-War Movement contributed in raising our soldiers' spirits to a large extent'.[59]

The will to battle of communist fighters certainly remained high in the first phase of the offensive. Although Westmoreland had been confident that American firepower would shatter enemy morale, a month into the Tet Offensive American officials in Saigon expressed the view 'that their "determination appears to be unshaken" despite the casualties inflicted on them'.[60] This allowed assaults to continue in a number of areas, and enabled the North Vietnamese to hold on in cities like Hué even when faced by the full force of American military might. Many American troops felt that enemy units would not give up unless wiped out, a sentiment later echoed by Giap:

> The spring 1968 offensive revealed abruptly to the Americans that the Vietnamese people do not give up easily and that their military strength has not been in any way impaired by United States aggression, no matter what its forms and its cruelty.[61]

The tenacity of well-motivated fighters was ultimately unable to prevail against an enemy with significantly more firepower and greater mobility – Hué was retaken in March, for example – but it allowed the North Vietnamese and Vietcong to strike a significant blow against the South Vietnam-US alliance.

Nevertheless, the scale of the offensive did begin to take its toll. Morale could quickly fade in urban infiltration units, which sometimes struggled with tactical confusion when cut off from commanders. The small squad that seized Saigon's radio station, for instance, found itself surrounded and without promised reinforcements. Unsure how to proceed, they detonated the building (with themselves inside) before further instructions could arrive.[62] Similar confusion and sacrifice happened in hundreds of other small actions across the country. Thousands of the most enthusiastic and best-trained soldiers were killed in the first weeks of combat, and those who remained eventually began to lose their enthusiasm for the costly struggle. By the time the offensive drew to a close, 'Senior Communist cadres expressed alarm at the erosion of morale among their comrades, many of whom had "lost confidence" in the cause and had become "doubtful of victory and pessimistic, and display shirking attitudes".'[63]

On the American and South Vietnamese side, things were not much better. The offensive beginning at a time of traditional truce took most by surprise; many ARVN soldiers were on leave, and American forces, although on alert, were not expecting anything on the scale of the nationwide offensive. The reaction at all levels was 'confusion, shock, dismay, and disbelief'.[64] Jeff Harvey, a company commander in 1/28 Infantry, could get no information on the first day aside from the stock response: 'All hell is breaking loose.'[65] Even when the situation calmed a little the lack of information could impair soldiers' ability and enthusiasm for combat. Nicholas Warr, a platoon commander in the Marines sent to recapture Hué in February, remembered being told very little about his mission: 'The briefing was short, no longer than a half hour, and did little to improve my morale.'[66] Things were apparently even worse in the ARVN, with the CIA worried that morale was collapsing and that it might, if pressed further, face disintegration.[67]

While taken by surprise, American forces retained a high degree of combat efficiency, and morale remained relatively high; men trusted to their training and to their buddies to see them through, and were encouraged by the support of an awe-inspiring amount of firepower. In ground combat veteran soldiers stiffened their comrades' resolve: one section leader recalled laconically that when coming under fire, 'a couple of my new soldiers started to panic. I got them settled down.'[68] Simonsen was glad of his 'grizzled combat veteran' of a platoon sergeant, who 'was instrumental in holding things together during tough times'.[69] There was a strong strand of professional pride that motivated the US forces and brought men together in even the worst of the fighting. Few places were worse than the close-quarter combat in the Citadel of Hué. Marine Myron Harrington said of his experiences there:

> After a while, survival was the name of the game as you sat there in the semidarkness, with the firing going on constantly … You went through the full range of emotions, seeing your buddies being hit, but you couldn't feel sorry for them because you had the others to think about. It was dreary, and still we weren't depressed. We were doing our job – successfully.[70]

The idea of fighting for the men around – known as primary group cohesion – was still a motivating factor for American troops, and it underpinned their strong combat performance. Although the unpopularity of the war and the prevalence of draftees changed this quite radically from about 1969, in the first months of Tet soldiers seem to have retained a strong bond at unit level, even if they were increasingly distrustful of their senior political and military leaders.[71] Instances of combat refusal and fragging were uncommon, certainly compared to the latter years of the war, and there is little evidence that drug use significantly impacted fighting ability.

While a major outcome of Tet was the solidification of American public opposition to the war, the motivation and morale of combatants was an important factor in the fighting throughout the offensive. Good motivation and high morale allowed an inferior force to land significant blows against a larger and better-armed opponent in the early stages of combat, just as the group cohesion, professional pride, and high morale of US and some ARVN forces allowed them to weather the storm and eventually push back.

Chapter 10

Non-Combatants

'[Mary Seacole] in the time of fearful distress, personally spared no pains and no exertion to visit the field of woe'
Lady Alicia Blackwood.[1]

While battles are ultimately decided by those who fight in them, they can also be influenced by people who are present but play no role in the actual combat. Non-combatants in and around battlefields have been a regular feature of conflict over the past millennium, and include military personnel, civilians loosely attached to the armies, and others caught up in the crossfire. The list is lengthy: engineers, pioneers, commissaries, military policemen, medical personnel, armourers, blacksmiths, wagon drivers, mechanics, technicians, priests, camp followers, guides, refugees, stragglers, war reporters – and many others who might find themselves on a battlefield without the purpose of fighting. By their nature non-combatants are likely to have a marginal role in most battles, but they can play a significant part in preparing soldiers for the fight, preparing the terrain on which a clash is fought, dealing with casualties, reporting on what happened – and sometimes simply getting in the way of those engaged in combat.

One of the most important roles of non-combatants is ensuring that fighting troops are prepared for battle. Indeed, the 'tail' of most modern armies is larger than the frontline 'teeth', as it takes a huge amount of effort to keep fighting soldiers and their equipment in the field. Historically, fighting troops have had a greater degree of self-reliance, but have still benefited from sizeable support networks, formal or informal, to keep them and their kit in fighting condition. Medieval and early modern armies were predominantly made of fighting men with a few formal supernumeraries, although there might be significant numbers of unofficial camp followers. By the twentieth century, support units had grown considerably. Four-tenths of the British army by 1944 were non-combatants, and the overwhelming majority of personnel in all air forces were not intended to go into battle.[2]

At the most basic level, a wide range of non-combatants are generally involved in making sure soldiers enter battle fed, watered, and in a degree of comfort. Where such assistance is absent, soldiers risk going into combat in poor physical and mental condition. Logistics networks are connected to frontline units by commissary officers or transport drivers, and in a more casual capacity camp followers might sell small comforts, prepare meals, offer laundry or mending services, or other services of a more intimate kind. From the seventeenth to the twentieth century, *cantinières* and *vivandières* – women, usually wives of soldiers, selling food, alcohol or luxuries – were a constant and semi-formal part of the French army, becoming 'a normal and expected source of supplies' for soldiers on campaign and even on the battlefield.[3] In other armies, the role was often less formal but no less important. Where non-combatants were able to ensure supplies it removed the need for foraging expeditions, which could see whole units degenerate into militarily useless gangs of hungry men for hours at a time. Historically, the efforts of commissaries and camp followers in maintaining soldiers have been vital in keeping up morale as well as physical efficiency. At Eylau in 1807, Jean-Roch Coignet claimed (hyperbolically) that the arrival of some Jewish traders with four enormous casks of brandy saved Napoleon's army, which had had almost no food and been exposed to brutal cold for several days.[4] In the Crimea, Mary Seacole became famous amongst the army for providing soldiers with comforts and sometimes even necessities, as well as ministering to the wounded. In the First World War, the commissariat and cooks performed a vital role in ensuring that men received a hot meal and drink before going over the top, which some general officers believed vital to their men's fighting ability.

The importance of non-combatants in supporting the physical needs of soldiers continues, although since the later nineteenth century, armies have rarely been accompanied by camp followers on the scale of early modern warfare, and where soldiers have found comfort with civilians it has generally been away from the front lines rather than in camp on the eve of battle. Where camp entertainments have been provided – for example in the USO shows of the Vietnam War – they have tended to be formal affairs divorced from the fighting, rather than the small comforts and services previously provided on a daily basis. Instead, armies have developed much larger service corps to ensure that the needs of soldiers going into battle are met. The commissariat (or equivalent) has remained important for providing troops with supplies, although increasingly in recent conflicts soldiers can rely on portable rations to sustain them through combat rather than requiring daily resupply.

Soldiers have often also relied on non-combatants for spiritual preparation. Armies of all kinds have found themselves accompanied by spiritual or religious figures who, for some soldiers at least, have been able to provide comfort and reassurance in the moments before combat. At Agincourt (1415), Henry V famously began the day by kneeling in prayer with his army, as one of his royal chaplains recalled:

> our king, after offering praises to God and hearing Masses, made ready for the field … then, indeed, and as long as the conflict lasted, I … and the other priests present, did humble our souls before God and, bringing to mind … which at that time the Church was reciting aloud, said in our hearts: 'Remember us, O Lord, our enemies are gathered together and boast themselves in their excellence. Destroy their strength and scatter them, that they may understand, because there is none other that fighteth for us but only Thou, our God.' And also, in fear and trembling, with our eyes raised to Heaven we cried out that God would have compassion upon us and upon the crown of England.[5]

Whether or not their pleas excited heavenly interest, collective prayer would certainly have provided comfort for men going into action, and for those left to watch the battle unfold. On a more personal level, in the First World War, Sergeant Daniels of the Royal Artillery remembered praying with a padre on the fire step of his trench, almost in the face of the enemy. Although several of his comrades mocked such spiritual comfort, Daniels was adamant: 'I really think without a doubt that praying to God did save my life.'[6] Prayer could be a very personal thing – especially when confronted with the prospect of imminent death – but the presence of clergymen has also been a comfort to countless soldiers down the centuries.

Soldiers are assisted in their preparation for battle in a more practical sense by the efforts of armourers, technicians, mechanics, farriers, and blacksmiths who have, in different eras, maintained weapons, horses, vehicles, and other paraphernalia of combat. Some of these tasks could be undertaken by fighters themselves, especially the more rudimentary duties such as sharpening bladed weapons, caring for horses, or basic vehicle maintenance, but in many armies support services were vital to maintain efficiency over any length of time. The dominance of the battlefield by mounted medieval knights was built on a shadow army of squires, farriers and armourers who maintained their weapons, armour, saddlery and steeds; some of these men may have also fought alongside their masters, but their non-combat role was arguably more important. Mechanised armies are kept in the field by whole corps of technicians whose skills are required to look after the increasingly complex equipment used in combat. The British Army's Corps of Royal Electrical and Mechanical Engineers, for example, created in 1942 for the maintenance of mechanised units, reached a strength of over 150,000 personnel only two years later.[7]

The training, work ethic, skill and morale of these men can be as important as that of the combat troops in maintaining a mechanised force in the field, but their impact is often most noticeable by their absence. Part of the inadequacy of First World War tanks stemmed from the lack of adequate maintenance facilities with trained technicians to prevent or repair mechanical faults. With air units, a lack of technicians could be even more problematic; the Luftwaffe's inadequacies at Stalingrad in the late autumn and early winter of 1942/3 were as much a function of the lack of adequately trained mechanics, ground crew and air controllers as a dearth of pilots, machines, or even precious fuel. Air units supporting ground forces in combat also need trained observers and forward controllers on the battlefield to ensure that they target the correct areas; the better the controllers, the more effective the airstrikes, and the less the likelihood of friendly fire.

Preparations for battle can also stretch to preparing the ground for combat, which has often been the role of engineers, sappers, pioneers, and sometimes even miners. In more modern armies engineering units have become part of the military establishment, with many twentieth-century militaries embracing the concept of the 'combat engineer'. Such units have often been at the forefront of fighting and cannot really be classed as non-combatants: in 1944, Larry Cane of the unexcitingly named US 582nd Engineers Dump Truck Company described his exploits in a letter to his wife:

I landed in France on D-Day, 6 June 1944, with the combat engineers in the assault wave. I was on the storming of the beach fortifications and since then have been right up in the thick of it with the parachute troops … A couple of nights ago we ferried paratroops across a river and I was placed in command of all heavy machine-guns assigned to provide overhead fire for the crossing.[8]

Even with the letter constrained by censorship from going into further detail, it is hard in this case to label Cane – and the thousands of engineers like him – as anything other than a combatant. Just as frequently, however, sappers perform key tasks in shaping the arena of combat without partaking in the actual fighting.

A key role of military engineers is the construction of earthworks or redoubts on a future battlefield to strengthen a defensive position. Field fortifications are by no means always the work of non-combatants, but sappers have done their fair share of constructing (or at least supervising the construction of) defensive positions. Extreme examples include elements of the trench systems of the First World War, which reshaped the terrain of the battlefield entirely, the Lines of Torres Vedras in Portugal in 1810, or the French Maginot Line of the 1930s, although the latter two were so strong as to deter serious assault. In a more subtle way, even quickly built field fortifications can act as a force multiplier for the defender, and also alter the shape of the battlefield to provide new points of pivot, anchor or enfilade. The construction of the rough earthen redoubts around Balaclava (1854) by British engineers, for example, gave their Ottoman allies a better-protected and more-defined line to defend against Russian assault. The positions not only allowed the Ottoman defenders to hold out for longer than might have been possible in the open field, but also concentrated initial Russian attacks onto the defensive emplacements, allowing time for Franco-British reinforcements to be rushed to the battlefield. A similar delaying effect was achieved in a very different way by American engineers caught in the path of the German onslaught at the Battle of the Bulge (1944). Quickly laid minefields, roadblocks, and demolition of key bridges and infrastructure helped to slow the German advance and bought time for the Allies to organise a more effective defence.[9]

Sappers are also crucial in getting armies past, across or over obstacles on the battlefield. Obstacles might be natural, such as rivers, valleys, or mountains, or they might be man-made, such as minefields or fortifications. Building temporary bridges over rivers or canals to help troops in battle has been a longstanding occupation of military engineers. During Napoleon's withdrawal from Moscow in 1812, the construction of two bridges over the river Berezina allowed the remnants of Napoleon's army to cross and scatter the Russian blocking forces, preventing the complete destruction of the emperor's command. It was, in the words of one eyewitness, 'an operation on which the fate of the army depended':

> The pontooneers and sappers worked at the construction of the bridges with a zeal and courage beyond all praise ... in spite of the drifting ice, they often went down to the armpits to place and hold the trestles until the beams were fixed on the caps ... From over one hundred who went down into the water to either build or maintain the bridges, only a small number survived.[10]

On the other hand, the failure of French bridges at Aspern-Essling outside Vienna three years earlier cut Napoleon's army in half mid-deployment, contributing directly to his defeat; only the stoicism of his troops and the unceasing efforts of engineers to get the bridges back in commission prevented a worse disaster.

The ability of engineers to overcome obstacles swiftly and securely is an important factor in mobile warfare. Removing impediments to manoeuvre might be more a matter of facilitating operational movement than directly impacting combat, but the availability of non-combatant engineers can be vital to assuring tactical advantage. In the Second World War, the role of engineers at the army's cutting edge was crucial to blitzkrieg tactics. To take just one example from the 1940 campaign, in the first few days of June the engineers of the German 6th Division were involved in 'clearing mine blocks', repairing roads, and creating detours around demolished bridges to facilitate the division's advance, before spearheading the vanguard in driving ferry and bridge crossings over the Seine.[11] As German success depended on the ability to maintain the advance to keep the enemy off balance, the role of engineers in ensuring the success of blitzkrieg should not be overlooked.

It is, however, in more static warfare that engineers have tended to come into their own. Through the early modern period, sieges were an engineer's natural habitat, at times in conjunction with miners who worked to undermine defences from beneath. This is by no means a modern phenomenon. At Melun in 1420, English miners dug beneath the French defences only to be met by a French counter-mine, leading to clashes between the two forces – including a somewhat dubious report of a joust between mounted knights in the tunnels. Such tactics were still familiar over six centuries later; during the First World War, both sides on the Western Front used corps of miners to dig towards and under enemy trenches, with the British especially building huge underground mines to be detonated at the beginning of an offensive, such as at the Somme (1916), Passchendaele (1917), and perhaps most famously Messines (1917). The military effect of these operations was ultimately rather marginal, not least because the explosions tended to destroy the landscape and make exploitation by advancing troops more difficult, although the nineteen simultaneous blasts at Messines are thought to have killed thousands of German defenders. The miners were an additional string to an army's bow, albeit one only useful in static warfare where combat could be planned long in advance.

Once in battle, armies have also tended to rely on a whole array of non-combatants to ensure communication between front and rear areas of the battle zone. Most important to an army's fighting ability were the drivers, waggoners, or runners whose job it was to bring up reserves of ammunition or spare equipment to replace that expended or destroyed. These individuals essentially connected the hardware of the army's logistical tail to its combat teeth, and their presence, organisation and courage could make a key difference in a clash. This has generally been less important in an army with less expendable munitions or fewer projectile weapons, and in medieval and early modern forces such systems would usually be organised on an ad hoc basis. Even well into the nineteenth century, troops can be found relying on improvised supply lines from whoever happened to be in camp. At Isandlwana in 1879, Lieutenant Horace Smith-Dorrien recalled:

> I, having no particular duty to perform in camp, when I saw the whole Zulu army advancing, had collected camp stragglers, such as artillerymen in charge of spare horses, officers' servants, sick etc., and had taken them to the ammunition boxes, where we broke them open as fast as we could, and kept sending out the packets to the firing line.[12]

These efforts were in vain as the firing line was soon overrun; Smith-Dorrien was one of only five British officers to survive the slaughter. The sheer quantity of ammunition required by modern firearms has meant that more recently armies have tended to have more formalised lines of supply from depots to frontline fighters. By the Second World War, the distribution of ammunition often fell to soldiers with a secondary combat role. Hans Rehfeldt was a mortarman in the German army on the Eastern Front, but won the Iron Cross for his role in ferrying forward ammunition:

> Under heavy enemy mortar fire he carried ammunition from the transfer point to the weapon without pause, allowing the mortar to wipe out a nest of enemy infantry ... Rehfeldt made an important contribution to the success of his mortar team.[13]

On the other side of things, non-combatants have often played a key role in the evacuation and treatment of the wounded, or in the burial of casualties. Although unlikely to influence the outcome of a battle directly, the efforts of military doctors, nurses, medics and stretcher-bearers can improve morale and soldiers' chances of survival following injury. Army medical services will generally find plenty of employment once battle is joined, and have often found themselves in the thick of the action, rescuing or treating wounded men while battle rages around them. It is no coincidence that two of the three men ever to receive two Victoria Crosses for valour in the British army were doctors – Arthur Martin-Leake and Noel Chavasse. Yet while army medics perform a vitally important task, they are likely to have little immediate effect on the course of combat, other than perhaps in bolstering the morale of troops who might feel better knowing that medical services are at hand. At times the need to evacuate the wounded has led to truces, official or unofficial, descending on battlefields, but this has tended to happen during natural lulls after particularly brutal action, such as on some sections of the Somme battlefield on 1–2 July 1916. Medical advances off the battlefield certainly played a vital part in maintaining military strength – before the twentieth century far more lives were lost to disease than to enemy action – but this was not necessarily an issue of non-combatant intervention on the battlefield. Army medical services have of course been crucial in preventing soldiers from falling out through illness, or in rehabilitating wounded men and returning them to combat duties, but their main achievement is simply in having saved the lives of countless combatants across the centuries.

Other non-combatants attached to fighting units who have played a crucial role in battle include military musicians. Military bands tended to develop during the early modern period, when marching in step required a collective rhythm throughout fighting units, and simple commands over expanding battlefields could be expressed by bugle or trumpet. Whether bandsmen are armed and expected to fight alongside their musical role depends largely on the force to which they belong. In the British army, for instance, bandsmen held a secondary role of stretcher-bearers in combat. Most eighteenth- and early nineteenth-century armies used drummer boys to keep time for men marching on the battlefield, clearly expecting them to have no combat role. Some armies marched into battle with bands playing, such as the Russians in the Crimea or the bagpipers of British Highland units right up to the First World War. The benefit of musicians in battle was not only in keeping rhythm or conveying orders, but in bolstering morale; according to one proponent of the bagpipes, stirring music was 'capable of stimulating men at the psychological moment when effort was failing'.[14] At Loos (1915):

> the heroism of the pipers was splendid. In spite of murderous fire they continued playing. At one moment, when the fire of the machine guns was so terrific that it looked as if the attack must break down, a Seaforth piper dashed forward in front of the line and started 'Caber Feidh'. The effect was instantaneous — the sorely pressed men braced themselves together and charged forward. The Germans soon got to realise the value of the pipes and tried to pick off the pipers.[15]

As this anecdote hints, military musicians may not have been engaged in actively fighting the enemy, but that did not prevent them from becoming targets or suffering casualties alongside the rest of their units.

While non-combatants within the military have been predictably active in supporting the efforts of fighting troops, civilians have also at times appeared in prominent positions on the battlefield. War reporters perhaps represent the group most likely to wilfully stray into combat zones. Reporters appeared in their modern sense during the Crimean War, but their antecedents might be traced in the heraldic chroniclers of the medieval battlefield. Witnesses of battle tend to play very little part in the actual outcome of fighting, although the knowledge that great deeds of arms (or examples of shirking) would be recorded may play a role in encouraging men to action. Heralds especially tended to record predominantly actions that fit with notions of chivalric honour. Jean Froissart, the noted fourteenth-century chronicler, began his account by hoping that in reporting famous deeds of arms 'brave men should be inspired thereby to follow such examples'.[16] More broadly, the greatest impact of reporters has been in shaping how combat is perceived and understood by news consumers at home, although any impact on morale, political support for the conflict, or pressure to change approach would take a long time to build. Perhaps the most obvious example of this is the Vietnam War, where the grinding combat of the Tet Offensive gradually increased criticism of the conflict among the mainstream news media, damaging both public and political backing for the intervention.

A final but perhaps vital role of non-combatants can simply be to distract or impede fighting soldiers on the battlefield. At its most altruistic this might include soldiers feeling the need to help civilians caught in the crossfire, or in holding back from attacking a target because of the risk of non-combatant casualties. The rules of engagement for most Western forces now take steps to limit the potential for collateral damage, especially in urban areas, which can at times hinder military operations. Anecdotal evidence from Iraq after 2003 suggested that such rules were sometimes ignored by coalition forces when fighting became heaviest, a clear indication that limitations imposed to prevent civilian casualties had a very real operational impact.[17] More prosaically, armies might find themselves hindered by refugees fleeing the fighting or even stragglers from their own forces, which might block crucial communications routes or disrupt formations moving forward to combat. In France in 1940, British commander Lord Gort found 'their presence on the roads was often a grave menace to our movement'.[18]

Prisoners of war can also prove a distraction from battle. Once captured, prisoners have to be disarmed, guarded, and their wounded treated, removing soldiers from frontline duties. An inability to secure prisoners can prevent them from being taken in the first place. At

Austerlitz (1805), French General Thiébault recalled: 'Up to the last hour of the battle we took no prisoners, it would just not do to take any risk; one could stick at nothing, and thus not a single living enemy remained to our rear.'[19] A lack of adequate protection for captives, or a fear that they may be liberated by a quick enemy raid, can cause grave concern for the rear areas of the army. At Agincourt, Henry V infamously ordered the killing of prisoners, possibly because he feared that they would join an attack on his baggage by a small band of locals. Attacks by non-combatants (or fleeing soldiers) on an army's baggage while it was busy fighting were not in fact uncommon. At Vitoria (1813), fleeing French soldiers, camp followers and some civilians joined victorious allied troops in rifling the accumulated plunder and collected magazines of the French occupation of Spain, 'liberating' over a million pounds in gold and vast quantities of other stores.[20] At Marston Moor (1644), the flight of some parliamentary troops led to the wholesale plunder of their army's baggage by some who assumed the battle lost, as chaplain Simeon Ash lamented:

> The runaways with other poore people, who attended the Army, did grievously plunder our Wagons, and other carriages, for the Wagoners, Carters &c, being affrighted with the flight of our owne souldiers, did leave their charge, in the hands of such, who love to spoyle.[21]

The ultimate impact of non-combatants will rarely be as important as that of the soldiers who fight, flee or die on the battlefield. Yet they have continued to play an important role in preparing troops for combat, in providing the technical and professional expertise needed to keep weapons and equipment in fighting order, and in ensuring that soldiers are fed, clad and comforted going into battle. At times, non-combatants have helped to prepare the terrain of battle, and at others their presence as civilians or refugees added an extra complication to the dynamics of the battlefield. In battle itself non-combatants can play a key role in bolstering morale or ensuring supply of munitions, along with smoothing the communication and mobility of forces at all levels. And whatever the course of combat, non-combatants have played their role in settling the aftermath, whether by treating the wounds of casualties or reporting the outcome of events. In this last way, at least, non-combatants have played a perennial role in shaping how battles are understood, interpreted, and ultimately remembered.

Was There a Man Dismayed? Balaclava (1854)

The scrappy action in defence of Balaclava harbour on 25 October 1854 is best remembered in the English-speaking world for the Charge of the Light Brigade, immortalised in the eponymous poem by Alfred, Lord Tennyson. The charge was of limited military value, questionable success, and led to the virtual destruction of the brigade, yet has been mythologised as one of the most famous single actions not just of the Crimean War, but of any war. This points us towards an important fact: that battles, and their memory, can very much be shaped by those who did not actually fight in them.

Tennyson of course was not at Balaclava, but read about the battle at home in the newspaper. Crimea was the first major European conflict in which war correspondents, chief amongst them William Russell of *The Times*, were present to report on military operations. Russell and fellow observers such as Frances Duberly, wife of the 8th Hussars' paymaster, were not to influence the outcome of Balaclava, but they did ensure that it became known in detail to the world at large. Duberly's published letters and journals gave the public fascinating insights into life at the front.[22] Russell's lengthy newspaper articles and later books gave his view on events.

At Balaclava, his view was very good indeed:

Alma was a long, straggling, smoky battlefield, of which the view was interrupted and broken ... Inkerman was fought in a fog and mist. But the field of Balaclava was as plainly seen from the verge of the plateau where I stood as the stage and those upon it are seen from the box of a theatre.[23]

Russell's clear and lurid account of the battle was instrumental in fixing the narrative in the public mind. It was his description of the 'thin red streak' of the 93rd Highlanders repulsing Russian cavalry that was the basis for the famous 'thin red line'. Written reports were even supplemented by photographs, such as those of Roger Fenton, although rudimentary photographic techniques meant that camps and landscapes rather than battle itself were the subject of the images. It is unlikely that approaches to combat were affected in any significant way by the additional scrutiny of these civilian war reporters, but soldiers were clearly aware of their presence. Some soldiers wrote home that reports in *The Times* could give a better account of progress in the war than they could themselves.

Other civilians at Balaclava could lay claim to a greater impact on the battle. John Blunt, for example, unofficially attached himself to Lord Lucan's staff as an interpreter for the Ottoman troops manning the forward redoubts, who took the brunt of the initial Russian assault.[24] While enough officers could speak French for Franco-British cooperation to run smoothly, coordination with their Ottoman allies proved more difficult. Civilians able to bridge the language barrier were worth their weight in gold. Despite the staunch defence of the redoubts, British soldiers did little more than hurl abuse at the Ottomans when they eventually withdrew in disorder. James Skene remembered seeing the wife of a Highlander belabouring fleeing Ottomans with a stick.[25] Her efforts were less effective than Blunt's, who managed to persuade the rallied Ottomans to form up next to the 93rd, where they held part of the line for the rest of the battle.[26]

As ineffective as the Scotswoman was at improving inter-allied relations, the presence of wives and camp followers on campaign was important to keep up morale and, in small ways, help the physical effectiveness of troops. Wives often did laundry, cooking, sewing and other small chores for soldiers, assisting in their general maintenance. Some even became temporary nurses in the field hospitals.[27] Duberly was able to find a servant among the wives of her husband's regiment.[28] Despite the relatively small numbers of camp followers in the Crimea, the small comforts of home made a difference to many men. So too did receiving actual comforts of home in the shape of letters or packages; the non-combatant troops that kept men connected to their families across the sea did a valuable service in maintaining spirits, as mails were sorely missed if they did not appear.[29]

More directly impacting on soldiers' effectiveness was the commissariat, whose adequate distribution of supplies and food was important to ensure that men going into combat would be less prone to physical and mental exhaustion. Although the Russian army as a whole was 'badly provisioned, owing to the systematic venality and cheating', those going into action at Balaclava were able to enjoy an early morning breakfast of 'Kasha porridge [and] their ration of spirits' before marching off.[30] Ottoman troops in the redoubts complained that they were poorly supplied, with 'nothing to eat but biscuit and little water to drink' for two days before the battle.[31] Hunger and thirst were unlikely to have helped their fighting abilities. The British commissariat had trouble distributing rations, not least because its locally recruited drivers 'displayed a remarkable aptitude for rapid desertion'.[32] For the troops stood-to in response to the Russian appearance at around 6 am, it appears to have been a hungry morning. No food reached the men of the Light Brigade at Balaclava, although after the infamous charge, Lord Paget, commanding 4th Light Dragoons, remembered 'profiting of the forethought of some commissariat officer, who sent us some rum and biscuit'.[33]

The surprise Russian advance meant that soldiers at Balaclava also went without other services in preparation for battle. Army chaplains were not called upon to give divine service, and troopers did not have time to visit blacksmiths or armourers to check equipment and hone weapons. The absence of armourers' services was especially damaging to the cavalry, as the horsemen's slashing blades struggled to pierce the thick coats of Russian soldiers. Russell caustically demanded, 'whose fault was that? Surely it was someone's business to see that the edges of the troopers' swords were sharp enough for work!', although Paget blamed the troopers for forgetting to use the point of the blade.[34] The Russians too seem to have omitted visiting the armourers, as several British cavalrymen found themselves bruised rather than cut by their blows. These non-combatants had little role in the day, although the cavalry's farriers were later called into action in the melancholy task of shooting horses unfit for further service.[35]

More involved in the preparations for the battle were the engineers. The Ottoman-held redoubts were prepared in advance by Colonel Stanton of the Royal Engineers, assisted by a Prussian named Waagmann and a host of sappers. The earthworks built by these non-combatants enabled the Ottoman troops to hold for some time against superior numbers, but they were rather too exposed and unsupported by the British lines. The engineers – and Lord Raglan's staff – appear to have been aware of this, but preferred to garrison the heights rather than leave them to the enemy.[36]

The defeat of the position was predictable, but the engineering works bought Raglan time to move more troops to the defence of Balaclava.

Other non-combatants did enter battle. Artillery drivers played a crucial role in positioning guns and whisking away captured pieces, but had no combat role. Paget recollected seeing Russian drivers 'let themselves fall off between the horses' to avoid engaging his cavalry.[37] One of General Liprandi's aims was to get into the British artillery and siege park at Kadikoi, disable the wagons and drivers, and then destroy the guns and stores at will.[38] It was fear of the Russians removing captured guns from the redoubts that spurred Raglan to order the Light Brigade forward; the lack of drivers left the horsemen unable to exploit their capture of the Russian gun line. Musicians also marched into action without being expected to fight; each Russian regiment boasted 155 musicians all told, while each British battalion had a complement of drummers and bandsmen. Trumpeters and buglers were used by both sides to relay commands; the 4th Light Dragoons lost every one of its trumpeters at Balaclava, impeding their officers' ability to give orders, especially during the retreat.[39] During action Russian bandsmen played to encourage their units, but the fourteen bandsman with each British infantry regiment served in combat as stretcher-bearers.[40]

Medical services more generally made a contribution to the battle. In October 1854, the conflict's most famous practitioners – Florence Nightingale, Mary Seacole, or Russian surgeon Nikolay Pirogov – had not yet arrived. Medical provision for both sides was inadequate. Lieutenant Colonel John Adye recalled that after the Battle of Alma in September, the Russians had made no provision for their wounded, declining to collect them under flag of truce, and sailors had been drafted from the fleet to carry away the British wounded on hammocks slung between oars. Military ambulances were so inefficient that their absence made little difference:

> the ambulance corps was on a small scale, and created in a hurry when the war began. Its waggons were few in number, heavy and cumbrous in form. The drivers were old pensioners … its means of usefulness [was] never very great or at all sufficient[41]

Few nurses were present near the battlefront, with most confined to base rather than field hospitals.[42] Military surgeons were present, however, and did their level best to treat casualties. Russell noted surgeons attending men on the field within two or three minutes of the Heavy Cavalry's charge, and the actions of Surgeon Mouat in going to the aid of Captain Morris of 17th Lancers under fire later in the day led to him becoming the first medical man awarded the Victoria Cross.[43] The work of surgeons on both sides, rudimentary as it may have been, did some good in reducing the death toll and allowing some men eventually to return to service.

The non-combatants at Balaclava thus did not dictate the course or outcome of the battle, but they did play a significant role in shaping the physical condition of men and weapons, the terrain over which the battle was fought, the fate of the casualties, and, perhaps crucially for military historians trying to understand the clash, how the battle was recorded, interpreted and remembered.

Chapter 11

The Clash of Arms

'It has been a damned nice thing – the nearest-run thing you ever saw in your life'
　　　　　　The Duke of Wellington after the Battle of Waterloo.[1]

For all that battles are influenced by preparation and planning, by the leadership of officers and generals, by the mental and physical state of troops, by terrain, weather and climate, and by the weapons and tactics employed by the combatants, it is only in the clash of arms that a battle can be decided. The coming together of countless factors on the battlefield, as the swords swing or the bullets fly, makes the field of combat a cruelly unpredictable arena, and understanding the experience of battle for fighters at the local level can be crucial to understanding the wider event.

The human factor is perhaps the hardest variable to pin down in the assessment of a battle. What soldiers do in battle cannot be explained solely by examining how they are trained, equipped, motivated, led or supplied. Half a century ago John Keegan set out to try to uncover something of the reality of combat – the 'face of battle', as he called it – arguing that to really understand a battle, one must understand the people in it. His approach differed starkly from writers who sought to explain battle only in structural terms of armies, weapons, logistics or tactics, and underlined the importance of attempting to capture soldiers' combat experience. Moreover, his work encouraged others to put the individual soldier back at the centre of the analysis of battle.

Battle has remained an extremely hostile environment, both mentally and physically, despite the enormous changes to battlespace over the past millennium. For those engaged, combat is an assault on the senses. Battlefields are noisy, disorienting places. Aside from any difficulties caused by atmospheric conditions, battles are frequently shrouded by smoke from weapons or fires started by the fighting, or by dust kicked up by thousands of men, horses or vehicles milling around. In many cases the thick air would seem choking to mouths and throats already dried out by nerves or fear. Even where the air is clear, soldiers in ranks might see little beyond the heads and weapons of the men in front; men in open order might see even less as they take cover or search for an enemy that has done likewise. Din in battle is constant. Moments of relative quiet might mark lulls in the fighting, but combat itself is cacophonous; not only the clashing of weapons or the percussive thump of guns, but the shouting of orders, yells of anger or fear, screaming of the wounded and dying, sounding of instruments, banging of equipment, roaring of engines, or thudding of horses' hooves. Combat is unruly; men pressed together in tight formation would be jostled, pushed and impeded by their neighbours, and even the neatest of alignments would be ruined by men flung about by projectile or explosion. In open order, soldiers can quickly lose a sense of the wider battlefield, and might feel disoriented or cut off. Soldiers protected by armour might feel insulated from some of the chaos around them, but would pay for their protection with reduced visibility and perhaps restricted movement. All men in battle also face exhaustion, from the weight of their weapons and equipment, the effort of wielding them and manoeuvring, and the tension of facing injury or death for hours or perhaps days on end.

Beyond the sensory experience, battles can be places of terror. Not all soldiers feel terror – for some there is exhilaration, while for others death in battle may hold no particular dread – but the possibility of death or maiming is generally enough to provoke a feeling of fear. How soldiers react to that fear is impossible to predict. As Polish general Stanislaw Sosabowski explained, 'no matter how hard or well a man is trained, it is impossible to tell his reaction until he has had his baptism of fire and felt the nearness of death, the involuntary shiver of fear.'[2] This can occur in veteran troops as much as novices; more so, perhaps, because veterans will have first-hand experience of what battle can do. After two years in the trenches, veteran French officer Henri Desagneaux wrote morosely in his diary in 1918: 'What hope is there? You can't always go on without copping it, won't the fatal moment come when our luck will turn? ... we are here waiting to die.'[3] Human physiology comes somewhat to the rescue once action begins, pumping adrenaline into the bloodstream to prevent the sensation of fear from becoming debilitating, but it will be a rare soldier who can turn their mind entirely from the prospect of injury or worse.

Physical and psychological sensations of battle build on the existing corporeal and mental state of the combatants. Societal structures and campaign logistics can inform whether men arrive on the battlefield malnourished or in good shape, but the few hours immediately before combat are also crucial in determining whether men are exhausted or rested, fed or hungry, watered or thirsty. Tired troops are more prone to moral and physical shocks, and are likely to be more brittle than better-rested soldiers – although high morale can to some extent overcome fatigue. Hunger and thirst will see men tire quicker, perhaps making it harder to withstand the physical exertions of combat. The health and happiness of animals – horses especially – is also important if they are to play a full role in combat. Armies that recognise this can give their troops an advantage in battle. In the First World War the British army eventually insisted that men should be given sleep and a hot meal before going into action wherever possible; Major General Bainbridge of 25th Division even suggested timing assaults to get the best out of the soldiers: 'dawn attacks are not to be recommended. The vitality of men is at its lowest and the best cannot be got out of them.'[4] Men's minds were prepared for the fray by prayer and alcohol, the age-old sources of courage.

The individual soldier therefore experiences battle as something of a sensory, mental and physical maelstrom. As we have seen, leadership, motivation, discipline, organisation, training and equipment can all help soldiers to overcome these disconcerting experiences, but they cannot fully explain why individuals act as they do at the moment of contact with the enemy. Moreover, they do not explain how each individual's actions add up to a unit overcoming an enemy, or becoming bogged down, or fleeing from the field. Calculations of numbers and firepower certainly play their part, but there are enough examples of victories of the outnumbered and outgunned to demonstrate that other factors can be equally important.

Perhaps the most prominent of these is the role of the individual soldier. Individual acts at the moment of contact, both big and small, affect battle in myriad ways. Exactly how this happens can be extremely difficult for the researcher of a battle to unpick. Sources to analyse in any detail the actual moment of contact are remarkably slim for most battles. Occasionally the acts of individuals are memorialised in word or image, remembered in the annals of combat as decisive moments that turned the tide of a battle. Occasionally, first-hand accounts of clashing forces provide us with an insight into one soldier's experience. Yet most such incidents go unrecorded.

On occasion the actions of a single soldier – often operating on their own initiative, without orders or a prepared plan – can significantly influence the course of a battle, from the lone Norseman who reputedly held the river crossing at Stamford Bridge (1066), or indeed the Saxon who is said to have swum downstream to stab him from below, to the German private opening a swing bridge over the Mons-Condé Canal to allow his comrades to cross at the Battle of Mons (1914). Morale or training might be factors in such actions, but are not sufficient in themselves to cause them; a better explanation perhaps lies in the indefinable and inexhaustible qualities of human ingenuity, initiative and courage. Such individual action might change a battle by deflecting an enemy advance, opening up a line of attack, or even putting a hostile force to flight. At Stamford Bridge, the Norseman's stand prevented Harold Godwinson's men from crossing the river and gave his fellows time to organise their forces, although they still lost the ensuing battle. At Mons, Private Oskar Niemeyer's actions in swimming the canal and opening the bridge, at the cost of his own life, helped to undermine the British defences and make their line untenable. Despite inflicting severe casualties on the German attackers, the BEF as a whole was forced to retreat once their enemies had crossed the canal.

Other personal actions may be decisive at a local level, rather than for the overall battle. The British retreat at Mons may have been more costly were it not for other individual acts of heroism, for example. With the Royal Fusiliers under heavy fire at Nimy railway bridge, Lieutenant Maurice Dease kept the covering machine gun operating despite the death of the other crew members. When he finally succumbed to severe wounds, Private Sidney Godley volunteered to take his place, keeping the gun in action to cover the Fusiliers' retreat until his weapon could fire no more.[5] The actions of these two men did little to help the BEF's overall predicament, but they almost certainly helped to prevent the death or capture of a number of their comrades.

Fighting at the local level is also affected by the example that individuals set for those around them. The tendency of soldiers to revert to crowd instincts can rouse men to attack or can quickly turn a reverse into a rout, especially if panic is exacerbated by a lack of information, discipline or leadership.[6] An instinct for self-preservation, wilfully suspended to allow soldiers to enter the storm of battle, pushes most to seek some kind of illusory safety in numbers. Once some begin to withdraw, the remaining men become unsettled. A few may attempt to strengthen their comrades' resolve by heroic example, and sometimes this might work. On other occasions, it might not. These boldest individuals may be cut or shot down, or they may simply be grossly outnumbered by those beginning to drift backwards. Either way, the mass of men will generally follow the strongest example, whether that is to attack, stand fast, or flee. The disorder caused by men following this crowd instinct, especially in retreat, makes it much harder to rally a breaking or broken force, although strong organisation and junior leadership can help.

The lack of cohesion and discipline typical of temporary medieval armies perhaps exacerbated this tendency to follow the crowd instinct and might explain the frequency with which beaten forces collapsed into rout, although the same phenomenon can be found in eyewitness accounts of battles through to the present day. Militiaman Garret Watts remembered running as his unit disintegrated at Camden in the American Revolutionary War (1780), writing, 'The cause of that I cannot tell, except that everyone I saw was about to do the same. It was instantaneous. There was no effort to rally, no encouragement to fight. Officers and men joined in the flight.'[7] At the Battle of the Somme over a century and a quarter later, British Lieutenant Sidney Rogerson witnessed some German troops flee from shelling:

> [As] the shells started falling all round the spot, first one and then another German, ludicrous in their coal-scuttle helmets, long coats and boots, emerged and floundered wildly into the nearest deep shell-hole … There must have been twenty or thirty Germans who bolted … those who were not casualties must have been severely frightened![8]

Even experienced and well-motivated troops can be affected by such instincts. As the Duke of Wellington reputedly said when asked if his troops had ever fled: 'all soldiers run away.'[9]

On the other side of things, soldiers can be encouraged and inspired to stand their ground or continue a punishing assault by the examples of others. Just as all soldiers can run, almost all can show hardiness or steadiness if their comrades appear to be doing likewise. Setting an example has always been a key part of battlefield leadership and is therefore to be expected from those of rank or status, but it is often the example of those not traditionally seen as leaders that can be most noteworthy. In a small skirmish at Neufchâtel in 1166, for instance, a young untested knight, unflatteringly nicknamed 'greedy guts', was instrumental in setting an example to the Norman knights; at one point, cut off during a lull in fighting, he undertook a lone charge in a bid to regain his lines, which spurred the rest of the Normans into renewing the action.[10] Such boldness is perhaps not surprising when we learn that the young man was William Marshal, whose later martial prowess earned him the moniker 'the greatest knight', yet to the men at Neufchâtel he was just a young and unknown, if rather eager, member of their company.

That Marshal's actions filtered down to posterity is due to his later fame, which encouraged retrospective recording of his youthful exploits. Yet most such micro-actions in battle are not recorded. Even when first-hand accounts of battle became more popular from around the 1600s, few writers mentioned anything beyond the most outrageously heroic individual actions, although it is clear that the role of individual example was important to troops as they crossed swords or exchanged fire with the enemy. To take one illustrative instance from the Battle of Gettysburg (1863), the famous bayonet charge of the 20th Maine in defence of Little Round Top probably would not have got far without the example of Lieutenant Holman Melcher and the colour party, who reputedly led the dash towards the Confederates. The fact that there was somebody to follow played a key role in encouraging others to charge. Advancing with the colours almost certainly helped; when carried into battle, a unit's colours were the focal point for many acts of inspiration, partly because their visual prominence allowed soldiers to actually see them being taken forward, and partly because of soldiers' attachment to their standards. Often, though, the example of a man on his own might be enough, even in more open-order combat. At Isurava in 1942, the hard-pressed Australians were rallied by Private Bruce Kingsbury's solo charge at the attacking Japanese positions.[11] Although Kingsbury was killed in the attack, the citation for his posthumously awarded Victoria Cross highlighted the importance of his actions:

> His initiative and superb courage made possible the recapture of the position which undoubtedly saved Battalion Headquarters, as well as causing heavy casualties amongst the enemy. His coolness, determination and devotion to duty in the face of great odds was an inspiration to his comrades.[12]

Kingsbury's charge may not have been able to win the battle, or even to turn its tide, but the inspiration and example he showed almost certainly helped to prevent the collapse of his unit.

The above are instances of relatively extraordinary behaviour which drew general attention because each man stood out from his comrades. In other instances, however, it was the collective example of comrades standing fast with a sense of togetherness, encouraged perhaps by regimental officers and NCOs, that induced soldiers to hold their ground under the most trying conditions. After the Battle of Albuera (1811), French commander Marshal Soult complained bitterly that his adversaries had failed to flee: 'I turned their right, and penetrated their centre; they were completely beaten; the day was mine, and yet they did not know it, and would not run.'[13] Although suffering grievous casualties, the British, Portuguese and Spanish soldiers stood firm and refused to acknowledge defeat, eventually carrying the day. The role of general officers in their stand was minimal; battalion officers were largely reduced to encouragement and exhortations, in the words of the gravely wounded colonel of the British 1/57th, to 'die hard'.[14] Collective guts and grit rather than tactics, generalship or any single act of heroism, held the line that day.

While the role of individuals is vital to understanding the progress and outcome of clashing armies, there can seemingly be an element of chance in how soldiers react to circumstances. Chance on the battlefield is a vague concept, but could be described as simply the occurrence of the incalculable. For an individual soldier this might include being hit by an arrow or bullet or piece of shrapnel; one can never predict where lumps of metal will fly, and being in the path of one of these projectiles – or conversely avoiding them – seems a matter of luck rather than judgement.

In hand-to-hand combat a warrior might have more certainty in his own skill and strength, but even there the intervention of a panicked comrade, a slippery patch of ground, or an obstacle unseen through the narrow slits of a helmet's visor might prove a man's undoing. There is a limited repertoire of things that a soldier might do to keep himself from harm on the battlefield; the rest is essentially left to luck.

For the wider army, some factors of chance can be calculated and planned for. As Frederick the Great commented, 'the more one foresees obstacles to his plans, the less one will find them later in the execution.'[15] Those with apparent good luck are often those best placed to deal with or take advantage of the unexpected. Yet even with contingencies in place, armies can suffer monstrous ill-fortune. At the Battle of Salamanca (1812), for example, the two senior French commanders, Marshal Marmont and General Bonet, were wounded in separate incidents near the start of the battle, leaving their forces rudderless for a crucial period.[16] Although we might take from Oscar Wilde to suggest that losing two commanders looked like carelessness, the infrequency of such events means that it can probably be placed in the bracket of misfortune.

In some cases, strokes of apparent luck come from accidents or mistakes on the part of the enemy. Leaving aside major tactical or operational blunders that any general should seek to exploit, chance circumstances can transform minor errors into more significant episodes. A Union soldier's discovery in a field of a stray copy of the Confederate army's operational plans in the lead-up to Antietam (1862), and the fact that the soldier had the wit to pass the papers up the chain of command rather than using them for kindling or on a visit to the latrine, was a rare slice of fortune for Union General McClellan, even if it might have been prevented by better staff work or information security from the Confederates.

One occurrence often put down to ill-fortune is the misidentification of friend and foe on the battlefield. The grave consequences of such errors make it important for armies to distinguish their own forces from those of the enemy. On medieval and early modern battlefields, livery, flags, and even rudimentary uniforms were used to allow men to distinguish one another in combat. At Evesham (1265), Simon de Montfort's men sported white crosses on their arms, while Prince Edward's wore red crosses. At Marston Moor (1644), as Parliamentarian chaplain Simeon Ash explained, 'our signal was a white paper or handkerchiffe in our hats; our word was *God with us*. The enemies signal was to bee without bands and skarfs; their word was *God and the King* [*sic*].'[17] By the eighteenth century, brightly coloured uniforms were universal and aided identification, although the unfortunate tendency of armies to use similarly coloured cloth could cause confusion.

Modern armies continued the tradition of visual distinctions; in the Second World War the Allied white star and German iron cross were blazoned across vehicles and aircraft to help to distinguish friend from foe. At times identifiers have also been used to allow individuals to stand out in battle. Medieval noblemen each had their own insignia for identification, which had the added benefit of allowing others to observe their glorious deeds, and allowing enemies to identify them as men worth capturing for ransom if the day went badly. Indeed, the failure to identify themselves could be fatal. At Agincourt (1415), the Duke of Brabant arrived late and charged into the fray 'wearing an improvised coat drawn from the flag of one of his trumpeters'; wounded in the face and unrecognised as a man worth ransoming, he had his throat slit.[18]

A failure to identify friend from foe creates confusion and can lead to significant unnecessary casualties. Mistaking hostile troops for friends at best causes problems with morale and at worst leaves a force wholly unprepared to receive an attack. Chronicler Jean Froissart recorded that on the day after Crécy a force of French levies unaware of the battle 'fell in with the English and went right up to them, thinking they were their own people … There was a sharp engagement and the French were soon fleeing in disorder.'[19] Shortly afterwards the same happened to another force under the Archbishop of Rouen and the Grand Prior of France, both of whom were killed in the ensuing slaughter. Froissart reckoned that more levies were killed in these incidents than in the battle itself.[20] Similar incidents could happen even in the age of distinctive uniforms and linear tactics. Over 500 years later, at Fredericksburg in the American Civil War, Brigadier General Gregg's brigade was routed after he mistook advancing Union troops for retreating Confederates; Gregg himself was killed in the brief ensuing action.

On the other side of things, the mistaking of friends for foes can lead to deadly and destructive incidents of what has come to be termed 'friendly fire'. Even approximate rates of attrition from friendly fire are impossible to calculate, as in the chaos of battle it is not always possible to tell who was shooting (or stabbing) at whom, but it is by no means uncommon. It might include units attacking one another in confusion – especially in the age of gunpowder, where clouds of smoke obscured vision, but there are plenty of examples of it happening before and since – and accidents from panicky or ill-trained troops shooting their own comrades. On occasion there also seems to be a degree of deliberateness in the targeting of friendly troops, as seen in the French knights riding over retreating Genoese allies at Crécy, or in the Soviet 'blocking battalions' firing on their own soldiers in the Great Patriotic War. Occasionally soldiers would use the chaos of battle to commit outright murder; men in Frederick the Great's army are known to have shot the odd unpopular commander, while in Vietnam, the threat of 'fragging' became commonplace for irksome officers.

The majority of friendly fire incidents are relatively small-scale, often because the mistake is quickly realised; such events rarely change the overall course of battle. At Gauche Wood during the Battle of Cambrai, for instance, British tanks hampered by poor visibility opened fire on an Indian cavalry regiment, killing three men before the horsemen's furious colonel rode up to remonstrate. The incident did not prevent the tanks, cavalry and some attached infantry from cooperating to launch a successful attack on the wood.[21] On occasion, though, even brief incidents of friendly fire could have more serious consequences: at Chancellorsville in 1863, 'Stonewall' Jackson was fatally shot by his own picket line who mistook his staff for a Union cavalry patrol, robbing the Confederacy of one of its best generals. Where larger units are involved, the consequences can also be more severe. In the fog-bound Battle of Germantown (1777), two American brigades blundered into one another and opened fire, each thinking that the other was the enemy. After a sharp firefight both broke and withdrew, leaving a significant gap in George Washington's line, and contributing to the ultimate defeat.[22]

All armies also suffer a degree of attrition through battlefield accidents, where friendly troops are hit through error rather than misidentification. Such incidents are endemic in armies festooned with lethal weapons and equipment, especially in lesser trained or experienced forces. Some might be due to weapons failure, such as the death of Scottish King James II when an artillery piece exploded next to him at the siege of Roxburgh in 1460. In the linear warfare of the seventeenth to nineteenth centuries, men were at some risk of being accidentally shot or even stabbed by the men in front or beside them in the chaos of battle. French Marshal Gouvion Saint-Cyr estimated that a quarter of all Napoleonic casualties were down to men unintentionally shooting those in the ranks in front of them, while the colonel of the 23rd Light Dragoons complained at Waterloo, 'we always lose more men by our own people than we do by the enemy.'[23] These figures may be exaggerations, but accidental killings were certainly rife.

The decision of a clash of arms comes down to many factors. Preparation for battle is certainly crucial, as are the decisions taken by army commanders on the day. Yet the countless decisions, exploits and actions of individual soldiers in the thick of the fighting are equally vital. Examples are important; heroic individual action might change the face of the contest, but more often individuals set an example – for good or ill – for those around them. Individual errors or inattention can lead to accidents and even the odd disaster, although luck can also play a part. Luck – the intervention of the imponderable – is a seeming constant in battle, although it tends to favour those who are best prepared.

The Nearest-Run Thing: Waterloo (1815)

The events of Sunday, 18 June 1815, on the gentle slopes of the ridge of Mont St Jean, just south of the village of Waterloo, saw almost 200,000 men of the armies of Napoleon, the Duke of Wellington and Prince von Blücher thrust into a tight arena of combat only four or five square miles in area. By the end of the day's maelstrom, nearly 50,000 of those men would be dead, wounded or dying, and the remainder of Napoleon's army would be in flight back towards the French frontier. It was the last major battle of the Napoleonic Wars.

As dawn broke on the fateful day, none of the three armies was immediately ready for combat. Blücher's force was still nowhere near the battlefield; beaten at Ligny two days earlier, he had withdrawn to Wavre, a dozen miles from where his ally Wellington now stood. Yet Blücher, that inveterate hater of Napoleon, was determined to march to Wellington's aid and to combine their forces against the French emperor. Napoleon's troops were also not fully concentrated on the field. The previous day and night had seen heavy rainstorms, and the ground over much of the future battlefield and its approaches was sodden. Thick mud meant that movement was difficult. The artillery and supply wagons especially struggled to move into position.

For many men of the French and allied armies on the field of Waterloo, it was a wet and hungry dawn. Some men lit fires to dry their sodden clothes and, if they were lucky, cook their meagre rations. Between 7 and 8 am, the sun came out, to the relief of the cold and damp soldiers, but many on both sides entered the battle in a state of exhaustion – not least because a good proportion of the troops had been engaged in fighting at Quatre Bras or Ligny only two days earlier. Ensign Edward Macready of 1/30th summed it up:

> We had been three days without rations, and the night of the 17th was dreadful, the mud was up to our ankles and it rained dreadfully, we had no cover but our clothes, and all arose in the most complete ague imaginable.[24]

Such exhaustion would play its role in the battle, although the terrifying exhilaration of combat seems to have given men the wherewithal to see the day through.

For all its fame as a battle, the grand tactical plans at Waterloo were not particularly distinguished. Wellington aligned his forces along the ridge of Mont St Jean, with his right anchored on the large, sturdy chateau, gardens and orchard of Hougoumont, his centre protected by the farm of La Haye Sainte, and his left, from where he expected the Prussians to appear, on the small settlements of Papelotte, La Haye and Frischermont. Unsure of the quality of his command, he interspersed his British, Germanic and Dutch-Belgian forces along the line, and used the reverse slope to conceal many of his troops from French artillery. The height of the crops also helped to shield his men from view. Captain Coignet, attached to Napoleon's staff, noted that at the eastern edge of the battlefield the allied infantry was hidden by a steep ravine, and the cavalry behind tall rye, with only the fire of the artillery showing their position.[25] On the opposite side of the battlefield, Major Llewellyn of the 28th Regiment complained that 'the rye in the field was so high, that to see anything beyond our own ranks was impossible.'[26] With his troops firmly ensconced, Wellington's plan was simply to hold Napoleon until Prussian reinforcements arrived.

Napoleon drew up his army on the low ridge opposite, with d'Erlon's I Corps on the right, Reille's II Corps on the left, and the Guard and VI Corps in reserve. He also created a grand battery of some ninety cannon opposite Wellington's centre-left. His plan, according to orders written on the morning of the battle, was simply to bludgeon Wellington out of the way, assaulting towards Mont St Jean (to the rear of Wellington's centre) with both frontline corps, intending to take it and split Wellington's army asunder. Due to the softness of the ground, which meant that some of his troops had not yet even arrived on the field, Napoleon ordered that the battle should commence at 1 pm. His plan showed little regard for the qualities of Wellington or his troops, even though several of Napoleon's senior officers who had faced Wellington in the Peninsular War (including his chief-of-staff Marshal Soult, and Marshal Ney) counselled caution.

Despite Napoleon's unsubtle grand tactical plan, the fighting at Waterloo began at around 11.30 am, when French artillery opened fire on Wellington's right. Shortly thereafter, a brigade of Reille's II Corps advanced against Hougoumont, either as a diversionary move to impel Wellington to weaken his centre, or simply in an attempt to neutralise this bulwark which might impede a French attack on the main lines. The assault stalled, however, and the divisional commander, Napoleon's brother Jérôme, fed in reinforcements until almost his whole division was engaged. The attackers cleared the woodland around the chateau but made no progress against the strong walls of the main building and garden. The decision to commit additional troops seems to have been a local one rather than emanating from army command, but it would become a drain on resources and compromise the reserves available to Napoleon at the later crisis of the battle.

At 1 pm, however, the main attack on the British centre-left began. The grand battery opened an intense bombardment, although the only visible target was Bylandt's Dutch-Belgian Brigade, which was stationed forward of the ridge. It took heavy casualties, but the majority of Wellington's infantry found some shelter on the reverse slope. With French artillery aiming by line-of-sight, they were unable to target most of Wellington's forces with any accuracy. Nevertheless, morale and discipline were crucial to withstand even such a bombardment. The inability to see the enemy or to strike back added to the terror of the artillery onslaught, and could do significant psychological damage to ill-led troops. At this stage, however, with casualties few and the majority of officers and NCOs still in place, the line held firm. Only Bylandt's brigade, exposed to the full force of the enemy's cannon, broke and withdrew.

The bombardment lasted perhaps half an hour before d'Erlon's I Corps advanced. Four divisions of infantry, nearly 20,000 men, made their attack across the valley. In a grand tactical sense, this assault was intended to hammer Wellington's centre into submission. It was, however, the minor tactics that first wrong-footed the advance. Two of the divisions chose to advance in divisional columns, with the battalions each deployed in three ranks and lined up one behind another. Whether this arose from a misunderstanding or as a response to the need to traverse the wet ground and chest-high crops, the decision placed the French troops at an immediate tactical disadvantage. The columns provided a superb target for the allied artillery, and created significant difficulties for deploying in the face of the enemy. The divisions on the left and right of the advance also ran into the garrisons of La Haye Sainte, Papelotte and Frischermont; they made some progress against these extemporised fortifications, but their advance against the main line stalled. Elements of the left-hand division that threatened the allied ridge were hurled back by a counterattack from part of Kempt's infantry brigade and a Hanoverian infantry battalion, the latter of which was in turn attacked and scattered by French cuirassiers. The two central divisions, however, came on solidly, despite their poor deployment. In sheer weight alone – nigh-on 10,000 men – they posed a major threat. Bylandt's absconding brigade had left a gap in Wellington's line just at the point where the two divisions would strike. It was quickly plugged by Lieutenant General Picton's 5th Division – the infantry brigades of Kempt and Pack.

Outnumbered three-to-one, it is easy to imagine that the thin red line of 5th Division faced almost certain defeat. But it is here that minor tactics, morale and human psychology must be taken into account. Each French division boasted a frontage of maybe 200 men and marched several battalions deep, apparently relying on weight of numbers to crunch through the enemy. Indeed, a charge would have plenty of impetus behind it, and in a straight firefight new men could step rapidly forward to replace casualties. However, despite the traditional vision of British tactics popularised in part by Charles Oman's work on the Peninsular War, it was rarely British practice to engage in prolonged musketry duels.²⁷ Instead, Picton's infantry met the column with an effective counterattack. Advancing through the tall rye to the top of the ridge, which was lined by a hedgerow, the two British brigades approached the oncoming French columns, stopped at close range, and unleashed a single volley before immediately charging with the bayonet. Kempt unequivocally narrated: 'I met it [the enemy division] at the charge with the 28th, 32nd, and 79th Regiments in line, and completely repulsed the Enemy's Column, driving it in a state of the greatest confusion down the slope of the position.'²⁸ Lieutenant Shelton of the 28th concurred that his regiment 'gave a very steady volley into the Enemy's Column, and charged', driving the enemy before them, while his fellow officer Ensign Mountsteven estimated that they fired once at a distance of only thirty to forty yards before charging.²⁹ Accounts agree that the French fled rather than waiting to receive the charge.

The explanation for this startling success lies as much in the individual's experience of the event as in any assessment of relative grand tactics. The French troops, assailed by artillery and skirmishers on their slow and difficult march across muddy, crop-covered fields, would already have been losing enthusiasm; their approach to the ridge and the exhortations of officers would have kept them going and maybe even given hope of swift success, but the sudden appearance of the previously unseen enemy to their front, followed by a volley from three regiments at short range, would have robbed their advance of all momentum. Eyewitnesses state that the columns were also attempting to deploy into line when the counterthrust arrived, which would simply have added to their disorder. Perhaps a few brave souls continued to move forward, but by this stage the leading formations would have been in significant disarray. The French certainly returned fire. One of the shots hit Picton in the head, killing him instantly, although the fact that it hit a horseman at head height indicates that many of the shots probably went high of the standing infantry.

At this stage the British troops would still have been well in hand of their officers, and able to respond to battalion-level tactical decisions; the French officers would be struggling to keep order, with regimental and battalion command structures in the van largely if not entirely fragmented. General officers would have had little influence at this stage of the clash, as simply making themselves heard over the noise or seen in the smoke would have been nearly impossible. The death of Picton seems to have had little immediate effect on the British troops; it is likely that few men outside the immediate vicinity were even aware of it, shrouded as they were in cannon and musket smoke, while facing front in ranks. The French fire certainly did little to stop the British counterattack, and the inability of the French to bring any artillery to bear (the grand battery's line of sight was blocked by their own infantry, and horse artillery had not been properly deployed) meant that there was no way of destroying the cohesion or command and control of the British units. The British had the advantage of order, leadership, momentum, and the higher ground. It is a phenomenon repeated time and again in military history that unformed men rarely stand against an organised attack. Some men will run, and others will be obliged to follow suit to avoid being isolated and slaughtered. The herd mentality takes hold, causing even the brave to follow their fellows to the rear. The downhill charge of almost 3,000 bayonet-wielding British infantrymen broke the deployed French battalions.

This did not, however, rout the whole French advance. Several battalions of the central divisions had been put to flight, and others disordered by their precipitous withdrawal, but the depth of the columns meant that there remained several largely formed units. Moreover, two brigades of French cavalry had been sent to support the infantry attack. With 5th Division temporarily leaderless, unformed after its charge, and its muskets empty, the British line was now vulnerable. There were no immediately available infantry reserves. At this juncture, however, the grand tactical decision swung back into play, for Wellington and his cavalry commander, the Earl of Uxbridge, had recognised the danger and launched a second counterattack with two brigades of heavy cavalry. The Household Brigade charged to the right of La Haye Sainte, sweeping aside the French cuirassier regiment that was disordered after overrunning the Hanoverian battalion. The brigade then smashed into the flank of the left and left-central French infantry divisions, causing those who might have renewed the attack on Kempt's brigade to flee in disorder. Further to the left of Wellington's line, the Union Brigade launched itself through gaps in Pack's brigade to strike the two central columns; with the foremost units already in flight from the British infantry counterattack, this fresh assault put both divisions to rout. Unable to see the cavalry until it was almost upon them, and unable to deploy easily into defensive formation, cohesion in the already rattled French ranks collapsed. Perhaps 3,000 men were taken prisoner, and nearly as many again were lost as casualties.

Wellington's line had survived the first crisis of the day, but he felt in no position to follow up the limited counterattacks of the two infantry and two cavalry brigades. Kempt and Pack quickly rallied their infantry and returned them to the reverse of the ridgeline, while the Household Brigade's troopers were, with rather more difficulty, reined in. The Union Brigade, however, flush with its own success, took the charge too far, chasing the fleeing French infantry across the valley and charging the guns of Napoleon's main battery. Although they managed to get in amongst the cannon, the tired men and blown horses were counterattacked by French lancers and dragoons, incurring severe losses. The cavalry's indiscipline and poor leadership meant that the brigade was, to all intents and purposes, destroyed as a fighting force; its commander, Sir William Ponsonby, was amongst the dead.

Despite this, Wellington's counterstroke had been successful in defeating the enemy's first main attack. Moreover, the Prussians of Bülow's IV Corps were now in the vicinity of the battlefield, and in contact (by messenger, at least) with Wellington's far left. Napoleon, however, was still unaware of this development, and ordered a renewal of the assault on Wellington's centre, beginning with the farmhouse of La Haye Sainte. Two brigades were launched against this bulwark, but were repulsed by the determined resistance of Major Baring's German garrison. Attacks also continued at Hougoumont, where a small force of Frenchmen managed to break through the main gates and into the chateau courtyard. In what Wellington later asserted was a pivotal moment of the battle, a group of ten officers and Guardsmen managed to close the gates against further French reinforcements. The action of these few men effectively prevented the fall of this vital position; those Frenchmen who had gained entry were slaughtered, aside from a single drummer boy.[30]

Despite these failures, it appeared to Napoleon's headquarters that the allied centre-right was under significant pressure. This certainly seems to have been the case from Ney's advanced command position; interpreting troop movements seen through the smoke as the beginnings of a general withdrawal, he launched forward a heavy cavalry division, hoping to turn retreat into rout. This was based on the sound principle that demoralised and disorganised troops might panic at the sight and sound of a cavalry charge, and the infectious panic might spread through the army, causing a more general disintegration.

In the event, Ney was wrong. The movement he saw was possibly Wellington reorganising his line following the repulse of I Corps, or maybe a stream of wounded and prisoners heading to the rear. Instead of units on the point of collapse, Ney's troopers were met by steady infantry who deployed into battalion squares to repel cavalry. These squares – four-sided hollow formations, in which the infantry in four ranks faced outwards, bayonets fixed – were largely invulnerable to horsemen, who nevertheless made a series of costly and unsuccessful frontal attacks. Determined to break the allied army, Ney threw in more and more units, until much of the cavalry reserve was committed to the attack. Here the musketry of the allied infantry was effective, as was the cool leadership of battalion officers. Time and again, for an hour or more, the French cavalry came forward with courage and tenacity, but made little impression on the solid infantry squares. Many British letters and reminiscences of the battle describe the cavalry attacks in relatively few words; more deadly, and therefore to them more noteworthy, were the actions of the French skirmishers and, eventually, supporting artillery, for whom the squares proved a tempting target. In the face of these attritional attacks, the ostentatious sangfroid of officers was crucial.

The example set by officers was indeed important throughout the battle. Napoleonic battle was a disorienting experience of noise, heat and thick acrid smoke assailing each individual. Soldiers on both sides of the valley took heart from the steadiness of their immediate officers, who were more than sensible of the example required of them. Under fire many officers strove to adopt a studied nonchalance; artilleryman Captain Mercer recalled forcing himself to remain unmoved as a French skirmisher took very deliberate aim at him, merely wagging a playful finger at the fellow when his musket ball flew wide.[31] Several officers refused to retire when wounded, or returned to the lines after cursory treatment, in order to inspire their men and prove their own courage. Where officer casualties were high, such as in d'Erlon's attacking divisions or in some of the British infantry units, morale could waver. Rifleman John Lewis of 2/95th admitted that 'seeing we had lost so many men & all our commanding officers my heart began to fail', although in the end his unit stood firm.[32] General officers were also of great importance setting an example at Waterloo; dozens of accounts mention Wellington's presence along the allied line as an inspiring influence, and on the French side Ney's presence in the front ranks became a matter of legend.

Despite his presence in the vanguard of the charge, Ney's cavalry attacks failed. Wellington's centre was hard-pressed, but at this critical juncture Napoleon had few troops to exploit the opportunity. Half of Reille's II Corps were now engaged fruitlessly against Hougoumont and could not be reformed to support the centre; Lobau's VI Corps and some Imperial Guard units had been diverted to provide a reserve against Bülow's Prussian corps, now ominously appearing towards the village of Plancenoit on Napoleon's right. Bülow's cautious advance enjoyed some initial success without threatening any serious breakthrough, but his growing force prevented Napoleon from concentrating his full attention on Wellington's army.

At this stage the emperor's battle plan was in tatters, but he still believed he could improvise a victory. Slowly extricating his cavalry from their debacle, he renewed the infantry assault against Wellington's centre. Under heavy fire from French skirmishers, and with the cavalry charges not long abated, the ammunition carts of Wellington's baggage park could not make it through to the beleaguered garrison of La Haye Sainte. One by one, Baring's men ran out of powder and shot, and by 6 pm the garrison was overrun; only one in ten escaped alive. A battery set up in the farmhouse ruins inflicted heavy casualties on the allied centre at short range. Shortly thereafter, Napoleon launched two battalions of his Old Guard against the Prussians at Plancenoit, ejecting their entire brigade from the village. With the right stabilised and success coming in the centre, Napoleon decided to deal Wellington's thinning line a death blow before any further Prussian intervention.

The final French reserve, the elite Imperial Guard, was therefore committed to assault the British centre-right, while d'Erlon's reformed divisions and the available elements of II Corps moved against the centre-left. The attack of the Guard has been mythologised, especially by British writers: the elite guardsmen of Britain and France, clashing head-on at the culmination of nigh-on a quarter-century of Anglo-French struggle. Romanticism aside, however, the attack proved a gamble too far for Napoleon. Already Bülow's Prussians had been reinforced by the corps of Pirch and Ziethen, which were visible beyond Wellington's left.

In order to bolster morale, Napoleon ordered word to be spread that this was Grouchy bringing French reinforcements.

The attack on Wellington's centre-left was not pressed home with any particular vigour and made little headway, although it pinned the allied forces in place. On the French left, the Imperial Guard attacked with greater intent in two shallow columns. Morale was high as they advanced against Maitland's guards and Halkett's infantry brigade, both of whom were exhausted after a day under artillery bombardment and cavalry attack. Wellington found it expedient to advance his remaining cavalry to line up behind the infantry to stiffen their resolve. As the Imperial Guard reached the allied slope, the British troops stood from their prone position, causing a check in the guardsmen's ranks; as they came closer, the British infantry poured volley fire into the head of the columns. The Frenchmen came on, accepting huge punishment, but their advance slowed. A short musket duel developed, inflicting casualties on both sides, but the need to fire and load robbed the columns of much of their forward momentum. Against the right-hand column, a British and a Hanoverian battalion swung out of the line to assault its flanks with musketry; against the left, the Footguards held firm. As against d'Erlon earlier, the British enjoyed the higher ground, and remained in good order despite the losses incurred throughout the day. With the Imperial Guard stalled, the allied troops launched a bayonet charge which drove them from the slope and back across the shallow valley.

As the Guard was pushed back, Prussian troops on the far left of the allied line began to break through the weak French flanking forces around Papelotte. Exhausted by a day's fighting, with their right flank and rear now threatened by supposed reinforcements that turned out to be enemies, and with the Guard defeated on the left, the fighting spirit of I and II Corps collapsed all along the line. A cry of treason went up through the ranks, and men began melting away towards the rear. Seeing the enemy wavering, Wellington ordered a general advance which, combined with the continued Prussian assault, swept away French resistance with remarkable rapidity. Not all was plain sailing for the allies – Prussian and British artillery briefly exchanged fire at the east of the battlefield, and British hussars inadvertently sabred some Prussian cavalry – but the joint assault was more than the French could stand.

Napoleon's army collapsed spectacularly, its morale vanished. Units gripped by panic disintegrated one after another. Wellington's remaining cavalry plunged into the retiring troops, breaking up resistance as soon as it could be organised. The remaining Imperial Guard battalions formed a rearguard behind which they hoped to rally the army, but it was a lost cause. Many men fled individually or in groups, while troops which retained leadership and discipline could do nothing but withdraw in the general rout. Wellington's exhausted troops were eventually able to overrun the French rearguard, but could do little more. The Prussians took up the pursuit, harrying the equally exhausted French through the warm summer's night. Napoleon himself was forced to flee south, the battle – and his empire – irretrievably lost.

Chapter 12

Sources of Conflict

'I wish to place on record these matters of great renown'
Jean Froissart.[1]

Many of the major battles in history already have an excellent bibliography of narrative and analytical accounts that tell us a great deal about how the events unfolded, how the battle turned out, and why. Yet to really understand a contest – or to unearth information about an unstudied battle – it can be enormously valuable to turn to the primary sources. This chapter will outline some of the sources that can be accessed and used to understand battle in Europe over the past millennium; not just written accounts, but administrative records, visual representations, physical artefacts, archaeological remains, and the battlefields themselves.

Eyewitness Narratives

Eyewitness accounts of battle exist for conflicts throughout the last millennium, both from combatants themselves and from those who witnessed battle but did not participate. These sources are enormously useful, but the researcher must approach them with a critical eye. As always, they must ask themselves the core questions that form the basis of any good analysis: who wrote this, and why? What is their aim in setting pen to paper? Who is the source for? And crucially, how might this affect the information they choose to include, to omit, or even to fabricate? Soldiers trying to remember events that took place in the heat of battle might easily make mistakes, especially if they are writing at a remove of several years. Senior officers would have a vested interest in emphasising their role in victory and deflecting blame for defeat; although even the most self-serving apologia can have value, if only to show what the commander considered important in retrospect. The role of censorship must also be taken into account by the researcher, particularly in regard to letters or communications from the front line.

Throughout the medieval period, narratives of battle were often provided by combatants themselves, or by others who claimed to have witnessed the events they described. The citation of eye-witnesses – including the narrators themselves – was relatively common in medieval narratives of battles, and was used in order to establish trustworthiness and expertise on the part of the narrator. Jean Le Févre, for example, who was himself a herald as King of Arms of the Troison d'Or, emphasised his own trustworthiness as a narrator in his work since he witnessed the events that he described.[2]

However, medieval and early modern narratives of battles composed by eyewitnesses contain myriad opportunities for partiality – whether conscious or unwitting. Often, eyewitness narratives were recorded for posterity with two primary motivations in mind: the desire to record and commemorate the glorious deeds of great individuals; and the need to inform and encourage young knights, the next generation of great individuals, to emulate the glorious deeds of their predecessors. Their concern was often therefore with reputation, not chronology. The time and the date of a battle were not important to them (often frustratingly so, for modern scholars), but narrators ensured that they included as full and correct a list as possible of the major participants and the deeds that they performed. In deciding what deserved to be committed to memory in this way, medieval writers made conscious judgements concerning the information that they would include, and also that they would omit. Researchers must therefore accept that these narratives will often be incomplete and will present a highly selective range of information.

The later medieval and early modern periods saw the emergence of an additional group of battlefield commentators: the heralds, whose roles expanded and became more codified during the fourteenth and fifteenth centuries. The role of heralds was diverse: they acted as chivalric messengers, diplomatic envoys and authorities on diplomatic missions. It is this detailed knowledge of the diplomatic polity of the time that marks heraldic accounts out as being particularly useful for gleaning detailed contemporary knowledge of the political context of a battle – but not necessarily its full narrative.

From roughly the seventeenth century we see increasing numbers of unofficial accounts written by people – generally men and generally soldiers, but with some exceptions – who were actually present on the battlefield. These could take the form of letters, diaries, memoires, or histories worked up for publication. These narratives are naturally patchy, often somewhat narrow in perspective, and can be difficult to trace, but where they do exist, they afford some interesting insights. Moreover, accounts increasingly appear from combatants at all levels, from army command down to individual soldiers. Accounts from senior officers can give an impression of the unfolding tactical situation, and may also show the commanders' thoughts, methods and justifications for their actions. First-hand accounts of soldiers are less likely to help with a metanarrative, but can show a whole range of experiences of the fighting men, from their routine on the day of a battle to what they ate, the junior command structures, the morale of the unit, the proficiency with weapons, the effects of 'fog of war', to the actual experience of the clash of arms itself – although it is rare to find a single account that does all of this.

In the modern era, eyewitness accounts can also be affected by literary style. Certainly by the Napoleonic Wars in the early nineteenth century, advances in printing and public taste for reading meant that soldiers' memoirs, and sometimes diaries, became widely available. However, as with any established genre, the informal rules of what the audience expected could sometimes skew the narrative. Tales of battle were expected to be heroic and to present examples of daring and sangfroid in the face of the enemy, and so this became the emphasis of many of the reminiscences, to the detriment of other aspects of the battle experience. The example of the Baron de Marbot, whose memoirs are a breathless gallop through the daring exploits of a Napoleonic cavalry officer, is highly illustrative. A great deal of first-hand information can still be gleaned from these notebooks and memoirs. Unlike medieval records, these accounts often do give the basic details of place, date, size of forces, and tactical evolutions. But the conventions of such writing can make some of the accounts quite formulaic, and can downplay individual experience and sentiment. This persists well into the twentieth century, although the reaction to the First World War especially led to a counter-narrative emerging, in which many war reminiscences focused instead (although often equally formulaically) on the horror, futility and destructive nature of conflict. This is not to suggest that the majority of these recollections are anything other than honest; the researcher must simply remember that there are reasons beyond the battlefield that participants emphasise some parts of the experience over others.

Contemporary Reporting

There are also plentiful accounts of battle produced contemporaneously by those who were not direct witnesses of conflict. These sources could be produced for a wide range of audiences – from small, private groups to international distribution – and for a wide range of motivations, from the author's personal glory to public information, or simple profit. Again, these sources can provide very useful information to the researcher, although they tend to focus on the narrative rather than the personal experience of battle.

Chronicles composed by non-eyewitness authorities provide the main corpus of narrative material regarding many medieval battles. These sources provide accounts of battles – often brief – although they rarely state where they find information. This category includes Thomas Walsingham's *Chronica Maiora* (1380–1422), which was almost entirely unknown beyond St Albans during the later medieval period yet provides detailed, dramatic narrative accounts of the battles of Shrewsbury and Agincourt. Chronicles composed by lay individuals also became increasingly common throughout the later medieval period as monastic narratives declined, but these can still suffer from a lack of information or unclear source material.

The simplest information regarding battle that is presented in these sources is that concerning the bare chronologies of events. This information is comprised of the date and location that a battle occurred, and a handful of named attendees – who are almost invariably well-known individuals. The rather terse entry in the Anglo-Saxon Chronicle (Worcester MS) for the Battle of Hastings (1066), for example, consists of a mere half-dozen sentences – yet this is the only contemporary English account of the battle to survive. Nevertheless, such brief information can provide a useful complement to eyewitness narratives, particularly in placing such combats into their wider historical context.

This brevity leads to the most obvious limitations of narratives of battle found in chronicles: the lack of certainty regarding the numbers of combatants provided. Furthermore, details that reflected poorly on some combatants could be omitted, while legendary acts of heroism or chivalry may be exaggerated or even created in order to reflect a particular message. Chroniclers and narrators often neglected to cite their sources, leaving the reader only guessing at where these writers acquired their information. For much of the medieval and early modern periods, word of mouth would have been crucial to the dissemination of this information and may account for the brevity of many accounts, reliant as they may have been on the briefest of news carried to their corner of the country. Occasionally, however, a narrator is at pains to identify sources of information: the Late Medieval chronicler Jean Froissart, for example, stated that he had searched out knights, esquires and heralds to ask them about the events he wished to narrate.[3]

The modern equivalent to historical chronicles could be seen to be media reports and newspapers – in that they disseminate information passed to them by third parties who may or may not have witnessed the combat personally. Newspapers can be useful for giving a basic narrative of battle, or for highlighting the most noteworthy or sensational elements of a combat. They often lean on official information and can therefore be relied upon to give their government's perspective on a confrontation. However, censorship or deliberate disinformation can mean that these reports may be fragmentary, erroneous or misleading. In the eighteenth and nineteenth centuries, endemic plagiarism meant that errors were easily repeated between publications. This problem is not unique to these centuries, or to newspapers – the persistently erroneous repetition of the English archers' 'v-sign' at Agincourt is a case in point.

The rise of the war correspondent – that is to say, someone who sends reports from a battlefront – led to a marked increase in the quality of reporting from roughly the Crimean War onwards. In modern conflicts, reporters have often been embedded with troops leading to detailed insights into operations and the soldiers' experience. Their experiences and the hazards they face often reflect those of combatants themselves, as evidenced by the tragic cases of war correspondent fatalities. Journalists have also been key in exposing combat atrocities, bringing to light issues that might have otherwise remained hidden.

Official Narratives

Official descriptions of battle are a hugely important resource for the researcher, especially for nineteenth- and twentieth-century conflicts. The more bureaucratic nature of armies and the more developed systems of archiving and record-keeping mean that for many conflicts we have extensive records of army orders, battlefield reports, casualty registers, medical reports, regimental war diaries, and despatches. The proliferation of material towards the modern day does tend to mean that a smaller proportion is digitised or published, although such is the continued interest in conflict of the past two centuries that huge strides are being made in making these records publicly available. Aside from using published collections, national archives or military archives of the various belligerent nations are often the best starting point for research. Most have easily navigable websites and searchable catalogues, often with links to digitised material, and archival staff can be wonderfully helpful.

The value of these collections to the researcher of battle is obvious. They give unique insights into the information being passed up and down the chain of command, the intentions of the commanders on either side, the movements and actions of different units, and the casualties they suffered. From this we can begin to extrapolate the leadership, strength, cohesion and effectiveness of the armies, and to understand the losses occasioned in men and materiel. There are of course gaps in the record. Regimental war diaries can be frustratingly vague at times (understandably – in the thick of the action, one can imagine that the officers' attention was elsewhere), and surviving written battlefield orders will tend to explain a tactical plan, rather than reflect the actual ebbs and flows of battle. Despatches and reports are also frequently tailored to reflect well on the writer. This reminds us that these sources must come with a caveat. 'Official' does not equate to either accurate or truthful, and we still need to read formal records with a critical eye.

Muster Rolls, Pay Records, Supply

Administrative records rarely provide much information about the narrative of a specific battle, but can tell the researcher an enormous amount of information about the size of armies, their weaponry, supplies and infrastructural support. For much of the medieval and early modern period, the sources available on battle administration are varied but inconsistent, with records from the period being incomplete, lost or destroyed. However, in the most positive of cases, there is a rich body of administrative material available for the researcher. As these records were usually compiled by clerks – either on campaign themselves or in the seat of government – many are likely to be located in national archives or central repositories of state documents.[4] While these records are an excellent – and underused – corpus of resources, they can present some challenges for researchers. Few are published or in translation, and therefore may require skills of palaeography or language to access, particularly those dating from the medieval period.

These records include memoranda on supplies, horses, and equipment, especially weaponry. Most of these records are simply lists of purchase orders for an entire campaign, which do not provide much detail on a particular battle but can nevertheless be used to extrapolate information about key confrontations – as Anne Curry and others have done with their reassessment of the English arrow volleys at Agincourt, based on arrow supplies for the campaign.[5]

These records also include details on combatant numbers and identities: garrison and muster rolls, and pay records. Many of these for the later medieval period have been collated, for example in the 'Soldier in Later Medieval England' project, whose database contains details of combatants serving in English armies between 1369 and 1453.[6] However, the researcher must be wary of using these records as evidence of battle participation: we do not know that these soldiers actually fought in battle, only that they were paid to be there – and of course, many individuals' names may not have been entered on lists of combatants, for instance if they were members of larger retinues.

Researchers can continue to use pay and muster records to explore the size and composition of armies into the eighteenth century and beyond. Since the nineteenth century, the bureaucracies of Europe have generally kept excellent records of the men enlisted in their armies, which include not only names but places of birth, domicile, previous occupation, and often a brief physical description. Many of these records are available to view in national or military archives. In the case of Napoleon's army, for example, the majority of these records have been scanned and made available online, providing a vast (and as yet underused) resource for researchers.[7] These particular records also provide a history of service for each enlisted man, complete with date and cause of their discharge from the unit (including death, illness, capture, desertion, or, occasionally, retirement). While such records are a little cumbersome for understanding the overall size and composition of an entire army, they can offer an interesting 'microhistorical' approach to a battle.

Administrative records for the twentieth and twenty-first centuries are far more detailed, and many have been put online and are searchable through military archives, museum records, and genealogical databases. The most recent records, however, will be inaccessible to researchers due to privacy and secrecy legislation.

Visual Sources

Alongside written descriptions of battle, images can tell the researcher a lot about the combats of the past – particularly details of weaponry, terrain, and the atmosphere of battle. Visual sources include artworks, statuary, memorials, photographs and film, and many are accessible through museums, collections, or online repositories. However, many remain in private hands or personal collections and access to these may be limited.

Visual representations of battle in the medieval and early modern periods were meant to tell stories. They often focused on individuals, crucial moments in battle, or the glorification of victory. Their illustrative function therefore depended heavily on the story that their creator wished to tell, whether reflecting military triumph as in the Armada portrait of Elizabeth I, or the eleventh-century Bayeux tapestry; heroic leadership as in the portrait of *Louis XIV with his Staff at the Siege of Cambrai* attributed to the studio of Adam-François van der Meulen (c.1680); or moralising criticism of war as evident in Pieter Bruegel the Elder's *Massacre of the Innocents* (1565–7). The researcher must therefore take pains to investigate the creator of these visual sources in order to assess how best to use their work. The novel information on specific battles provided in visual sources is often relatively small, and depictions of armour, weaponry and terrain vary in accuracy, so such representations are often best used in conjunction with written accounts or other sources.

The development of photography has given researchers new insights into battle. Quite simply, it allows us to visualise elements of battle as it actually was, which in many cases can be worth more than the proverbial thousand words. Still photographs can be used to view snapshots of battlefield terrain, the soldiers involved, their equipment and weaponry, and occasionally their experiences. Early photographs tend to focus on post-combat scenes, such as the famous images of casualties at Gettysburg or Spion Kop, but nineteenth-century 'in action' pictures are almost universally staged, and do little to show the realities of battle. Later photographs, especially from the First World War and beyond, do more to capture the dynamism of combat.

The battlefield of the twentieth century is also uniquely accessible to researchers through film. Film imagery of battle is often sanitised and moments of actual fighting on camera are relatively rare, but the footage can give insights into soldiers' morale and emotions, how they manoeuvred or used their weapons, or how their equipment affected combat performance. Photography and film can be a fascinating resource, especially for detail not evident from official sources or written accounts, although they will rarely give a full or balanced overview of a battle.

Much of the available footage originates from official photographers or filmmakers, or from newsreels. In 1916, the British army actually invited filmmakers to document the opening moves of the Battle of the Somme.[8] Second World War newsreels often contained live-action footage, and researchers can benefit from hours of such source material, much of it now digitised and available online, for example from British Pathé or United Newsreels. Conflicts of the later twentieth century tend to be well documented in visual imagery, often by reporters or film crews officially sanctioned by the military and allowed access to the front lines. The rise of the television documentary has also led to the creation of thousands of hours of recorded reminiscences from soldiers and civilians involved in conflicts, providing another hugely valuable resource.

Artefacts

Artefact resources include any physical remnants of battles or equipment used in them. Some of these are found in museums or private collections; others are uncovered in situ as archaeological finds.

Weapons of course provide invaluable information for the researcher of the technology of battle. A study of the physical artefacts can provide detail on the destructive capacity of weapons; their composition and durability; their reach and range; and their penetrative power and accuracy. Armour and equipment remains provide insight into the level of protection available and actually attained during combat. Weapons and equipment also provide crucial insight into the combatants themselves: their physical size and strength, and the nature of injuries that they might have suffered. Weapons in their original state – from swords to tanks and aircraft – can be examined in collections and museums across the globe. Where the provenance of these objects is known, they can be used to gain an in-depth understanding of the tools of combat. Remains of weaponry may also be found on battlefields from all periods, from bodkins at Crécy to twentieth-century ordnance in the fields of northern France. Archaeological surveys of battles can provide key details regarding the location, intensity and scale of fighting, and can fill in gaps in museum collections by placing the weapons into their battlefield context.

The deadly impact of these weapons can of course be observed on skeletal remains. An analysis of these can give ideas of the age, physical stature, likely profession, and even diet of men killed in the battle. An assessment of wound patterns can also be used to extrapolate information about weaponry, armour, tactics and training. However, while skeletal remains can tell us much about the general realities of warfare, they rarely tell us much about the events or narrative of a specific battle. Assessment of an individual skeleton leaves an enormous amount regarding the combat down to interpretation. For the researcher, archaeological reports on skeletal remains are most effectively used in conjunction with surviving records or other artefacts.

Battlefields

While narratives, accounts and artefacts tell us a great deal, the battlefield itself remains a useful source for the study of combat. While chapter four explored how terrain could affect the outcome of battle, it is also worth considering how we might look at sites of battle as a source to try to put together a fuller picture of events.

The first order of business in using battlefields as a source is finding where a battle took place. Pinning down the location is important as it allows us to gain an understanding of the wider context of a battle: not only topography (more on that below) but its strategic location near roads, rivers, cities, or other sites of importance; the general climate of the area; and any conditions that might impact the advance, retreat, reinforcement, or resupply of either force. In some cases, identifying a battle site is straightforward: the field of Waterloo, for example, became famous with tourists almost as soon as the smoke cleared. In other cases, tracking down the cockpit of combat can be more difficult. To take one extreme example, the site of the Battle of Brunanburh (937) remains a mystery, despite being arguably the most important British military event in the centuries before the Conquest, with suggestions of its location ranging from the Wirral to County Durham, Lancashire, Yorkshire, and southern Scotland.

Locating an elusive battlefield is largely only possible through the triangulation of a variety of sources, such as written accounts, archaeological finds, churchyard burials, contemporary memorialisation, or, if you are exceptionally lucky, contemporary maps. Even with such information, however, pinpointing the exact location of action can be difficult, as evidenced by the lengthy debates over the site of the Battle of Bosworth (1485) – with the general consensus now being that the expensively constructed battlefield visitors' centre is some way from the actual battle site.

Fortunately, there is relatively extensive secondary evidence available detailing the sites of many battles, often including thorough maps and surveys, which can prove extremely valuable starting points in a battlefield analysis. In Britain, for example, the Battlefields Trust works to conserve and explore the country's battlefields, and publishes useful survey information.[9] In some cases, archaeological reports can also offer additional unique insights – which is discussed in more detail in the 'artefacts' section above.

An examination of the physical battlefield can also prove fruitful for understanding a battle. Perhaps most importantly, the terrain of the battlefield can be used to understand the relative positions of the respective armies. Even when there has been sometimes quite significant change in the landscape, a battlefield can afford us an impression of the key contours of terrain and strategic strongpoints: high ground, natural features that could anchor a flank or mask an attack, rivers or bodies of water that, depending on conditions, could act as barriers, avenues of transport, or sources of hydration. Where a battlefield remains largely untouched, it is through a study of the terrain that we are best able to understand lines of sight, folds in the ground, areas of exposure or concealment, fields of fire, and the gradients of sloping ground. This can help us to assess command decisions, or evaluate the difficulties faced by troops in carrying or holding their objectives. While some of these issues could also be assessed from a map, the battlefield itself allows the researcher to grasp them with greater clarity. A map may tell us that there is a slope; but only the battlefield can tell us how firm or soft, rocky or smooth, constant or changeable that slope might be. It is also only by visiting the terrain that the researcher can better understand the acoustics of a battlefield, should that seem relevant to their analysis.

The basic composition of the ground is another point of interest. Although again we would need to take into account any changes in climate or land use since the battle, a site visit can give clues as to whether the ground underfoot was mostly soil, sand, clay, rock, or other material – which will help with any analysis of aspects such as movement, field fortification, or the likely effects of artillery bombardment. A site visit may also give a broad impression of climatic conditions or, if necessary, give an insight into the local flora – although the researcher would have to take into account the sometimes significant climatic changes over the past millennium.

Change is indeed the biggest drawback of using the physical landscape. While documents and artefacts exist in a form of stasis, the battlefield is subject to erosion, enclosure, development or, in some cases, deliberate alteration (the building of the Lion Mound at Waterloo, which required the defacing of much of Wellington's ridge, springs to mind). The researcher must proceed with care, and if possible should try to ascertain just how much any battlefield has changed before committing to it as a source. But even with this in mind, there is much that they can still tell us.

Afterword: Understanding Battle

How then can we understand a battle? How can we explain why a combat turns out the way it does, why one side is a victor, why another is vanquished? There is clearly no formula; neither numbers nor training, tactics nor technology can guarantee victory. It may seem odd to conclude a book with questions, but the aim of this work has always been to prompt enquiry. There are common themes that this book has explored that can be used to analyse any battle, to help throw some light on proceedings. Every battle is, of course, different. Battles within the same war or campaign can differ markedly – in fact, even clashes within the same battle can have widely different outcomes. It is almost never any single factor that determines the outcome of a battle, but the interplay of myriad details that we can often only begin to unpick.

When approaching the study of battle, it is always worth thinking of our sources of information. What do we know about the battle, and how do we know it? How do historians know what they claim to know? If possible, it can be useful (and always fascinating!) to go back to the primary sources – the accounts of men and women present on the field of combat whose words tell us something of what they saw, thought, and felt. We can read the dispatches and reports of generals, or the semi-literate reminiscences of the lowest of private soldiers; all will illuminate something of the battle. Such sources allow us, albeit in a distant way, to meet those who actually took part in the object of our study.

We can also step back a little and look at the bigger picture. What were these societies that were going to war, and why did they think fighting was worthwhile? Who did they choose to fight for them, and why? What values or codes would be likely to influence their men – or women – on the battlefield? We can ponder how each society viewed its soldiers, how it organised them, and how it armed them. In this we might stray into considerations of grand strategy – to what end did the country or society arm soldiers, and how would that help it achieve its aims? For the 'why' of it, we can stroll a little further down the path of strategy: what were the political or grand strategic events leading up to the specific conflict? What pressures or influences were brought to bear to make the armies want to fight? For some battles these issues might not seem too relevant, but for most there are grains of knowledge that can add to our understanding of why people, armies or machines acted the way they did in combat.

Zooming in from the bigger picture to the theatre of operations, we really should consider the armies that are to do battle – their numbers, organisation and command structures certainly, but also their training, cohesion, equipment and professional ethos. We can think about the condition of the troops as they prepare to fight, supplied perhaps by logistics networks and non-combatants attached to the army: are they fed, watered and well-clad; sheltered or exposed; rested or exhausted? And we can further contemplate the effect that this might have on the bodies and minds of soldiers going into combat; slowness of movement or thought, increased brittleness of spirit, and a greater likelihood of mistakes all accrue from hunger, fatigue or cold. An army marches on its stomach, as Napoleon famously said – and so too does it fight. The condition of animals we should consider too. Horses are almost ubiquitous in battle until the mid-twentieth century, either as beasts of burden or mounts for cavalry, and their health or weariness can impact their use.

And while we are here with the army, around its campfires, examining its food and clothing, we can take note of the soldiers' emotions. How do they feel on the eve of battle? What motivates them to fight? How is their morale? Have they been into battle before? Will the morrow bring entirely new terrors, or have they already been into battle too often; are they all-too familiar with the horrors to come? Writers too frequently treat soldiers as automata, as things to be moved around a battlefield. Perhaps in our consideration of society we find that the soldiers *would* act like automata, because of their social conditioning – but more probably not.

Staying with the army, we can cast an eye over the weapons that they carry and armour they use – and importantly, compare these to the tools of their enemy. A swordsman is a battle-winning weapon if fighting people armed with sticks and rocks; he is not so handy against a machine gun. Weapon types and combinations are important. We can try to calculate the theoretical lethality of the weapons, but we should also consider the condition of the actual pieces to be carried into combat. Are they well maintained or not? Are blades sharpened, moving parts oiled, and mechanisms checked – have the mechanics and armourers done their jobs? Have the logistics networks ensured that there is enough ammunition for bows or firearms, and if not, can the deficiency be remedied? Have political failures starved the army of supplies, or has the task of moving food and munitions and all the other paraphernalia of combat simply proved too much for the supply train? We can also consider how appropriate the weapons are to the soldiers we have just examined; do they have the strength and the skill to wield their tools of war, or at least to wield them better than the enemy?

The weapons that the army has at its disposal will naturally affect how it lines up to fight. And when we see the army arrayed for battle, it is worth pausing to think of whether the formations and tactical systems adopted are really appropriate for the troops and weaponry on offer. The grand tactics are important; where are the forces concentrated, are they in position to attack or defend, are the army's flanks covered, and do they have clear lines of advance or retreat? And will these dispositions actually allow them to strike effectively at the enemy? Yet too often histories are written of grand tactics – a division did this, or a corps did that – without focusing in on the actual tactics used at small unit level (should our battle have small units) to bring the weapons to bear on the enemy. Such minor tactical detail is not always available to us, especially in lesser-known or lesser-recorded clashes, but is nevertheless important. Our consideration of an army's organisation, doctrine and training can be useful here, as it will give us some idea of what an army is structured to do, what it should do, and what it can actually do.

Tactics will also be heavily affected by the terrain on which the battle is fought; good tactics are those that make best use of weapons in the landscape of the battlefield to affect the enemy. And it is worth pausing for more than a cursory glance at that landscape. Key features must be noted – high ground, water, woodlands and so on – but the nature of the ground itself is important. Wet or dry, sandy or boggy, can make a big difference to movement, the effect of weapons, and even visibility. Such considerations of course go hand in glove with the prevailing conditions; it is always important to glance upwards at the weather, as well as considering general climatological data, as these factors can affect ground conditions, weapon performance, visibility, carry of sound, the effect of smoke, rapidity of troops tiring, and a host of other vital issues.

Of course, good commanders will have taken all of this into account when making their dispositions, and in our consideration of a battle we should assess the qualities of the men or women leading the forces before us. Their professional skill is important: are they experienced or green, respected or reviled, a frontline fighter or chateau commander? Are they used to commanding a force of this size or complexity, or is it all rather new? Their personality is equally important: rash or cautious, ambitious or coy, bombastic or open to advice, a general's personality will inevitably intrude on their command. But our leader is just one person – and we must consider how their orders are passed down the chain of command, if indeed such a chain exists. Here again we return to army organisation, and perhaps must consider influences of political thinking and social hierarchies in understanding whether, how, and how effectively an army is staffed.

But the troops are now moving, the battle is engaged. We now understand how it came to this point; we have a good idea of the conditions of the armies, their weapons and equipment; we have given the general and perhaps his staff a thorough examination, and have critiqued his formations and their appropriateness to weapons and weather and landscape. But now the action commences, perhaps punctuated by thuds of cannon, almost certainly pierced by screams of the wounded and dying. We must try to understand why one army will win, and why the other will run. We see the troops moving forward towards the enemy, and we notice those who lead them. Junior officers or NCOs, or perhaps men who command through social rather than formal military status. How well do they inspire, and motivate, and lead by example? How do they manoeuvre, and how do they react to tactical changes? Are the formations rigid, awaiting orders, or do soldiers show initiative? Is the army organised to allow that? Do some men inspire their comrades, or do they, as a group, start to shy away? And now the clash of arms is upon us; weapon on weapon, soldier on soldier. Why do some stand and some run? Why do some triumph and some fall?

Perhaps our sources will tell us. From historians' works to military reports, soldiers' accounts or civilian records, to the battlefields and artefacts of battle themselves, combat has left a trail of information for us to follow. Perhaps we will pick up hints of an answer when these sources discuss tactics or weapons, or the terrain on which battle was fought, or the conditions of the day, or the influence of leaders, or the state of troops' morale, or their physical condition. But in truth, all of these factors are vital to understanding the nature of the clash, to understanding why soldiers fight or flee, live or die; fundamentally, to understanding battle.

Notes

Introduction
1. Sidney Rogerson, *Twelve Days on the Somme* (Barnsley, 2020), p.60.
2. Jean Froissart, *Chronicles*, ed. & trans. Geoffrey Brereton (London, 1978), p.87.
3. John Keegan, *The Face of Battle* (2nd edn., London, 2014), p.97.
4. William Russell, *The Great War with Russia* (London, 1895), p.138.
5. Russell, *Great War*, p.169.

Chapter 1: Society
1. Olivier de Laborderie, J.R. Maddicott & D.A. Carpenter, 'The Last Hours of Simon de Montfort', *The English Historical Review*, 115:461 (2000), p.410.
2. Erin Finley, *Fields of Combat* (Ithaca, 2011), p.23.
3. John Keegan, *A History of Warfare* (London, 2004), p.227.
4. V.L. Ménage, 'Some Notes on the Devshirme', *Bulletin of the SOAS*, 29:1 (1966), p.72.
5. Gregory Liebau, 'Barbarossa and his Bishops', *Medieval Warfare*, 3:2 (2013), p.15.
6. Philippe Contamine, *War in the Middle Ages* (Oxford, 1984), pp.77–80.
7. *Calendar of Close Rolls, Edward III: Volume 11, 1360–1364*, ed. H.C. Maxwell Lyte (London, 1909), pp.534–5.
8. Clifford Rogers, 'Tactics and the Face of Battle', *European Warfare 1350–1750*, eds. Frank Tallett & D.J.B. Trim (Cambridge, 2010), p.206.
9. Contamine, *War*, p.80.
10. Elizabeth Longford, *Wellington: the Years of the Sword* (New York, 1969), pp.321–2.
11. Tom Hickman, *The Call-Up* (London, 2005), p.232.
12. Max Arthur (ed.), *Forgotten Voices of the Great War* (London, 2002), p.135.
13. J.M. Winter & Antoine Prost, *The Great War in History* (Cambridge, 2005), p.94.
14. *The Somme Times* (31 July 1916), p.2.
15. Max Arthur (ed.), *Forgotten Voices of the Second World War* (London, 2005), p.161.
16. Arthur (ed.) *Forgotten Voices of the Second World War*, p.210.
17. Liebau, 'Barbarossa and his Bishops', pp.14–15; Michael Prestwich, *Armies and Warfare in the Middle Ages* (New Haven, 1996), p.168.
18. Ron Hassner, *Religion on the Battlefield* (Ithaca, 2016), p.53.
19. Cousinot, *Chronique de la Pucelle*, ed. M. Vallée de Viriville (Paris, 1864), p.296.
20. Matthew Bennett, 'Legality and Legitimacy in War and its Conduct, 1350–1650', *European Warfare*, eds. Tallett & Trim, p.265.
21. Rory Cox, 'A Law of War? English Protection and Destruction of Ecclesiastical Property during the Fourteenth Century', *The English Historical Review*, 128:535 (2013), pp.1381–417.
22. Michael Glover, *The Peninsular War* (London, 2001), p.187.
23. *Flores Historiarum*, ed. H.R. Luard (3 vols; Rolls Series, 1890), vol.2, p.481.
24. D.A. Carpenter, 'Simon de Montfort: the First Leader of a Political Movement in English History', *History*, 76:246 (1991), p.4.

25. William Rishanger, 'Cronicon de Duobus Bellis de Lewes et Evesham', *Ypodigma Neustriae*, ed. H.T. Riley (London, 1876), p.539.
26. *Calendar of Close Rolls, Henry III: Volume 13, 1264–1268*, ed. A.E. Stamp (London, 1937), pp.124–5.
27. de Laborderie et al., 'Last Hours', p.410.
28. *The Song of Lewes*, ed. C.L. Kingsford (Oxford, 1890), 1.370; Rishanger, 'Chronicon', p.543.
29. Carpenter, 'Simon de Montfort', p.14.
30. F.M. Powicke, *King Henry III and The Lord Edward* (2 vols; Oxford, 1947), vol.2, p.484.
31. de Laborderie et al., 'Last Hours', p.411.
32. C.S. Watkins, *History and the Supernatural in Medieval England* (Cambridge, 2007), p.48.
33. de Laborderie et al., 'Last Hours', p.411.
34. de Laborderie et al., 'Last Hours', p.411.
35. D.A. Carpenter, 'A Noble in Politics', *Nobles and Nobility in Medieval Europe* ed. A.J. Duggan (Woodbridge, 2002), p.201.
36. M. Strickland, *War and Chivalry* (Cambridge, 1996), p.185.
37. Pierre Langtoft, *The Chronicle of Pierre de Langtoft*, ed. Thomas Wright (2 vols; London, 1868), vol.2, pp.144–5.
38. *The Metrical Chronicle of Robert of Gloucester*, ed. W.A. Wright (London, 1887), 1.736.
39. de Laborderie et al., 'Last Hours', p.412.
40. Stephen Miller, 'The British Way of War', *Journal of Military History*, 77:4 (2013), p.1332.
41. Miller, 'British Way of War', p.1336.
42. Eliza Riedi, 'The Women Pro-Boers', *Historical Research*, 86:213 (2013), pp.92–115.
43. *Manchester Guardian* (3 January 1900).
44. Vanessa Heggie, 'Lies, Damn Lies, and Manchester's Recruiting Statistics', *Journal of History of Medicine*, 63:2 (2008), pp.179–82.
45. Thomas Pakenham, *The Boer War* (London, 1992), p.248
46. Spencer Jones, 'Shooting Power: A Study of the Effectiveness of Boer and British Rifle Fire, 1899–1914', *British Journal for Military History*, 1:1 (2014), p.32.
47. Hugh Rethman, *The Natal Campaign* (Stroud, 2017), p.69.
48. Jones, 'Shooting Power', p.37.
49. Jones, 'Shooting Power', p.35.
50. S. Attridge, *Nationalism, Imperialism and Identity in Late Victorian Culture* (Basingstoke, 2003), p.2.
51. Miller, 'British Way of War', p.1336.
52. Rethman, *The Natal Campaign*, pp.226–7.
53. Pakenham, *Boer War*, pp.235–6.
54. Pakenham, *Boer War*, p.230.

Chapter 2: Grand Strategy and Politics
1. Carl von Clausewitz, *On War*, trans. Michael Howard & Peter Paret (Princeton, 2008), p.87.
2. Wolfgang Schivelbusch, *The Culture of Defeat* (London, 2004), pp.14–15.
3. Harry Summers, *American Strategy in Vietnam* (Mineola, 2012), p.1.
4. Paddy Griffith, *Forward Into Battle* (New York, 1990), p.68.
5. Linda Racioppi, *Soviet Policy Towards South Asia Since 1970* (Cambridge, 1994), pp.114–15.
6. Geoffrey Hoskins, *A History of the Soviet Union* (London, 1992), pp.454–5.
7. Michael Glover, *Wellington as a Military Commander* (London, 1973), p.79.

8. *The Dispatches of Field Marshal the Duke of Wellington* (8 vols, London, 1844–7), vol.3, p.812.
9. Christopher Duffy, *The Military Experience in the Age of Reason* (Ware, 1998), p.250.
10. Frank McLynn, *Napoleon* (London, 1998), p.558.
11. John Grehan & Martin Mace (eds), *The BEF in France* (Barnsley, 2014), p.106.
12. Duffy, *Military Experience*, pp.189–90.
13. John Keegan, *The First World War* (London, 1999), p.300.
14. Keegan, *First World War*, pp.300–301.
15. Jacques Frémeaux & Bruno Reis, 'French Counterinsurgency', *Insurgencies and Counterinsurgencies*, eds. Beatrice Heuser & Eitan Shamir (Cambridge, 2016), pp.63–5.
16. Neville Lawley, *The Battle of Marston Moor* (Uckfield, n.d.), p.23.
17. William Seymour, *Battles in Britain: Volume II, 1642–1746* (Ware, 1997), p.88.
18. *A Letter from Generall Leven, the Lord Fairfax, and the Earl of Manchester; To the Committee of Both Kingdoms* (London, 1644), p.3.
19. Simeon Ash, *A Continuation of True Intelligence from the English and Scottish Forces in the North* (London, 1644), p.3
20. Seymour, *Battles*, p.87.
21. Lawley, *Marston Moor*, p.21.
22. *Letter from Generall Leven*, p.4.
23. Lion Watson, *A More Exact Relation of the Late Battell Neer York* (London, 1644), pp.4–5; *Letter from Generall Leven*, p.4.
24. Watson, *A More Exact Relation*, p,7.

Chapter 3: Leadership
1. Dwight D. Eisenhower, *The President's News Conference*, 14 November 1956.
2. Keith Stewart, 'The Evolution of Command Approach', paper presented at the International Command and Control Research and Technology Symposium, Santa Monica (June 2010), p.4.
3. Correlli Barnett, *The Lords of War: From Lincoln to Churchill* (London, 2012), p.229.
4. Christopher Duffy, *The Military Experience in the Age of Reason* (Ware, 1998), p.244.
5. Andrew Roberts, *Leadership in War* (London, 2019), p.14.
6. General James Mattis to 1st Marine Division, 'Commanding General's Message To All Hands', March 2003.
7. Cathal Nolan, *The Allure of Battle* (New York, 2017), p.150.
8. *The Life and Campaigns of the Black Prince*, ed. & trans. Richard Barber (Woodbridge, 1986), p.77.
9. John Steane, *The Archaeology of the Medieval English Monarchy* (London, 2004), p.35.
10. Nolan, *Allure of Battle*, p.152.
11. John Grehan & Martin Mace (eds.), *The BEF in France* (Barnsley, 2014), p.107.
12. Marc Morris, *A Great and Terrible King* (London, 2008), p.303.
13. *The Chronicle of Walter of Guisborough*, ed. H. Rothwell (London, 1957), p.299.
14. The National Archives (London), WO 158/234, Orders 22 June 1916.
15. Alan Clark, *The Donkeys* (London, 1961).
16. John Keegan, *The First World War* (London, 1999), p.314.
17. John Keegan, *The Face of Battle* (2nd edn.; London, 2014), p.222.

Chapter 4: Conditions of Landscape
1. Katrin Möbius & Sascha Möbius, *Prussian Army Soldiers and the Seven Years' War* (London, 2019), p.50.
2. J.W. Castellani et al, 'Cardiovascular and Thermal Strain During 3–4 days of a Metabolically Demanding Cold-Weather Military Operation', *Extrem Physiol Med*, 6:2 (2017).

3. Alan Forrest, *Conscripts and Deserters* (Oxford, 1989), p.68.
4. Frank McLynn, *1066: The Year of the Three Battles* (London, 2011), p.194.
5. Kelly DeVries, 'The Implications of the *Anonimo Romano* Account of the Battle of Crécy', *The Medieval Way of War*, ed. Gregory Halfond (London, 2015), pp.309–22.
6. Max Arthur (ed.), *Forgotten Voices of the Great War* (London, 2002), pp.236–7.
7. Donald Olsen et al., 'Perfect Tide, Ideal Moon: an Unappreciated Aspect of Wolfe's Generalship at Quebec, 1759', *William and Mary Quarterly*, 59:4 (2002), pp.957–74.
8. Carl von Clausewitz, *On War*, trans. Michael Howard & Peter Paret (Princeton, 1989), p.348.
9. With Prussians on higher ground surrounding the French army at Sedan in 1870, French General Ducrot complained, '*nous sommes dans un pot de chambre, et nous y serons emmerdés*' (we're in a chamber pot and we're going to get shit on).
10. Kelly DeVries, 'Implications', pp.316–17.
11. *The Carmen de Hastingae Proelio of Guy, Bishop of Amiens* ed. & trans. Frank Barlow (Oxford, 1999), p.5.
12. C. Grainge & G. Grainge, 'The Pevensey Expedition: Brilliantly Executed Plan or Near Disaster?', *The Battle of Hastings: Sources and Interpretations*, ed. S. Morillo (Woodbridge, 1996), p.142.
13. *The Gesta Guillelmi of William of Poitiers*, trans. R.H.C. Davis & Marjorie Chibnall (Oxford, 1998), pp.126–7.
14. Christopher Hewitt, *The Battle of Hastings: A Geographic Perspective* (2016). Electronic Thesis and Dissertation Repository. 3628. https://ir.lib.uwo.ca/etd/3628, p.181.
15. Hewitt, *Geographic Perspective*, p.210.
16. *Gesta Guillelmi*, p.129.
17. S. Morillo, *The Battle of Hastings: Sources and Interpretations* (Woodbridge, 1996), pp.xxviii–xxix.
18. *The Chronicle of Battle Abbey*, trans. E. Searle (Oxford, 1980), p.39.
19. *Henry, Archdeacon of Huntingdon Historia Anglorum: The History of the English People*, trans. D. Greenway (Oxford, 1996), p.395.
20. *Carmen de Hastingae*, p.31.
21. James Marshall-Cornwall, *Napoleon as a Military Commander* (New York, 1998), p.145.
22. David Gates, *The Napoleonic Wars 1803–1815* (London, 2003), pp.28–9.
23. David Chandler, *The Campaigns of Napoleon* (London, 1966), p.424.
24. Chandler, *Campaigns of Napoleon*, pp.430–1.

Chapter 5: Tactics
1. Quoted in Herman Hattaway, *Reflections of a Civil War Historian* (Columbia, 2004), p.200.
2. Brent Nosworthy, *Battle Tactics of Napoleon and his Enemies* (London, 1997), p.xvii.
3. Stephen Biddle, *Military Power: Explaining Victory and Defeat in Modern Battle* (Princeton, 2006), p.5.
4. Stephen Morillo, *Warfare under the Anglo-Norman Kings, 1066–1135* (Woodbridge, 1994), pp.169–70.
5. Paul Hill, *The Norman Commanders* (Barnsley, 2015), pp.142–3.
6. David Caldwell, 'Scottish Spearmen, 1298–1314', *War in History*, 19:3 (2012), p.280.
7. *The Chronicle of Geoffrey le Baker of Swinbrook*, trans. David Preest (Woodbridge, 2012), p.46.
8. Clifford Rogers, 'Edward III and the Dialectics of Strategy, 1327–1360', *Transactions of the Royal Historical Society*, vol.4 (1994), p.89.
9. Clifford Rogers, 'Tactics and the Face of Battle', *European Warfare, 1350–1750*, eds. Frank Tallett & D.J.B. Trim (Cambridge, 2010), pp.205–10.

10. James Lucas, *War on the Eastern Front* (London, 2014), p.31.
11. Bernd Horn, *No Lack of Courage: Operation Medusa, Afghanistan*, EasyRead Large edn. (Toronto, 2010), p.110.
12. *Napoleon's Maxims of War* (New York, 1861), p.85.
13. Frederick II, *Military Instruction from the Late King of Prussia to His Generals*, trans. T. Foster (5th edn., London, 1818), p.49.
14. Christopher Duffy, *The Military Experience in the Age of Reason* (Ware, 1998), p.190.
15. Philippe Contamine, *War in the Middle Ages* (Oxford, 1984), p.231.
16. Rogers, 'Edward III', p.86.
17. Katrin Möbius & Sascha Möbius, *Prussian Army Soldiers and the Seven Years' War* (London, 2019), p.50.
18. Tamás Pálosfalvi, *From Nicopolis to Mohács* (Leiden, 2018), pp.61–3.
19. Amy Griffin, Bob Hall & Andrew Ross, 'The Australian Counterinsurgency Campaign in the Vietnam War: the Ambush Battle', *Journal of Maps*, 10:1 (2014), p.61.
20. Robert Wolff & Harry Hazard, *A History of the Crusades* (Madison, 1969), vol.2, pp.301–302.
21. Max Hastings, *The Korean War* (New York, 1988), p.159.
22. Edwin Westrate, *Forward Observer* (Philadelphia, 1944), pp.109–17.
23. *Reaching Globally, Reaching Powerfully*, USAF Report (Washington, 1991), p.19; Kevin Kennedy, 'Stealth', *Naval War College Review*, 46:2 (1993), p.124.
24. *Reaching Globally*, p.21.
25. Bevin Alexander, *How Great Generals Win* (New York, 1993), p.306.
26. Tito Livio Frulovisi, 'Vita Henrici Quinti', *The Battle of Agincourt. Sources and Interpretations*, ed. Anne Curry (Woodbridge, 2000), p.62.
27. Kelly DeVries, 'Catapults are not Atomic Bombs', *War in History*, 4:4 (1997), pp.545–70.
28. Anne Curry, *Agincourt: A New History* (Stroud, 2010), p.228.
29. Christopher Phillpotts, 'The French Plan of Battle During the Agincourt Campaign', *The English Historical Review*, 99:390 (1984), p.60.
30. Curry, *Agincourt*, p.233.
31. John Keegan, *The Face of Battle* (2nd edn., London, 2014), p.79.
32. Pierre Cochon, 'Chronique Normande', *Battle of Agincourt*, ed. Curry, p.113.
33. Le Religieux de Saint-Denis, 'Histoire de Charles VI', *Battle of Agincourt*, ed. Curry, p.106.
34. Saint-Denis, 'Histoire de Charles VI', pp.106–107.
35. Anonymous, 'The Brut', *Battle of Agincourt*, ed. Curry, p.92.
36. Anne Curry, *Great Battles: Agincourt* (Oxford, 2015).
37. Keegan, *Face of Battle*, p.83.
38. Saint-Denis, 'Histoire de Charles VI', p.107.
39. 'Gesta Henrici Quinti', *Battle of Agincourt*, ed. Curry, p.37.
40. 'Gesta Henrici Quinti', p.37.
41. Adam Day, 'Operation Medusa: The Battle for Panjwai', *Legion Magazine* (2007), https://legionmagazine.com/en/2007/09/operation-medusa-the-battle-for-panjwai/.
42. Andrew Feickert, *U.S. and Coalition Military Operations in Afghanistan: Issues for Congress* (December 2006), p.3.
43. Horn, *No Lack of Courage*, p.29.
44. Horn, *No Lack of Courage*, p.39.
45. Horn, *No Lack of Courage*, p.125.
46. Horn, *No Lack of Courage*, pp.110–11.
47. Kenneth Finlayson & David Meyer, 'Operation Medusa', *Veritas*, 3:4 (2007).
48. Horn, *No Lack of Courage*, p.136.

49. Feickert, *Military Operations*, p.4.

Chapter 6: Logistics
1. Ernest King, *First Report to the Secretary of the Navy* (Washington, 1946), p.34.
2. S. Attridge, *Nationalism, Imperialism and Identity in Late Victorian Culture* (Basingstoke, 2003), p.2.
3. H.J. Hewitt, *The Organisation of War under Edward III* (2nd edn; Barnsley, 2004), pp.65–6.
4. Michael Prestwich, *Armies and Warfare in the Middle Ages* (New Haven, 1999), p.119.
5. Geoff Mortimer, *Eyewitness Accounts of the Thirty Years War 1618–48* (Basingstoke, 2002), p.57.
6. Prestwich, *Armies and Warfare*, p.254.
7. 'Gesta Henrici Quinti', *The Battle of Agincourt: Sources and Interpretations*, ed. Anne Curry (Woodbridge, 2000), p.33.
8. David Chandler, *The Campaigns of Napoleon* (London, 1966), p.386.
9. Jean-Roch Coignet, *The Notebooks of Captain Coignet* (Barnsley, 2016), p.120.
10. Walter Scott Dunn, *The Soviet Economy and the Red Army, 1930–1945* (Westport, 1995), p.225.
11. Dunn, *Soviet Economy*, p.229.
12. Bernard Bachrach, 'On the Origins of William the Conqueror's Horse Transports', *Technology and Culture*, 26:3 (1985), pp.505–31.
13. Martin van Creveld, *Supplying War* (2nd edn.; Cambridge, 2004), p.111.
14. Van Creveld, *Supplying War*, p.255.
15. Office of the Under Secretary of Defence (Comptroller) / Chief Financial Officer, *Program Acquisition Cost by Weapon System* (February 2020), p.6.
16. Zhang Hui, 'PLA Tibet Military Command Adopts Drones for Logistics Support', *Global Times* (11 September 2020).
17. J.S. Miselli, 'The View from my Windshield: Just-in-Time Logistics Just Isn't Working', *Armor*, 112:4 (2003), pp.11–12.
18. Timothy Carter & Daniel Veale, 'Weather, Terrain and Warfare: Coalition Fatalities in Afghanistan', *Conflict Management and Peace Science*, 30:3 (2013), p.222.
19. Van Creveld, *Supplying War*, pp.199–200.
20. Rhys Crawley, *Climax at Gallipoli* (Norman, 2014), p.364.
21. T.H.E. Travers, 'Command and Leadership Styles in the British Army: The 1915 Gallipoli Model', *Journal of Contemporary History*, 29:3 (1994), pp.403–42.
22. Peter Antill, 'Defence Logistics: an Historical Perspective', *Defence Logistics*, ed. Jeremy Smith (London, 2018), p.45.
23. D.A. Fulghum, 'Bomb Shortage Crimps Air War', *Aviation Week and Space Technology*, 150:18 (1999), p.22.
24. John France, 'The Battle of Carcano', *War in History*, 6:3 (1999), p.254.
25. 'Foe in Vietnam Blows Up Another Munitions Depot', *New York Times* (15 August 1972), p.3.
26. C.P. Melville & M.C. Lyons, 'Saladin's Hattin Letter', *The Horns of Hattin*, ed. B.Z. Kedar (Jerusalem, 1992), p.211.
27. Imad al-Din, *Conquête de la Syrie et de la Palestine par Saladin*, trans. H. Massé (Paris, 1972), pp.25–6.
28. *Chronique d'Ernoul*, ed. M.L. de Mas Latrie (Paris, 1871), pp.43–4.
29. John France, *Hattin* (Oxford, 2015), p.92.
30. Eracles, 'L'Estoire de Eracles Empereur et la Conqueste de la Terre d'Outremer', *Recuil des Historiens des Croisades* (Paris, 1859), vol.2, pp.62–5.

31. Antony Beevor, *Stalingrad* (London, 2007), p.44.
32. Joel Hayward, *Stopped at Stalingrad* (Lawrence, 1998), p.183.
33. Beevor, *Stalingrad*, p.97.
34. Hayward, *Stopped at Stalingrad*, p.184.
35. Beevor, *Stalingrad*, p.147.
36. John Erikson, *The Road to Stalingrad* (Boulder, 1984), p.392.
37. Erikson, *Road to Stalingrad*, pp.411–12.
38. Beevor, *Stalingrad*, p.182.
39. Robert Kaplan, 'Medicine at the Battle of Stalingrad', *Journal of the Royal Society of Medicine*, 93 (2000), p.97.
40. Beevor, *Stalingrad*, p.204.
41. Beevor, *Stalingrad*, p.55.
42. Hayward, *Stopped at Stalingrad*, p.310.
43. Prit Buttar, *On a Knife's Edge* (Oxford, 2018), p.276.

Chapter 7: Weapons and Armour
1. Blaise de Montluc, *Commentaires de Messire Blaise de Montluc Mareschal de France* (Bordeaux, 1592), f.6r.
2. Gareth Williams, 'The Mace', *Medieval Warfare*, 4:4 (2014), pp.34–5.
3. Stanley Karnow, *Vietnam* (London, 1994), p.552.
4. Giovanni Villani, 'New Chronicle', *The Battle of Crécy. A Casebook*, eds. Michael Livingston & Kelly DeVries (Liverpool, 2015), p.119.
5. W. Mark Ormrod, *Edward III* (New Haven, 2012), p.279.
6. Sidney Rogerson, *Twelve Days on the Somme* (Barnsley, 2020), pp.6–7.
7. Rogerson, *Twelve Days*, p.52.
8. John Grehan & Martin Mace (eds.), *The BEF in France* (Barnsley, 2014), p.92.
9. Trevor Dupuy, 'Military Weaponry: How Lethal?', *Army*, 29:2 (1979), pp.23–7.
10. I.-D. Salavrakos, 'A Reassessment of the British and Allied Economic and Military Mobilization in the Revolutionary and Napoleonic Wars', *Res Militaris*, 7:1 (2017), p.4.
11. *Statistics of the Military Effort of the British Empire During the Great War, 1914–1920* (London, 1922), pp.358, 485.
12. John Keegan, *The Face of Battle* (2nd edn., London, 2014), p.275.
13. Trevor Dupuy, *Numbers, Predictions and War* (New York, 1979).
14. George Raudzens, 'War-Winning Weapons', *Journal of Military History*, 54:4 (1990), p.420.
15. Arthur Gullachsen, 'Destroying the Panthers', *Canadian Military History*, 25:2 (2016), pp.1–29.
16. Anthony Tucker-Jones, *The Iraq War* (Barnsley, 2014), p.82.
17. Edward Martin, 'Characteristics of the Future Battlefield and Deployment', *Strategies to Protect the Health of Deployed U.S. Forces: Workshop Proceedings, National Research Council* (2000), pp.26–7.
18. Harlan Ullman, 'Slogan or Strategy?: Shock and Awe Reassessed', *The National Interest*, 84 (2006), pp.43–9.
19. Gábor Ágoston, 'Firearms and Military Adaptation: The Ottomans and the European Military Revolution, 1450–1800', *Journal of World History*, 25:1 (2014), p.90.
20. Michel de Lombarès, 'Castillon (17 Juillet 1453), Dernière Bataille de la Guerre de Cent Ans, Première Victoire de l'Artillerie', *Revue Historique des Armées* (1976), pp.7–31.
21. Jean-Claude Brunner, 'The Halberd', *Medieval Warfare*, 3:5 (2013), p.40.
22. Erich Anderson, 'The Battle of Arbedo: The Rise of the Swiss Pike', *Medieval Warfare*, 2:3 (2012), p.22.

23. Walter Emil Kaegi, 'The Contribution of Archery to the Turkish Conquest of Anatolia', *Speculum*, 39:1 (1964), p.105.
24. Olivier Bangerter, 'The Swiss Pike', *Medieval Warfare*, 5:1 (2015), pp.46–8.
25. Desmond Seward, *The Hundred Years' War* (London, 2003), p.67.
26. Andrew Ayton, 'English Army at Crécy', *The Battle of Crécy, 1346*, eds. Andrew Ayton & Philip Preston (Woodbridge, 2005), pp.189–90.
27. Bertrand Schnerb, 'Vassals, Allies and Mercenaries: The French Army before and after 1346', *Battle of Crécy*, eds. Ayton & Preston, p.269.
28. Michael Livingston 'Location of the Battle', *Battle of Crécy*, eds. Livingston & DeVries, pp.432–3.
29. Livingston, 'Location', p.437.
30. Jonathan Sumption, *The Hundred Years War* (London, 1990), p.528.
31. Kelly DeVries & Niccol Capponi, 'The Genoese Crossbowmen at Crécy', *Battle of Crécy*, eds. Livingston & DeVries, p.442.
32. Anna Comnena, *The Alexiad*, eds. Peter Frankopan, trans. E.R.A. Sewter (London, 2003), p.109.
33. Jean Froissart, *Oeuvres de Froissart: Chroniques*, ed. Kervyn de Lettenhove (26 vols; Paris, 1867–77), vol.5, p.8.
34. Kelly DeVries, 'The Implications of the *Anonimo Romano* Account of the Battle of Crécy', *The Medieval Way of War*, ed. Gregory Halfond (London, 2015), pp.309–22.
35. Balázs Tihanyi et al., 'Investigation of Hungarian Conquest Period Archery', *Acta Biologica Szegediensis*, 59:1 (2015), pp.65–77; Christopher Knüsel, 'Activity-related Skeletal Change', *Blood Red Roses*, eds. Veronica Fiorato, Anthea Boylston, & Christopher Knüsel (Oxford, 2014), p.109.
36. Roland Thomas Richardson, *The Medieval Inventories of the Tower Armouries 1320–1410*. PhD Dissertation, University of York (2012), p.257.
37. Kelly DeVries, 'Introduction and Use of the Pavise', *Arms and Armour*, 4 (2007), pp.93–100.
38. Villani, 'New Chronicle', p.119; Ormrod, *Edward III*, p.279.
39. Jean le Bel, *Chroniques*, eds. J. Viard & E. Deprez (2 vols; Paris, 1904–5), vol.2, p.109.
40. Clifford Rogers, *War Cruel and Sharp. English Strategy under Edward III* (Woodbridge, 2000), p.270.
41. Max Arthur (eds.), *Forgotten Voices of the Great War* (London, 2002), p.247.
42. Paddy Griffith, *Forward into Battle* (New York, 1990), p.120.
43. Arthur (ed.), *Forgotten Voices*, p.249.
44. Bryn Hammond, *Cambrai 1917* (London, 2008), chapter 2.
45. John Keegan, *The First World War* (London, 1999), pp.396–7.
46. Arthur (ed.), *Forgotten Voices*, p.251.
47. Arthur (ed.), *Forgotten Voices*, p.250.
48. Hammond, *Cambrai*, chapter 2.
49. Arthur (ed.), *Forgotten Voices*, p.247.
50. Brian Bond, *Britain's Two World Wars Against Germany* (Cambridge, 2014), p.136.
51. Arthur (ed.), *Forgotten Voices*, p.251.
52. Bond, *Britain's Two World Wars*, p.136.
53. Griffith, *Forward*, p.104.
54. *Statistics of the Military Effort of the British Empire*, pp.410, 414.
55. Gordon Corrigan, *Mud, Blood and Poppycock* (London, 2004), pp.152–5.
56. Griffith, *Forward*, pp.100–101.

Chapter 8: Armies, Personnel, and Training
1. David Chandler, *Waterloo* (London, 1997), p.62.
2. C.T. Atkinson, '"An Infamous Army"', *Journal for the Society for Army Historical Research*, 32:130 (1954), pp.48–53.
3. James Taylor, 'Optimal Commitment of Forces in Some Lanchester-Type Combat Models', *Operations Research*, 27:1 (1979), pp.96–114.
4. N.J. MacKay, 'Lanchester Combat Models', *Mathematics Today*, (2006), p.3.
5. Jean Froissart, *Chronicles*, ed. & trans. Geoffrey Brereton (London, 1978), p.87.
6. Matthew Bennett, 'The Development of Battle Tactics in the Hundred Years War', *Arms, Armies and Fortifications in the Hundred Years War*, eds. Anne Curry & Michael Hughes (Woodbridge, 1999), pp.12–18.
7. Christopher Duffy, *The Military Experience in the Age of Reason* (Ware, 1998), pp.17–18.
8. Brian Hall, *Communications and British Operations on the Western Front* (Cambridge, 2017), p.1.
9. Owen Connelly, *On War and Leadership* (Princeton, 2002), p.105.
10. Christopher Allmand, *The De Re Militari of Vegetius* (Cambridge, 2013), p.5.
11. John Grehan & Martin Mace (eds.), *The BEF in France* (Barnsley, 2014), p.90.
12. Max Arthur (ed.), *Forgotten Voices of the Second World War* (London, 2005), p.55.
13. Jean-Roch Coignet, *The Notebooks of Captain Coignet* (Barnsley, 2016), p.177.
14. Duffy, *Military Experience*, p.253.
15. Arthur (ed.), *Forgotten Voices of the Great War*, p.89.
16. Dennis Showalter, *Frederick the Great* (Barnsley, 2012), p.190.
17. G.P. Gooch, *Frederick the Great* (London, 1947), p.42.
18. Connelly, *On War and Leadership*, p.12.
19. David Ogg, *Europe of the Ancien Regime* (London, 1965), p.156.
20. Duffy, *Military Experience*, p.143.
21. Duffy, *Military Experience*, p.33.
22. Christopher Tozzi, *Nationalizing France's Army* (Charlottesville, 2016), p.41.
23. Katrin Möbius & Sascha Möbius, *Prussian Army Soldiers and the Seven Years' War* (London, 2019), pp.28–30.
24. Möbius & Möbius, *Prussian Army Soldiers*, p.28–9.
25. Möbius & Möbius, *Prussian Army Soldiers*, p.21.
26. Möbius & Möbius, *Prussian Army Soldiers*, p.20.
27. Duffy, *Military Experience*, p.244.
28. D. George Boyce, *The Falklands War* (Basingstoke, 2005), pp.125–6.
29. Robert Bolia, 'The Battle of Darwin-Goose Green', *Military Review* (2005), p.46.
30. Bolia, 'Battle of Darwin-Goose Green', pp.49–50; also footnotes 33–4.
31. Tom Hickman, *The Call-Up* (London, 2005), pp.216–18.
32. Max Hastings & Simon Jenkins, *The Battle for the Falklands* (London, 1997), pp.206–207.
33. Hastings & Jenkins, *Battle for the Falklands*, p.273–5.
34. Bolia, 'Battle of Darwin-Goose Green', pp.47–9.
35. Hastings & Jenkins, *Battle for the Falklands*, p.276.
36. Boyce, *Falklands War*, p.130.
37. Bolia, 'Battle of Darwin-Goose Green', p.49.
38. Spencer Fitz-Gibbon, *Not Mentioned in Dispatches* (Cambridge, 1995).

Chapter 9: Motivation and Morale
1. Joshua Chamberlain, *The Passing of the Armies* (New York, 1915; repr. 1992), p.15.
2. Anthony Kellett, *Combat Motivation* (Boston, 1982), p.6.

3. Kellett, *Combat Motivation*, p.7.
4. Marcus Schulzke, *Pursuing Moral Warfare* (Washington, 2019), p.49.
5. Gary Sheffield, *Leadership in the Trenches* (London, 2000), p.180.
6. Philippe Contamine, *War in the Middle Ages* (Oxford, 1984), p.79.
7. Contamine, *War*, p.151.
8. Contamine, *War*, p.89.
9. Sheffield, *Leadership*, p.182.
10. Simeon Ash, *A Continuation of True Intelligence from the English and Scottish Forces in the North* (London, 1644), p.8.
11. Maarten Otte, *The Franco-Prussian War, 1870–1871* (Barnsley, 2020), p.67.
12. Michael Glover, *Wellington's Peninsular Victories* (Moreton-in-Marsh, 1996), pp.105–106.
13. Rémy Ambühl, 'A Fair Share of the Profits? The Ransoms of Agincourt', *Nottingham Medieval Studies*, 50 (2006), p.130.
14. 'Chronique du Religieux de Saint-Denys', *The Battle of Agincourt. Sources and Interpretations*, ed. Anne Curry (Woodbridge, 2000), p.108.
15. John Keegan, *The Face of Battle* (2nd edn.; London, 2014), p.90.
16. Jonathan Sumption, *Trial by Battle* (London, 1990), p.248.
17. Francis Steckel, *Morale and Men* (Ann Arbor, 1990), p.300.
18. J. Glenn Gray, *The Warriors* (Lincoln, 1959), p.40.
19. Alexander Watson, *Enduring the Great War* (Cambridge, 2008), p.91.
20. Max Arthur (ed.), *Forgotten Voices of the Great War* (London, 2002), p.201.
21. Erin Finley, *Fields of Combat* (Ithaca, 2011), p.37.
22. Craig Taylor, *Chivalry and the Ideals of Knighthood* (Cambridge, 2013), p.169.
23. Contamine, *War*, p.255; *The Black Book of the Admiralty*, ed. T. Twiss (London, 1871), vol.1, pp.453–4.
24. Geoffroi de Charny, *The Book of Chivalry*, eds. R.W. Kaeuper & E. Kennedy (Philadelphia, 1996), p.129.
25. Charny, *Book of Chivalry*, p.133.
26. Arthur (ed.), *Forgotten Voices of the Great War*, p.19.
27. Charny, *Book of Chivalry*, p.91.
28. Le Religieux de Saint-Denis, 'Histoire de Charles VI', *The Battle of Agincourt*, ed. Curry, p.106.
29. Frank McLynn, *Napoleon* (London, 1998), p.260.
30. Josiah Marshall Favill, *The Diary of a Young Officer* (Chicago, 1909), p.13.
31. Dana Carleton Munro, 'The Speech of Pope Urban II At Clermont', *American Historical Review*, 11:2 (1906), p.238.
32. *The Deeds of Count Roger of Calabria*, trans. Kenneth Wolf (Ann Arbor, 2005), pp.85–6.
33. Michael Horowitz, 'Long Time Going: Religion and the Duration of Crusading', *International Security*, 34:2 (2009), p.168.
34. Effie Karageorgos, *Australian Soldiers in South Africa and Vietnam* (London, 2017), p.111
35. W. Mark Ormrod, *Edward III* (New Haven, 2011), p.165.
36. Jonathan Fennell, *Combat and Morale* (Cambridge, 2011), p.78.
37. Robert Mackay, *Half the Battle* (Manchester, 2002), p.95.
38. Michael Hicks, *Richard III: The Self-made King* (New Haven, 2013), p.211.
39. *Ingulph's Chronicle of the Abbey of Crowland*, ed. H.T. Riley (London, 1854), p.501.
40. Chris Skidmore, *Bosworth: The Birth of the Tudors* (London, 2013), pp.245–6.
41. *Paston Letters*, ed. A. Ramsay (London, 1859), vol.2, p.154.
42. David Candlin, 'A Proclamation Against Henry Tudor, 23 June 1485', *Ricardian Bulletin* (Summer 2007), pp.22–4.

43. Candlin, 'A Proclamation', p.23.
44. Glenn Foard & Anne Curry, *Bosworth 1485* (Oxford, 2013), pp.34–5.
45. Edward Hall, *Union of the Two Illustre Families of Lancaster and York*, ed. H. Ellis (London, 1809), p.423.
46. A.J. Pollard, *The Wars of the Roses* (New York, 1988), pp.78–9.
47. Leslie Boatwright, 'The Buckinghamshire Six at Bosworth', *The Ricardian*, 13 (2003), p.57
48. Foard & Curry, *Bosworth*, p.31.
49. Polydore Vergil, *Three Books of Polydore Vergil's 'English History'*, ed. H. Ellis (London, 1844), pp.223.
50. Skidmore, *Bosworth*, pp.333–4.
51. James Willbanks, *The Tet Offensive* (New York, 2008), p.11.
52. Merle Pribbenow, 'General Vo Nguyên Giáp and the Mysterious Evolution of the Plan for the 1968 Tet Offensive', *Journal of Vietnamese Studies*, 3:2 (2008), p.4.
53. Owen Connelly, *On War and Leadership* (Princeton, 2002), p.196.
54. Willbanks, *Tet Offensive*, p.13.
55. Ron Hassner, *Religion on the Battlefield* (Ithaca, 2016), p.45.
56. Robert Simonsen, 'When the Luckiest Marines' Luck Ran Out', *Vietnam*, 22:5 (2010), p.32.
57. Stanley Karnow, *Vietnam* (London, 1994), pp.547–8.
58. Willbanks, *Tet Offensive*, p.27.
59. James Gillam, 'Historical, Social, and Personal Effects of a War and a Battle', *Journal of Third World Studies*, 12:2 (1995), p.36.
60. David Schmitz, *The Tet Offensive: Politics, War and Public Opinion* (Lanham, MD, 2005), pp.66, 110.
61. Connelly, *On War and Leadership*, p.209.
62. Karnow, *Vietnam*, p.541.
63. Karnow, *Vietnam*, p.557.
64. Willbanks, *Tet Offensive*, p.31.
65. Jeff Harvey, 'All Hell is Breaking Loose', *Vietnam*, 28:5 (2016), p.27.
66. Nicholas Warr, *Phase Green Line: the Battle for Hué, 1968* (Annapolis, 1997), chapter 4.
67. Schmitz, *Tet Offensive*, p.127.
68. Harvey, 'All Hell', p.28.
69. Simonsen 'Luckiest Marines', p.32.
70. Karnow, *Vietnam*, p.546.
71. Jon Balkind, 'A Critique of Military Sociology: Lessons from Vietnam', *Journal of Strategic Studies*, 1:3 (1978), pp.237–59.

Chapter 10: Non-Combatants
1. Alicia Blackwood, *A Narrative of Personal Experiences* (London, 1881), p.263.
2. Alan Allport, *Browned Off and Bloody Minded* (New Haven, 2015), pp.206–207.
3. Andrew Orr, *Women and the French Army* (Bloomington, 2017), p.3.
4. Jean-Roch Coignet, *The Notebooks of Captain Coignet* (Barnsley, 2016), p.145.
5. Anne Curry (ed.), *The Battle of Agincourt: Sources and Interpretations* (Woodbridge, 2000), pp.34–5.
6. Max Arthur (ed.), *Forgotten Voices of the Great War* (London, 2002), p.140.
7. Allport, *Browned Off*, p.207.
8. Lawrence Cane, *Fighting Fascism in Europe* (New York, 2003), p.84.
9. William Baldwin, 'The Battle of the Bulge', *The Military Engineer*, 86:567 (1994), p.68.
10. *Passage de la Beresina* (Uckfield, n.d.).
11. Paul Thompson, 'Engineers in Battle', *The Military Engineer*, 33:189 (1941), pp.210–14.

12. Ian Knight, *Voices from the Zulu War* (Barnsley, 2011), p.81.
13. Hans Rehfeldt, *Mortar Gunner on the Eastern Front* (London, 2019), entry 3 April 1943.
14. Bruce Seton & John Grant, *The Pipes of War* (Glasgow, 1920), p.3.
15. Seton & Grant, *Pipes of War*, p.21.
16. Jean Froissart, *Oeuvres*, ed. Kervyn de Lettenhove (25 vols; Brussels, 1867–77), vol.2, p.1.
17. Alexander Downes, *Targeting Civilians in War* (Ithaca, 2008), p.234.
18. John Grehan & Martin Mace (eds.), *The BEF in France* (Barnsley, 2014), p.76.
19. David Chandler, *Austerlitz 1805* (London, 1990), p.83.
20. Michael Glover, *Wellington's Peninsular Victories* (Moreton-in-Marsh, 1996), pp.104–105.
21. Simeon Ash, *A Continuation of True Intelligence from the English and Scottish Forces in the North* (London, 1644), p.6.
22. Frances Isabella Duberly, *Journal Kept During the Russian War* (London, 1855).
23. William Russell, *The Great War with Russia* (London, 1895), p.138.
24. Candan Badem, *The Ottoman Crimean War* (Leiden, 2010), p.270.
25. James Skene, *With Lord Stratford in the Crimea* (London, 1883), p.105.
26. Badem, *Ottoman Crimean War*, p.272.
27. Carol Helmstadter, 'Class, Gender and Professional Expertise', *One Hundred Years of Wartime Nursing Practices*, eds. Jane Brooks & Christine Hallett (Manchester, 2015), p.32.
28. Duberly, *Journal*, p.123.
29. Holly Furneaux, *Military Men of Feeling* (Oxford, 2016), p.149; Daniel Lysons, *The Crimean War* (London, 1895), p.125.
30. Lascelles Wraxall, *Hand-book to the Naval and Military Resources of the Principal European Nations* (London, 1856), pp.85–6; Robert Kershaw, *24 Hours at Balaclava* (Stroud, 2019), p.30.
31. Badem, *Ottoman Crimean War*, p.272.
32. John Sweetman, 'The Crimean War and the Formation of the Medical Staff Corps', *Journal for the Society of Army Historical Research*, 53:214 (1975), p.116.
33. George Paget, *The Light Cavalry Brigade in the Crimea* (London, 1881), p.171.
34. Russell, *Great War*, p.159; Paget, *Light Cavalry*, p.183.
35. Paget, *Light Cavalry*, p.171.
36. John Adye, *Review of the Crimean War* (London, 1860), p.98.
37. Paget, *Light Cavalry*, p.183.
38. Kershaw, *24 Hours*, p.27.
39. Paget, *Light Cavalry*, p.71.
40. Albert Seaton, *The Crimean War: a Russian Chronicle* (London, 1977), p.96; 'Regimental Bands', *The Musical Times*, 54:839 (1913), p.28.
41. Adye, *Review*, pp.62–4.
42. Helmstadter, 'Class', p.29.
43. Russell, *Great War*, p.152; Ross Lawrenson, 'Sir James Mouat', *Journal of Medical Biography*, 12:4 (2004), p.197.

Chapter 11: The Clash of Arms
1. John Gore (ed.), *The Creevy Papers* (London, 1970), p.150.
2. Stanislaw Sosabowski, *Freely I Served* (Barnsley, 2013), chapter 2.
3. Henri Desagneaux, *A French Soldier's War Diary, 1914–1918* (Barnsley, 2014), p.67.
4. Wellcome Collection (London), RAMC/1218/1/1, 'Diary 25th Division – Somme Battle', p.10.

5. *London Gazette* (16 & 24 November 1914).
6. John Keegan, *Face of Battle*, (2nd edn., London, 2014), pp.149–51.
7. Christopher Duffy, *The Military Experience in the Age of Reason* (Ware, 1998), p.255.
8. Sidney Rogerson, *Twelve Days on the Somme* (Barnsley, 2020), p.50.
9. Andrew Roberts, *Napoleon and Wellington* (London, 2010), p.185.
10. Thomas Ashbridge, *The Greatest Knight* (London, 2015), pp.55–6.
11. William Russell, *The Second Fourteenth Battalion* (Sydney, 1948), pp.138–9.
12. *Supplement to the London Gazette* (9 February 1943), p.695.
13. Robert Southey, *History of the Peninsular War* (London, 1837), vol.5, p.241.
14. Michael Glover, *The Peninsular War* (London, 2001), pp.161–2.
15. Owen Connelly, *On War and Leadership* (Princeton, 2002), p.15.
16. Glover, *Peninsular War*, p.203.
17. Simeon Ash, *A Continuation of True Intelligence from the English and Scottish Forces in the North* (London, 1644), p.5.
18. Anne Curry, *Agincourt: a New History* (Stroud, 2010), p.263.
19. Jean Froissart, *Chronicles*, ed. & trans. Geoffrey Brereton (London, 1978), p.94.
20. Froissart, *Chronicles*, p.95.
21. Gordon Corrigan, *Mud, Blood and Poppycock* (London, 2004), p.153.
22. Bob Drury & Tom Calvin, *Valley Forge* (New York, 2019), p.80.
23. John Keegan & Richard Holmes, *Soldiers* (London, 1985), p.66; Keegan, *Face of Battle*, p.169.
24. Gareth Glover (ed.), *The Waterloo Archive* (London, 2010), vol.1, p.163.
25. Jean-Roch Coignet, *The Notebooks of Captain Coignet* (Barnsley, 2016), p.278.
26. H.T. Siborne (ed.), *Waterloo Letters* (London, 2015), p.348.
27. Paddy Griffith, *Forward into Battle* (New York, 1990), pp.12–49.
28. Siborne (ed.), *Waterloo Letters*, p.347
29. Siborne (ed.), *Waterloo Letters*, pp.349–50.
30. Julian Paget & Derek Saunders, *Hougoumont* (London, 1992), pp.45–6.
31. Cavalié Mercer, *Journal of the Waterloo Campaign* (London, 1927), pp.173–4.
32. Glover (ed.), *Waterloo Archive*, vol.1, p.159.

Chapter 12: Sources of Conflict
1. Jean Froissart, *Chronicles*, ed. & trans. Geoffrey Brereton (London, 1978), p.37.
2. Jean le Févre, *Chronique de Jean le Févre*, ed. F. Morand (2 vols; Paris, 1876–81), vol.1, p.1.
3. Jean Froissart, *Oeuvres*, ed. Kervyn de Lettenhove (25 vols; Brussels, 1867–77), vol.2, pp.1–2.
4. David Bachrach, 'Edward I's Centurions: Professional Soldiers in the Era of Militia Armies', *The Soldier Experience in the Fourteenth Century*, eds. Adrian Bell & Anne Curry (Woodbridge, 2011), p.110.
5. Anne Curry, *Agincourt 1415: The Archer's Story* (Stroud, 2008).
6. Online at www.medievalsoldier.org
7. Found at https://www.memoiredeshommes.sga.defense.gouv.fr/
8. The resulting film, *The Battle of the Somme*, became Britain's most watched film, retaining the accolade until the release of *Star Wars* in 1977.
9. http://www.battlefieldstrust.com/resource-centre/

Further Reading

This is a short selection of suggested resources for further study. It is by no means comprehensive or exhaustive. For ease of use it has been divided broadly chronologically, with a section on more general works. The lists include both secondary scholarship and some of the most interesting or accessible primary sources. Full references for other sources cited in this book can be found in the endnotes.

General works
Alexander, Bevin, *How Great Generals Win* (New York, 1993)
Clausewitz, Carl von, *On War*, trans. Michael Howard & Peter Paret (Princeton, 2008)
Connelly, Owen (ed.), *On War and Leadership* (Princeton, 2002)
Dupuy, Trevor, *Numbers, Predictions and War* (New York, 1979)
Gat, Azar, *A History of Military Thought* (Oxford, 2001)
Griffith, Paddy, *Forward into Battle* (New York, 1990)
Heuser, Beatrice, *The Evolution of Strategy* (Cambridge, 2010)
Heuser, Beatrice & Athena Leoussi, *Famous Battles* (Barnsley, 2018)
Holmes, Richard (ed.), *The Oxford Companion to Military History* (Oxford, 2003)
Keegan, John & Richard Holmes, *Soldiers* (London, 1985)
Keegan, John, *A History of Warfare* (London, 2004)
Keegan, John, *The Face of Battle* (2nd edn., London, 2014)
Kellett, Anthony, *Combat Motivation* (Boston, 1982)
Krimmer, Elisabeth & Patricia Simpson (eds.), *Enlightened War* (Woodbridge, 2011)
Lynn, John, *Battle: a History of Combat and Culture* (New York, 2008)
Nolan, Cathal, *The Allure of Battle* (New York, 2017)
Seymour, William, *Battles in Britain* (Ware, 1997)
Sullivan, Patricia, *Who Wins? Predicting Strategic Success and Failure in Armed Conflict* (Oxford, 2012)
van Creveld, Martin, *Supplying War* (2nd edn., Cambridge, 2004)

Medieval (up to c.1500)
Allmand, Christopher, *The De Re Militari of Vegetius* (Cambridge, 2013)
Asbridge, Thomas, *The Crusades* (New York, 2012)
Ayton, Andrew, & Philip Preston (eds.), *The Battle of Crécy, 1346* (Woodbridge, 2005)
Bell, Adrian, & Anne Curry (eds.), *The Soldier Experience in the Fourteenth Century* (Woodbridge, 2011)
Bennett, Matthew et al., *Fighting Techniques of the Medieval World* (London, 2005)
Charny, Geoffroi de, *The Book of Chivalry*, eds. R.W. Kaeuper & E. Kennedy (Philadelphia, 1996)
Contamine, Philippe, *War in the Middle Ages* (Oxford, 1984)
Curry, Anne (ed.), *The Battle of Agincourt. Sources and Interpretations* (Woodbridge, 2000)
Curry, Anne, & Michael Hughes (eds.), *Arms, Armies and Fortifications in the Hundred Years War* (Woodbridge, 1999)

Curry, Anne, *Agincourt: a New History* (Stroud, 2010)
Curry, Anne, *Great Battles: Agincourt* (Oxford, 2015)
Foard, Glenn & Anne Curry, *Bosworth 1485* (Oxford, 2013)
France, John, *Hattin* (Oxford, 2015)
Froissart, Jean, *Chronicles*, ed. & trans. Geoffrey Brereton (London, 1978)
Halfond, Gregory (ed.), *The Medieval Way of War* (London, 2015)
Hewitt, H.J., *The Organization of War under Edward III* (2nd edn.; Barnsley, 2004)
Hill, Paul, *The Norman Commanders* (Barnsley, 2015)
Jones, Dan, *Crusaders* (London, 2019)
Keen, Maurice (ed.), *Medieval Warfare* (Oxford, 1999)
Keen, Maurice, *Chivalry* (New Haven, 2005)
Livingston, Michael, & Kelly DeVries (eds.), *The Battle of Crécy. A Casebook* (Liverpool, 2015)
McLynn, Frank, *1066: The Year of the Three Battles* (London, 2011)
Morillo, S., *The Battle of Hastings: Sources and Interpretations* (Woodbridge, 1996)
Morillo, Stephen, *Warfare under the Anglo-Norman Kings, 1066–1135* (Woodbridge, 1994)
Oakeshott, Ewart, *European Weapons and Armour* (Woodbridge, 2000)
Pollard, A.J., *The Wars of the Roses* (New York, 1988)
Prestwich, Michael, *Armies and Warfare in the Middle Ages* (New Haven, 1999)
Rogers, Clifford, *War Cruel and Sharp: English Strategy under Edward III* (Woodbridge, 2000)
Seward, Desmond, *The Hundred Years War* (London, 2003)
Skidmore, Chris, *Bosworth: The Birth of the Tudors* (London, 2013)
Strickland, M., *War and Chivalry* (Cambridge, 1996)
Sumption, Johnathan, *The Hundred Years War* (4 vols; London, 2011–15)
Tallett, Frank & D.J.B. Trim (eds.), *European Warfare, 1350–1750* (Cambridge, 2010)
Taylor, Craig, *Chivalry and the Ideals of Knighthood* (Cambridge, 2013)
The Song of Lewes, ed. C.L. Kingsford (Oxford, 1890)

Early Modern (c.1500–1900)
A Letter from Generall Leven, the Lord Fairfax, and the Earl of Manchester; To the Committee of Both Kingdoms (London, 1644)
Ash, Simeon, *A Continuation of True Intelligence from the English and Scottish Forces in the North* (London, 1644)
Badem, Candan, *The Ottoman Crimean War* (Leiden, 2010)
Chandler, David, *Marlborough as a Military Commander* (London, 1973)
Chandler, David, *The Campaigns of Napoleon* (London, 1966)
Chandler, David, *Waterloo* (London, 1997)
Coignet, Jean-Roch, *The Notebooks of Captain Coignet* (Barnsley, 2016)
Donagan, Barbara, *War in England, 1642–1649* (Oxford, 2008)
Duberly, Frances Isabella, *Journal Kept During the Russian War* (London, 1855)
Duffy, Christopher, *The Military Experience in the Age of Reason* (Ware, 1998)
Esposito, Vincent & John Elting, *A Military Atlas and History of the Napoleonic Wars* (London, 1999)
Favill, Josiah, *The Diary of a Young Officer* (Chicago, 1909)
Fletcher, Ian (ed.), *Voices from the Peninsula* (Barnsley, 2016)
Frederick II, *Military Instruction from the Late King of Prussia to His Generals*, trans. T. Foster (5th edn.; London, 1818)
Gates, David, *The Napoleonic Wars 1803–1815* (London, 2003)
Glover, Gareth (ed.), *The Waterloo Archive* (multiple volumes; London, 2010–21)

Glover, Michael, *The Peninsular War* (London, 2001)
Goodwin, George, *Fatal Rivalry: Flodden 1513* (London, 2014)
Hibbert, Christopher, *Redcoats and Rebels* (new edn.; London, 2001)
Holmes, Richard, *Redcoat* (London, 2002)
Kershaw, Robert, *24 Hours at Balaclava* (Stroud, 2019)
Knight, Ian, *Voices from the Zulu War* (Barnsley, 2011)
Lipscombe, Nick, *The English Civil War* (Oxford, 2020)
Markham, David, *Imperial Glory: the Bulletins of Napoleon's Grande Armée* (London, 2003)
Marshall-Cornwall, James, *Napoleon as a Military Commander* (New York, 1998)
Mikaberidze, Alexander (ed.), *Russian Eyewitness Accounts of the Campaign of 1814* (London, 2013)
Möbius Katrin & Sascha Möbius, *Prussian Army Soldiers and the Seven Years' War* (London, 2019)
Mortimer, Geoff (Ed.), *Early Modern Military History* (Basingstoke, 2004)
Mortimer, Geoff, *Eyewitness Accounts of the Thirty Years' War* (Basingstoke, 2002)
Napoleon's Maxims of War (New York, 1861)
Nosworthy, Brent, *Battle Tactics of Napoleon and his Enemies* (London, 1997)
Otte, Maarten, *The Franco-Prussian War* (Barnsley, 2020)
Paget, George, *The Light Cavalry Brigade in the Crimea* (London, 1881)
Parrott, David, *Richelieu's Army* (Cambridge, 2001)
Seaton, Albert, *The Crimean War: a Russian Chronicle* (London, 1977)
Showalter, Dennis, *Frederick the Great* (Barnsley, 2012)
Tallett, Frank & D.J.B. Trim (eds.), *European Warfare, 1350–1750* (Cambridge, 2010)
The Dispatches of Field Marshal the Duke of Wellington (8 vols, London, 1844–7)
Watson, Lion, *A More Exact Relation of the Late Battell Neer York* (London, 1644)

Modern (post-1900)
Allport, Alan, *Browned Off and Bloody Minded* (New Haven, 2015)
Arthur, Max (ed.), *Forgotten Voices of the Great War* (London, 2002)
Arthur, Max (ed.), *Forgotten Voices of the Second World War* (London, 2005)
Beevor, Antony, *Stalingrad* (London, 2007)
Biddle, Stephen, *Military Power: Explaining Victory and Defeat in Modern Battle* (Princeton, 2006)
Black, Jeremy, *Strategy and the Second World War* (London, 2021)
Bond, Brian, *Britain's Two World Wars Against Germany* (Cambridge, 2014)
Boyce, D. George, *The Falklands War* (Basingstoke, 2005)
Busch, Reinhold (ed.), *Survivors of Stalingrad* (London, 2014)
Caddick-Adams, Peter, *Snow and Steel* (Oxford, 2015)
Corrigan, Gordon, *Mud, Blood and Poppycock* (London, 2004)
Desagneaux, Henri, *A French Soldier's War Diary, 1914–1918* (Barnsley, 2014)
Erikson, John, *The Road to Stalingrad* (Boulder, 1984)
Finley, Erin, *Fields of Combat* (Ithaca, 2011)
Grehan, John & Martin Mace (eds.), *The BEF in France* (Barnsley, 2014)
Hall, Brian, *Communications and British Operations on the Western Front* (Cambridge, 2017)
Hammond, Bryn, *Cambrai 1917* (London, 2008)
Hastings, Max & Simon Jenkins, *The Battle for the Falklands* (London, 1997)
Hastings, Max, *The Korean War* (New York, 1988)
Hayward, Joel, *Stopped at Stalingrad* (Lawrence, 1998)
Heuser, Beatrice & Eitan Shamir (eds.), *Insurgencies and Counterinsurgencies* (Cambridge, 2016)

Horn, Bernd, *No Lack of Courage: Operation Medusa, Afghanistan* (Toronto, 2010)
Karageorgos, Effie, *Australian Soldiers in South Africa and Vietnam* (London, 2017)
Karnow, Stanley, *Vietnam* (London, 1994)
Keegan, John, *The First World War* (London, 1999)
Lucas, James, *War on the Eastern Front* (London, 2014)
Macdonald, Lyn, *1914–1918: Voices and Images of the Great War* (London, 1991)
Macdonald, Lyn, *They Called it Passchendaele* (London, 1993)
McCartney, Helen, *Citizen Soldiers* (Cambridge, 2005)
Pakenham, Thomas, *The Boer War* (London, 1992)
Rogerson, Sidney, *Twelve Days on the Somme* (Barnsley, 2020)
Sheffield, Gary, *Leadership in the Trenches* (London, 2000)
Sloan, Elinor, *Modern Military Strategy* (2nd edition; London, 2017)
Sosabowski, Stanislaw, *Freely I Served* (Barnsley, 2013)
Statistics of the Military Effort of the British Empire During the Great War, 1914–1920 (London, 1922)
Steckel, Francis, *Morale and Men* (Ann Arbor, 1990)
Summers, Harry, *American Strategy in Vietnam* (Mineola, 2012)
The Wipers Times (London, 2013)
Thompson, Julian, *Dunkirk: Retreat to Victory* (London, 2009)
Tucker-Jones, Anthony, *The Iraq War* (Barnsley, 2014)
Watson, Alexander, *Enduring the Great War* (Cambridge, 2008)
Willbanks, James, *The Tet Offensive* (New York, 2008)
Winter, J.M. & Antoine Prost, *The Great War in History* (Cambridge, 2005)

Journals and periodicals
Journal of Military History
British Journal for Military History
Armor
Medieval Warfare

Online resources
www.battlefieldstrust.com/resource-centre/
www.medievalsoldier.org
www.memoiredeshommes.sga.defense.gouv.fr/

Index

Abyssinia, 35, 136–7
Accidents, 224–5
Afghanistan, 33, 92, 101–106, 115
Airpower, 6, 18, 86, 95–6, 135, 138
   air support, 36, 73, 87, 103, 104–105, 175
   difficulties for, 65–6, 73, 104, 202
   helicopters, 33, 71, 113
   psychological effect, 133, 187–8
   transport, 113–14, 115, 128
   see also Drones
Albigensian Crusade, 37
Albret, Constable Charles d', 98, 101
Alcohol, 11, 109, 128, 187, 200, 217
Alexander I (Rus.), 29
Alliances, 32–3, 156, 169, 211
Ambush, 37, 92, 95, 102, 103, 106, 177
Ammunition, 57, 108, 116, 125, 126, 205–206
   attacks on supply, 118
   shortages, 27, 116, 124, 127, 233
Amphibious assault, 69, 88, 203
Archaeology, 147, 244–5
Archers, 76, 96, 97, 98, 120, 122, 145, 147–8, 240
   arrow supply, 50, 100, 147
   damage inflicted by, 85, 99–100, 131, 135–6, 147
   effect of weather, 65, 73
   physique, 147
   rate of shot, 143, 147
   recruitment, 10, 179
   tactics, 83–4, 89, 99–100, 143
   training, 9–10, 162, 163
Armour (personal), 63, 85, 131, 135–6, 216
Armoured vehicles, 86, 91, 103, 104, 131, 135, 136
   see also Mechanical reliability
Army organisation, 8–12, 43–4, 155, 157–60, 162, 249

Army size, 155–6, 159, 160, 241
   see also Numerical advantage
Array, 179, 189, 192
Arrière-Ban, 9
Artillery, 56, 57, 71, 126, 150–1, 153, 162
   barrage, 56, 59, 86
   combined arms, 46, 59, 86, 90, 103, 154, 161, 168, 173
   development of, 134, 138, 139–40, 148, 164
   effect of conditions, 66–7, 68, 227
   ineffective use, 27, 32, 57, 230
   lethality, 57, 67, 134, 135
   movement of, 68, 127, 128, 139, 145, 170, 213, 226
   psychological impact of, 57, 132–3, 148–9, 166, 227
   tactics, 88, 104, 105–106
Ash, Simeon, 41, 209, 222
Atrocities, 15, 17–18, 22–3, 27, 37, 240
Augereau, Marshal Charles-Pierre, 67
Australian army, 92, 220–1
Austria, 77, 160
Axes, 131

Baggage, 42, 107, 111, 115, 120, 209
Bainbridge, Major General Guy, 217
Barbarossa, Frederick, 117
Barons' War, 19–23, 31
Battle (medieval formation), 43, 157
Battle, sensory experience of, 133, 166, 177, 215–16
Battlefields:
   as sources, 245–7
   conditions on, 67–8, 73
   location of, 74, 137–8, 145, 245
   size of, 44, 56, 138
   see also Terrain
Battles:
   Adowa (1896), 35, 137

Index

Agincourt (1415), 30, 110, 158, 185, 201, 223, 239, 240
  armies, 97, 159
  English archers at, 97, 98, 99–100, 135–6, 242
  killing of prisoners at, 17, 101, 181–2, 209
  leadership at, 48, 49, 50
  tactics, 88, 96–101
  terrain and conditions, 68, 73, 92, 93, 97–8
Albuera (1811), 221
Antietam (1862), 222
Arbedo (1422), 142
Aroge (1868), 136–7
Aspern-Essling (1809), 166, 204
Austerlitz (1805), 77–80, 209
  conditions, 78–9, 80
  leadership, 48, 77
  tactics, 78, 80, 91
  terrain, 78, 80
Balaclava (1854), 4–5, 203, 210–14
  medical services, 213–14
  rations, 211–12
  reporting, 210
Bannockburn (1314), 83–4, 89, 164
Barnet (1471), 37, 189
Berezina (1812), 73, 204
Bosworth (1485), 31, 37, 44, 73, 157, 188–94
  armies, 191, 192
  death of Richard III, 37, 73, 193
  location, 192, 246
  morale, 192–3
  recruitment for battle, 189–91
  role of Stanley, 47, 157, 192, 193
Bourgthéroulde (1124), 83
Bulge, the (1944–5), 63, 66, 203
Cambrai (1917), 149–54, 224
  aircraft, 150, 153
  artillery, 150–1, 153, 154
  combined arms, 86, 150, 152–3, 224
  tactics, 152, 153–4
  tanks, 150, 151–2, 153
  terrain, 137, 150
Castillon (1453), 84, 139–40
Chancellorsville (1863), 91, 224
Chosin Reservoir (1950), 94
Colenso (1899), 23, 26, 27
Courtrai (1302), 164

Crécy (1346), 4, 48, 49, 110, 144–9, 224, 245
  armies, 144–5
  battle the day after, 223
  casualties, 149, 223
  indiscipline, 157, 158, 166
  tactics, 88, 93, 145–6, 148
  terrain, 70, 73, 145, 148
  weapons at, 64, 132, 140, 143, 144, 146–7, 148
  weather at, 65, 146–7
  see also Genoese crossbowmen
Culloden (1746), 66
Darwin–Goose Green (1982), 172–6
  armies, 173–4, 176
  inter-service cooperation, 173, 174, 176
  supplies, 173, 174, 175
  tactics, 174–5
  training, 173–4
D-Day (1944), 46–7, 66, 69, 88, 203
Dunkirk (1940), 36, 50, 188
Evesham (1265), 19–23, 37, 52, 222
  armies, 20
  atrocities, 22–3
  background, 19, 20
  leaders, 19–20, 21–2, 31
  religion, 20–1, 22–3
Eylau (1807), 67, 88, 200
Fallujah (2004), 137–8, 177
Fleurus (1690), 159
Flodden (1513), 32, 71
France (1940), 30, 91, 92, 133, 165, 204, 208
Friedland (1807), 160
Gallipoli (1915), 63, 116
Germantown (1777), 224
Gettysburg (1863), 92, 220, 244
Goose Green *see* Darwin–Goose Green
Halidon Hill (1333), 84, 147
Hastings (1066), 30, 73–7, 112, 141, 166, 239
  conditions, 64, 73–4, 75
  leaders, 44, 74, 76–7
  tactics, 74, 75–6, 95
  terrain, 74, 75, 76, 77
Hattin (1187), 118–23
  armies, 119
  campaign, 119–22
  conditions, 63, 118, 121, 122

logistics, 115, 118–23
tactics, 122–3
Hué (1968), 196, 197
Ia Drang (1965), 140–1
Isandlwana (1879), 137, 205
Isurava (1942), 220–1
Jena-Auerstädt (1806), 67, 160
Kasserine Pass (1943), 95
Leipzig (1813), 48, 51, 157
Lewes (1264), 19, 20, 31, 52
Ligny (1815), 49, 225, 226
Loos (1915), 64, 207
Lützen (1632), 49
Magersfontein (1899), 23, 27
Majuba (1881), 23, 72
Manzikert (1071), 142
Marignano (1515), 85
Marston Moor (1644), 38–42, 180, 209, 222–3
  alliances, 39, 42
  armies, 41–2
  command structures, 39, 41
  relief of York, 39–40, 41
Mogadishu (1993), 73
Mons (1914), 165, 218
Morat (1476), 36
Muret (1213), 93–4
Myton-on-Swale (1319), 16
Nancy (1477), 85, 141
Nashville (1864), 96
Neville's Cross (1346), 141
Nicopolis (1396), 90
Omdurman (1898), 26
Panjwai (2006), 101–106
  air support, 103, 104, 105
  tactical plans, 102, 103, 105, 106
  Taliban defences, 102–103, 105
  terrain, 102, 105
Passchendaele (or Third Ypres, 1917), 68, 151, 205
Patay (1429), 88, 184
Peipus, Lake (1242), 63, 68
Poitiers (1356), 49–50, 109, 110, 158, 182
Poltava (1709), 34
Prague (1757), 159
Prestonpans (1745), 72
Quatre Bras (1815), 73, 226
Quebec (1759), 68–9
Rorke's Drift (1879), 137
Rossbach (1757), 90, 168–72

armies at, 168, 169–70
casualties, 168
influence of training, 169–70, 171
tactics, 90, 168, 170, 171
Rouvray (1429), 32
Salamanca (1812), 34, 46, 222
Somme (1916), 14, 55–60, 151, 163, 206, 219, 244
  army command, 55, 56–7, 58, 59–60
  casualties, 56, 183
  junior leadership, 58–9, 60
  tactics, 55, 135
  terrain, 55, 72, 73
  weapons, 56, 57, 133, 135, 205
Spring Offensive (1918), 86
Spurs (1513), 31
Stalingrad (1942–3), 62, 123–9
  approach to city, 123–4
  German air resupply, 128, 202
  Soviet counteroffensive, 117, 127–8
  strategic value, 37, 123
  supply shortages, 125–9
  tactics, 126
Stamford Bridge (1066), 74, 218
Stirling Bridge (1297), 51–5
  armies, 53
  strategic situation, 51–3
  tactics, 54–5
St Privat (1870), 30
Tanga (1914), 61
Tet Offensive (1968), 16, 194–8, 208
  aims, 194–5
  casualties, 196
  leadership, 197
  morale, 196–8
  political motivation, 195
Tinchebray (1106), 83
Towton (1461), 63, 65, 67, 93, 159
Tsaritsyn (1774), 159
Ulm (1805), 72, 77, 111
Ulundi (1879), 26
Varna (1444), 139
Verdun (1916), 38, 57
Vitoria (1813), 34, 181, 209
Waterloo (1815), 68, 134, 166, 168, 225–35, 246
  armies, 155, 225–6
  attacks, 227–31, 232, 233–4, 235
  eyewitness testimony, 226, 229, 232
  Hougoumont, 92, 96, 227, 231, 233

Index 273

leadership, 49, 227, 229–30, 232–3
legacy, 25, 58, 246, 247
morale, 47, 227, 232–3, 234–5
tactics, 71, 226–7, 228, 230, 234
terrain, 225–6, 227, 229
Battlespace, 138–9, 162, 215
Bernadotte, Marshal Jean, 67
Biological weapons, 132
Blitzkrieg, 87, 91, 204
Blücher, Prince Gebhard von, 49, 168, 225
Boer Republics, 13–14, 23, 24, 25
Boer War (Second), 12, 15, 23–8, 108, 163, 187
Brabant, Duke of, 99, 223
Britain, 23–8, 35, 38, 117, 172–3, 246
  airpower, 36, 187–8
  alliances, 32–3, 211
  army, 23, 25, 26, 34, 48, 155, 161, 163, 172, 181, 244
    equipment, 33–4, 116, 162, 165, 183
    in battle, 26–7, 46, 55–60, 133, 136–7, 150–4, 173–6, 218, 221, 224, 225–35
    medical services, 206, 207, 213–14
    'Pals' battalions, 182–3
    recruitment, 12, 13, 24–5, 174, 180, 185
    supplies, 63, 108, 116, 174, 205–206, 212
    support services, 199, 202, 203, 206, 207, 212, 217
    training, 13, 165, 174
    views on enemy soldiers, 15, 24, 27–8
    weaponry, 64, 134, 136–7, 150–4, 205
  'shell scandal', 116
  society, 12, 13, 14, 24
Buller, General Sir Redvers, 26, 27
Burgundy, 84, 85
  army, 36, 90, 141
Byzantium, 142, 146

Camp followers, 199, 200, 209, 211
Canadian army, 87, 101–106
Casualties, 35, 63, 156, 223, 224–5, 241
  treatment of, 17, 18, 206
  see also Wounded; Medical services
Casualty rates, 134, 135
Cavalry, 83–4, 85, 86, 88, 142, 161
  movement, 68, 112
  tactics to counter, 85, 89, 91

Chance, 166, 221–2
Charles I (Eng.), 39–40
Charles the Bold (Burg.), 36
Charles XII (Swe.), 34, 35
Chevauchée, 17, 107, 110, 144, 180
Chivalry, 17, 31, 182, 208, 237, 240
Chronicles, 50, 73, 159, 208, 239–40
Chuikov, General Vasily, 126
Citizenship, 8, 11
Civil War, American, 115, 186, 223
Civil Wars, British, 38–42
Civilians, 17, 27, 32, 106, 127, 208
Clausewitz, Carl von, 29, 45, 70
Clergymen, 16, 201
Coignet, Jean-Roch, 166, 200, 226
Cold, effect of, 69, 115, 187
  on people, 62–3, 79, 128, 249
  on weapons, 64
Colours, 220
Combined arms, 83–7, 90, 153, 158, 224
Commissariat, 200, 201, 211–12
Communication, 45, 56–7, 86, 161
Concentration of troops, 87–8, 156, 157
Conscription, 8, 10–13, 33, 174, 180, 186
Cossacks, 13
Counterinsurgency, 30, 33, 38, 102
  supply difficulties, 115
Cowardice, 126, 167, 184–5
Crimean War, 115, 200, 207, 208, 210–14, 240
Cromwell, Oliver, 39, 42
Crossbow, 10, 65, 100, 143, 146–7, 163
Crusades, the, 15, 36, 115, 118, 186–7

Davout, Marshal Louis-Nicolas, 160
Defection in battle, 47, 157
Desagneaux, Henri, 216
Desertion, 166, 192, 195, 212, 243
Discipline, 26, 45, 158, 166–7, 169, 171
  enforcement, 166–7, 171, 183–4
  importance in battle, 85, 100, 104, 144, 164
  see also Indiscipline
Doctrine, 162–3, 170, 250
Drones, 95, 113–14, 138
Duberly, Frances Isabella, 210, 211
Dupuy, Trevor, 134–5

Earthworks *see* Field fortifications
Education, 7, 12

Edward I (Eng.), 19, 20, 22, 31, 51–2, 179
Edward II (Eng.), 84, 118
Edward III (Eng.), 9, 73, 109, 187
   leadership, 48, 49
   Order of the Garter, 182
   tactical innovations, 84, 89, 147, 148
Edward of Woodstock, the Black Prince, 49, 50, 148, 182
Eisenhower, General Dwight, 46–7
Engineers, 106, 114, 202–205, 212
England, 23, 32, 51–2, 98, 182, 193
   army, 10, 53, 73, 144–5, 184, 223
      in battle, 97–101, 147–9
      prisoners, 17, 101, 181–2, 209
      records of, 242
      recruitment, 8, 10, 179, 187, 191–2
      supply, 108, 109, 110, 118, 147
      tactics, 83–4, 93
      training, 9–10
      weapons, 64, 135–6, 140, 143, 147, 148
   battles in, 16, 19–23, 32, 73–7, 188–94, 246
   Civil War, 38–42
   Norman Conquest, 73–4
   political instability, 19–20, 188, 190
Envelopment, 71, 90–1
Eugene, Prince, 32
Eyewitness accounts, 236–9, 248
   reliability, 236–7, 238

Falkenhayn, General Erich von, 38
Falklands War, 31, 172–6
Fastolf, John, 184
Fatigue, 62–3, 79, 211, 216, 217, 226, 249
Fear, 48, 132–4, 166, 167, 177, 216–17, 249
Field fortifications, 71, 93, 203, 212
First World War, 18, 29, 66–7, 93, 149, 203
   attitudes to, 3, 12, 14, 238
   casualties, 56, 58, 134, 182
   Christmas Truce (1914), 16
   comfort of troops, 200, 201, 217
   comradeship, 182–3
   eyewitness testimony, 3, 68, 133, 151–2, 238–9
   leadership, 44, 49, 55–60, 161
   logistics, 108, 112, 113, 116
   morale, 183, 207, 216
   mutinies, 14, 183
   on film, 244

recruitment, 13, 180, 185
'shell shock', 167
tactics, 55–7, 59, 88, 134, 149–50, 163, 205
   combined arms, 86, 150
   innovation, 140, 151, 153–4
   weapons, 64, 86, 132, 134, 135, 140, 149–54, 202
   see also Trenches
Fitness, 12–13
Flanks, 71, 82, 89–90, 91
Food, 13, 64, 69, 110, 200, 249
   importance in battle, 211–12, 217
   morale, 187, 200
   shortages at Stalingrad, 124–9
   supply, 69, 108–109, 111
Foraging, 69, 110, 111, 124, 200
France, 11, 19, 30, 38, 72, 191
   army, 97, 144–5, 168–9, 181, 225–35
   cantinières, 200
   casualties, 101, 134, 149, 185, 223
   disorganisation, 3, 157, 158, 166, 169–70
   foreign regiments, 169
   health of soldiers, 12–13
   innovation, 160
   leadership, 45, 46, 48, 157, 169
   movement, 111, 145
   mutinies, 14, 183
   recruitment, 9, 11, 169, 179
   supply, 111, 116, 117
   tactical innovation, 84, 85, 139–40
   tactics, 38, 88, 98, 146, 148, 163, 228
   weaponry, 30, 84, 140
   chevauchées in see Chevauchée
   cooperation with allies, 32, 211, 224
   society, 9, 10–11, 12–13
   wars in, 16, 17, 31, 38, 110
Franco-Prussian War, 30, 31, 160, 180
Fraser, Brig. Gen. David, 102, 103, 104
Frederick II, the Great (Pruss.), 35, 47, 48, 159, 168, 171
   maxims, 87, 89, 169, 222
   tactics, 88, 168
French Revolution, 11, 63, 111
   Wars of the, 160
Friendly fire, 67, 79, 104, 202, 223–5, 234
Froissart, Jean, 4, 146, 157, 208, 223, 240
Fuel, 113, 116, 202
   shortages at Stalingrad, 124, 125, 127, 128

Gaunt, John of, 179
General Staff, 25, 57, 160–1, 163
Geneva Conventions, 18
　see also Laws of war
Genoese crossbowmen, 65, 93, 109, 132, 143, 146–9, 224
Germany, 17, 29, 30, 124
　armies (pre-1871), 85, 141, 157, 158, 164, 169, 231
　army (post-1871), 17, 57, 66, 92, 150, 165, 218
　　against tanks, 95, 151, 153
　　blitzkrieg *see* Blitzkrieg
　　casualties, 134, 205
　　defeat, 14, 129
　　engineers, 204
　　morale, 128, 183
　　strategy, 37, 38
　　supply, 112–13, 116, 117, 123–9, 206
　　tactics, 59, 86–7, 94, 126, 153–4
　　weapons, 64, 66–7, 125, 133, 136, 153–4
　Luftwaffe, 128, 133, 202
　medieval, 9, 16
　　weapons, 130, 142
　see also Prussia
Giap, General Vo Nguyen, 194–5, 196
Glory, 31–2, 185, 208, 237
Gort, Lord, 133, 165, 208
Gribeauval artillery, 140
Gulf War (1991), 87, 113
Gunpowder, early use of, 64, 131–2, 148
Gustavus Adolphus (Swe.), 49

Haig, Field Marshal Douglas, 57, 150
Halberd, 142
Hamilton, General Ian, 116
Handguns, 84, 130, 131–2, 139, 140
Heat, 63, 64, 118–23
Helmand, 102
Henry II (Eng.), 108, 119, 179
Henry III (Eng.), 19–23, 31
Henry V (Eng.), 30, 92, 96–101, 110, 201
　killing of prisoners, 17, 101, 181, 209
　leadership, 48, 49, 50
Henry VII (Eng.), 31, 37, 44, 47, 157, 188, 190–4
　raising army, 190–1
Henry VIII (Eng.), 31–2
Heralds, 208, 237, 240

High ground, 71, 93, 247
　examples of, 54, 74–6, 78–80, 103–105, 212, 230
Hindenburg Line, 150, 152
Honour, 31–2, 50, 117, 184–5, 208, 237
Horses, 71, 132, 142, 148, 201–202, 249
　requirements of, 108, 110, 112, 120, 122
　used for transport, 110, 111–12, 127, 128
Hundred Years' War, 4, 10, 17, 110
　tactics, 84, 89, 163
Hungary, 90, 127, 139, 147
Hussites, 139

Identification, 21, 50, 222–4
　mistaking enemies for friends, 223
　see also Friendly fire; Uniforms
Impact of individuals in battle, 217–21
　example, 218–21, 229
　initiative, 218
　self-sacrifice, 218, 220–1
Indiscipline, 27, 50, 166, 170, 181, 231
　disobeying orders, 18, 183
　fleeing battle, 219
　of French knights, 100, 158
　see also Discipline
Industrial production, 35, 117, 124, 188
Infantry, 9, 30, 71, 162
　battlefield role, 83–6, 87, 88, 89, 91, 161
　weapons, 9, 141–2, 143–4
Insurgency, 101–102
Intelligence, 57, 102, 114
Iraq War (2003), 48–9, 63, 137–8, 183, 208
　technology in, 33–4, 136, 139
Israel, 35–6, 114
Italy, 10, 35, 72, 127, 136–7, 180

Jackson, Thomas, 91, 96, 224
James II (Scot.), 224
James IV (Scot.), 71
Japan, 15, 117, 220
Jerusalem, 36, 115, 118, 119, 120
Joan of Arc, 16
Jones, Lt Colonel Herbert 'H', 174, 175

Keegan, John, 7, 8, 57, 134, 215
Kitchener, Lord Herbert, 26, 55
Knights, 8, 9, 22, 43, 109, 179, 202
　armour, 122, 135–6
　brotherhood, 23, 182
　gaining honour, 184, 185, 193, 223, 237

identification, 22, 50, 223
  in battle, 122, 142, 220
  obligations, 8, 9, 179, 189
  tactics, 75, 83–4, 98, 148
  training, 20, 163
Korean War, 94, 117

Lanchester, Frederick, 156
Landsknecht, 85–6, 141, 158, 164
Language, problems with, 32, 156, 211
Lannes, Marshal Jean, 160
Laws of war, 16–18
Leadership, 43–60, 229, 251
  command structures, 43–4, 157–8
  inspiration, 48–50, 58–9, 76, 219, 220, 232–3
  loss of leader, 31, 37, 44, 46, 49, 58, 222
  negotiating with enemy, 47
  personality of leader, 44, 251
  tactical decision-making, 45–7, 58, 159
  welfare of troops, 47, 58, 217
  see also General Staff
Lee, Robert E., 91
Lethality *see* Weapons
Leven, Lord, 39–42
Light Brigade, Charge of (1854), 5, 210, 212, 213
  see also Battles, Balaclava
Lines of communication, 33, 78, 90, 111, 114, 117–18
  need to protect, 33, 87, 127, 157
Logistics, 107–29, 200, 249
  centralised stores, 108–109, 111, 147, 206
  collecting supplies, 107–10, 242
  effect on morale, 107, 110, 117, 128, 187, 200
  magazine system, 111
  private contractors, 109
  shortages, 109, 111, 115, 125–6
  transporting supplies, 69, 111–13, 115–16, 124, 128, 205–206, 250
  waterborne transport, 112, 113, 116, 118, 126
  see also Airpower, transport; Industrial production; Lines of communication
Longbow, 65, 96–7, 100, 101, 135–6, 147
Looting of bodies, 180–1
  see also Plunder
Luck *see* Chance
Lusignan, Guy de, 115, 118, 119–23

Mace (medieval), 131
Machine guns, 86, 135, 136, 143, 150, 154
Maginot Line, 92, 203
Maingre, Jean le, 98, 101, 181
Marksmanship, 25, 26, 164–5
Marlborough, Duke of, 32, 49, 111
Marmont, Marshal Auguste, 46, 222
Marshal, William, 220
Maurice of Nassau, 113
McClellan, General George B., 222
Mechanical reliability, 124, 136, 153, 202
Medals, 185
  awarded, 27, 206, 214, 221
  citations, 206, 221
Medical services, 116, 126, 206–207, 213–14
Melcher, Lieutenant Holman, 220
Memoirs, 238–9, 248
Mercenaries, 8, 10, 109–10, 120, 156, 179–80, 194
Mercer, Cavalié, 232
Militia, 8, 10, 155
Mines, 205
Ministeriales, 8–9
Mission command, 45, 163, 175
Montfort, Simon de, 19–23, 31, 37, 222
Montfort, Simon de (Elder), 93–4
Moon, effects of, 68–9
Morale, 37, 38, 196–8, 206, 249
  and training, 165, 197
  civilian, 36, 188, 194, 198, 208
  comforts, 108, 180, 187, 200, 211
  comradeship, 171, 182–3, 197–8
  definition, 177–8
  effect of operations on, 47, 95, 183, 187–8, 196
  effect of weapons on, 104, 133, 196
  effect of weather on, 63–4, 187
  effect on combat willingness, 178, 196, 197, 217
  role of leaders, 48, 49, 188, 189, 193, 197, 232
  see also Logistics, effect on morale
Morality, 14–15, 16–18
Mortimer, Roger de, 20, 21–2
Motivation, 177–87, 248
  compulsion, 179, 187
  comradeship, 182, 197–8
  definition, 177
  monetary reward, 179–82

Index   277

patriotism, 185–6
religion, 186–7
Motorised transport, 112–13, 116, 127
  maintenance, 202
  see also Mechanical reliability
Murder of officers, 224
Musicians, 207, 213
Muskets, 64–5, 132, 136, 158
  lethality, 144, 164
  tactics, 86, 91, 144, 164, 228–9
  training, 137, 164, 170
Mutiny, 14, 183
  See also Murder of officers

Napoleon Bonaparte, 11, 35, 47, 235
  army corps system, 111, 160
  as inspiration, 47, 48, 51
  atrocities, 17, 18
  battles of, 67, 68, 73, 77–80, 157, 204, 225–35
  maxims, 87, 185, 249
  plundering by armies, 17, 180
  speed of movement, 111
  strategy, 29, 30, 78
  supply problems, 111, 117, 200
  tactics, 35, 78–80, 88, 91, 93, 226–7
Napoleonic Wars, 17, 18, 160, 162
  experience of battle, 133, 166, 232
  friendly fire, 225, 234
  later influence, 25, 27
  records of, 238, 242–3
  recruitment, 12–13
  tactics, 78–80, 88, 226–7
  weapons, 134, 140
NATO, 66, 102, 104
Netherlands, the, 72
  army, 32, 155, 226, 227
Newcastle, Earl of, 39–42
Newspapers, 210–11, 240
Ney, Marshal Michel, 67, 227, 231–2, 233
Norman army, 73–7, 220
  tactics, 75–6, 83, 95
  transport, 112, 113
Nuclear weapons, 132
Numerical advantage, 34, 92, 155–6, 157, 163

Officers, 43–4, 50, 58, 158, 159
  ignorance of, 169
  social background, 10–11, 12, 44, 58
  see also Leadership

Ottoman army, 8, 90, 139, 159, 203, 211, 212

Panic, 15, 76, 118, 123, 219, 224
  causes, 90, 94, 118, 231–2
Paratroopers, 87, 91, 162
Patton, General George, 46
Paulus, Field Marshal Friedrich, 62, 123, 127, 128,
Pay, 9, 10, 11, 110, 171, 189, 242
Peninsular War, 17, 18, 34, 227, 228
Philip IV, the Fair (Fr.), 179
Philip VI (Fr.), 146, 147
Photography, 210–11, 244
Pikes, 10, 84, 89, 141–2
  combined arms, 85–6, 136, 158, 162
  tactics, 85–6, 88, 91, 144, 164
Plunder, 17, 18, 110, 124, 180–1, 209
Poison gas, 18, 64, 132, 153, 154
Portuguese army, 46, 221
Prisoners of War, 15, 17, 18, 208–209
  see also Agincourt; Henry V
Prussia, 10, 45, 180
  army, 30, 47, 160, 167, 168–72, 225–35
  casualties, 35, 168
  discipline, 167, 171, 224
  esprit de corps, 171
  leadership, 45, 48
  recruitment, 10, 170, 171
  tactics, 90, 168
  training, 170–1
Punishment see Discipline

Radios, 161–2, 173, 174, 175
Raglan, Field Marshal Lord, 212, 213
Railways, 112, 114, 117, 124, 125, 127
Ransoms, 17, 22, 181–2, 223
Rates of fire, 136, 142–3, 144, 151
Rawlinson, General Henry, 57
Recruitment, 8–13, 20, 158, 169, 178–80, 186
  for Bosworth, 188–91
  in Prussia, 170, 171
  'Pals' battalions, 182
Recruits, unfitness of, 12–13, 24–5
Religion, 14, 15–16, 17, 20–1, 186–7
  prayer, 201, 217
Ribauds, 140, 148
Richard I (Eng.), 36, 117
Richard II (Eng.), 17

Richard III (Eng.), 31, 44, 47, 157, 188–94
  death, 37, 73, 193
  military prowess, 189, 193
  summoning army, 189–90
Rifles, 26, 71, 86, 91, 136–7, 143
  lethality, 27, 30, 50, 132, 135, 150
  reliability, 64, 65, 136
  training, 26, 137, 164–5
Robertson, Field Marshal William, 12
Rogerson, Lieutenant Sidney, 3, 133, 134, 219
Rommel, Field Marshal Erwin, 116, 161
Roses, Wars of the, 84
Rupert, Prince, 39–42
Russell, William, 4–5, 210, 212, 214
Russia, 29, 77, 111
  army, 14, 34, 44, 159, 207
  in battle, 67, 77–80, 160, 204, 210–14
  logistics, 115–16, 211–12
  recruitment, 8, 10, 180
  Napoleon's invasion of, 29, 30, 47, 111
  society, 8, 10, 13, 180
  see also USSR
Russo–Japanese War, 116

Saladin, 36, 63, 118–19, 120, 121–3
Schiltron, 84, 141, 164
Scotland, 13, 17, 32, 39, 51–5, 224
  army, 41–2, 53–4, 84, 141, 164
  campaigns against, 51–5, 118, 187, 189
  claymore, 130
Seacole, Mary, 200, 213
Second World War, 15, 17, 32–3, 123–9, 223
  logistics, 35, 112–13, 116, 206
  on film, 244
  tactics, 86–7, 204
  weaponry, 133, 136, 140
  see also Blitzkrieg
Seljuk Turks, 142
Seven Years' War, 88, 167, 169
Seydlitz, Lieutenant General, 168, 172
Shelling *see* Artillery
Sieges, 117, 138, 204–205
  Melun (1420), 205
  Orléans (1429), 16, 36
  Roxburgh (1460), 224
  Vienna (1683), 159
Smith-Dorrien, General Horace, 205–206
Sobieski, John, 159
Sosabowski, General Stanislaw, 216

Soubise, Prince, 168, 169, 171
Soult, Marshal Jean-de-Dieu, 79, 221, 227
Spain, 17, 18, 110, 111, 209
  army, 85, 113, 141, 158, 164, 221
Spanish Succession, War of, 111, 159
Spears, 141
Strategy, 248–9
  definitions, 29, 82
  effect of battle on, 29–32
  effect on battle, 32–8
Streltsy, 8
Support services, 114, 138, 156, 199–200, 201–202, 205
Sweden, 10, 17, 34, 49
Switzerland, 10, 142, 169, 184
  pikemen, 85, 141, 158, 164
Swords, 130, 131, 143–4, 212
  combined arms, 86

Tactics, 81–106, 228, 250
  and weapons, 83, 84–6, 97, 134, 137, 139, 142–4, 149–50, 153
  counterattack, 94
  deception, 95–6
  defensive, 70–1, 92–6, 103
  definition, 82
  effect of conditions on, 68–9, 78, 79
  effect of terrain on, 70–3, 75–7, 78–80, 91–2, 93
  offensive, 72, 88–92, 105
Taliban, 101–103, 104, 105, 106
Tanks, 86, 135, 137, 150, 151–2, 224
  anti-tank tactics, 95, 153
  reliability, 128, 136, 153, 162, 202
Tercios, 85–6, 141, 158, 164
Terrain, 61, 70–3, 75–7, 78–80, 246–7, 250
  advantages for attacker, 71–2
  advantages for defender, 70–2, 74, 91–2
  and movement, 73, 92
  and supply, 114, 115, 124
  built up, 73, 103, 126
  see also High ground; Tactics; Weapons
Theoretical Lethality Index, 134–5
Thirty Years' War, 17, 49, 109, 110, 158
Torres Vedras, Lines of, 203
Training, 9, 10, 13, 162, 163–6, 169–71
Transport *see* Logistics
Trauma, 167
Trenches, 56, 92, 93, 152, 161, 167, 203
  tactics in, 55, 88, 150, 163

Uniforms, 26, 50, 222–3
USA, 11, 12, 29, 30, 132, 139
 Air Force, 95–6, 104, 114, 117, 140–1
 allies, 33, 35
 Army, 63, 102, 136, 137–8
  friendly fire, 224
  in combat, 95, 105, 140–1, 202–203, 219
  indiscipline, 183
  supplies, 112, 114
  Tet Offensive, 194–8
 Civil War *see* Civil War, American
 Marines, 49
USSR, 17, 35, 64
 invasion of Afghanistan, 33, 92
 logistics, 112, 123–9
 Red Army, 86, 117, 123–9, 184, 224
 see also Stalingrad (1942–3)

Vassalage, 8–9, 179
Vietnam War, 29, 30, 118, 139, 194–8, 200
 combat, 92, 140–1, 196–7
 fragging, 224
 unpopularity, 12, 195, 198, 208
Visibility, 66–7, 71, 79, 161, 250, 251
 impact of armour on, 135, 216, 224
Volunteering, 10, 11, 12, 24–5, 178

Wagon fortifications, 93, 139, 145, 148
Wales, 19, 20, 188, 191, 192
Wallace, William, 51, 53–5
War correspondents, 207–208, 210, 240
Wars of Religion, 15
Washington, General George, 224
Water supply, 69, 75, 77, 117, 120
 shortages, 63, 114, 115, 116, 121–3, 125, 212

Weapons, 130–54, 245, 249–50
 and terrain, 70–1, 137
 development, 134–6, 139–43, 149
 effect of weather on, 64–6, 79
 lethality, 134–6, 249
 preparation for battle, 212, 250
 prohibited, 18
 purpose, 130–1
 reliability, 136, 250
 role in shaping battlefield, 137–8, 149
 supply of, 25, 35–6, 108, 109, 147
 technological advantage, 136–7
 see also Tactics
Weather, 61–70, 79, 187, 250–1
 effect on movement, 68, 73, 74, 80, 115
 effect on soldiers, 62–4, 115, 187
 effect on supply, 69–70, 115, 124, 126–7
 effect on weapons, 64–6, 79
 see also Cold; Heat; Visibility
Wellington, Duke of, 18, 34, 181
 in Waterloo campaign, 73, 92, 155, 168, 225–35
 leadership, 46, 233
 quotations, 4, 11, 51, 155, 181, 219
Westmoreland, General William, 132
William I, the Conqueror (Eng.), 30, 73–7, 83, 112
Wolfe, General James, 68–9
World wars *see* First World War; Second World War
Wounded, 63, 124, 126, 128, 200, 206–207, 213–14
 treatment of enemy, 15, 17–18
 see also Medical services

Yom Kippur War, 16, 35–6

Zulus, 15, 26, 137, 205